D1280098

EDINBURGH UNIVERSITY PUBLICATIONS

History, Philosophy and Economics

No. 20

Overleaf: First page of The Laws of Æthelberht
from the *Textus Roffensis*

Þis syndon þa domas þe æðelbiriht cyning
asette on Agustinus dæge.

GODES FEOH. 7 CI
riceam .xii. gylde. Biscopes feoh.
.xi. gylde. Preostes feoh .ix. gylde.
Diacones feoh .vi. gylde. Clero
ces feoh .iii. gylde. Ciric friþ.
.ii. gylde. M friþ .ii. gylde. Gif cyning his
leode to him gehateþ 7 heom mon þær yfel gedo.
.ii. bote. 7 cyninge .l. scillinga. Gif cyning æt
mannes ham drincæþ 7 ðær man lyswæs hwæt
gedo. twi bote gebete. Gif frigman cyninge
stele .ix. gylde forgylde. Gif in cyninges tu
ne man mannan ofslea .l. scill gebete. Gif man
frigne mannan ofsleahþ. cyninge .l. scill. to
drihtin beage. Gif cyninges [illegible] smið oþþe
laadrinc mannan ofslehð [illegible] meduman leodgelde
forgelde. Cyninges mundbyrd .l. scillinga. Gif
frigman freum stelþ .iii. gebete. 7 cyning age þ
wite 7 ealle þa æhtan. Gif man wið cyninges mæg
denman geligeþ .l. scillinga gebete. Gif hio grin
dende þeowa sio .xxv. scillinga gebete. Sio þridde
.xii. scillingas. Cyninges fedesl .xx. scillinga
forgelde. Gif on eorles tune man mannan

LAW AND LEGISLATION

from Æthelberht to Magna Carta

H. G. RICHARDSON F.B.A AND

G. O. SAYLES F.B.A

EDINBURGH

at the University Press

EDINBURGH UNIVERSITY PRESS
22 George Square, Edinburgh 8
North America
Aldine Publishing Company
320 West Adams Street, Chicago
Australia and New Zealand
Hodder & Stoughton Ltd.
Africa, Oxford University Press
India, P. C. Manaktala & Sons
Far East, M. Graham Brash & Son

printed in Great Britain by
T. & A. CONSTABLE, LTD, EDINBURGH
Printers to the University of Edinburgh

CONTENTS

FOREWORD

IN this volume we have endeavoured to trace, with as little discussion of technical detail as is compatible with reasoned argument, the story of law-making and legislation in England from the obscurity of the sixth century to the year 1215 when our sources begin to be copious. We have planned the book in especial for readers who are likely to be repelled by discussions of the minutiae of the law. The detail will be found easily enough elsewhere by those who are interested, for example, in the evolution of particular writs and legal processes. But though we have restricted our text and our footnotes accordingly, yet even so we may have trespassed here and there upon the reader's patience. Nevertheless our hope is that this book will be read by many who would not in the ordinary course open a book of legal history and that they will be convinced that the history of the law is not necessarily dull and that it is quite essential for an understanding of history as a whole.

The present volume, though complete in itself, may be regarded as a companion to our *Governance of Mediaeval England from the Conquest to Magna Carta*. The history of both administration and law-making will be continued in the second volume of the *Governance of Mediaeval England*, which is already in preparation. Once more we remember with gratitude the Rockefeller Foundation of New York: it is quite certain that without its munificence this book would not have appeared so soon, if at all. The views we express are our own, founded upon a study of the documents themselves, in print and in manuscript. Certain of our conclusions cannot fail to appear heterodox, if not heretical. We have even felt impelled to differ from Felix Liebermann, though without in the least losing our admiration for his industry and learning, for that devoted scholarship of his which has made so much easier the path of all those who tread the tangled byways of Anglo-Saxon and Norman England. From Maitland too we have ventured to differ : but we need not express once more our devotion to his memory. Now and again we may perturb our older contemporaries by our lack of respect for conventional teaching, but our experience encourages us to hope, and indeed to anticipate, that a younger generation will find many of our arguments and conclusions persuasive. We are greatly indebted to Mr J. M. Wallace-Hadrill who has been good enough to read the first chapter and the first appendix in manuscript and to give us the benefit of his learned criticisms. We have sought to meet effectively the difficulties he felt in our interpretation of the scanty and sometimes conflicting evidence for the events of the sixth and seventh centuries. Whether we have penetrated the darkness better than our predecessors others must decide. We have done our best, without conscious bias or preconception.

H. G. R.
Goudhurst,
Kent

G. O. S.
Institute of Advanced Legal Studies,
University of London

I

LEGISLATION IN THE OLD ENGLISH KINGDOMS

THE record of legislation in England is one of the longest in Europe. It is often said to have begun in the early years of the seventh century, but there is reason to believe that it began before the end of the sixth century under King Æthelberht of Kent. His laws have no known model, though comparison has sometimes been made with the *Lex Salica* attributed to Clovis. There is, however, little resemblance in style and form, and while the Frankish laws are in Latin, the Kentish laws are in English. It was at one time conjectured that behind the *Lex Salica*, as it has come down to us, there may have lain a vernacular text, but here again the suggestion lacks any real evidence and it appears to have been abandoned.[1] Nor is it possible to suppose that the English text of Æthelberht's laws is a translation or adaptation of a Latin original.[2] Not only have we the express word of Bede that they were written in English, but they come to us in association with the laws of Æthelberht's successors, which likewise bear no trace of translation. Bede indeed tells us that Æthelberht's laws were made 'juxta exempla Romanorum'; but what these words meant to him or what he intended to convey is very uncertain.[3] We can, we think, question the grounds of Charles Plummer's assertion that they show 'that the reduction of native custom to writing was, like so much else, the result of Christianity, bringing Roman civilisation in its train'.[4] On the contrary, the evidence, in our view, points in the opposite direction. Æthelberht's legislation was in no sense Christian but, if an offensive word may be used inoffensively, pagan.

Since this view is in opposition to that generally held and since, if it is true, it is important, we must set out our arguments carefully. Let us begin by declaring our belief that the Kentish laws, as they have come down to us, are authentic. They exist in but a single manuscript, the *Textus Roffensis*, written in the twelfth century, that is, as Liebermann said, half a thousand years from the time the earliest were made.[5] The

[1] That Clovis, in fact, promulgated laws rests upon much later tradition. In any case his contribution, if such there was, cannot be distinguished from later accretions. S. Stein maintained that the *Lex Salica* was a fabrication of the time of Charles the Bald (*Speculum*, xxii.115-34, 395-418). He has been answered by J. M. Wallace-Hadrill, *The Long-haired Kings*, pp. 110-19, and by R. Buchner in *Deutsches Archiv*, ix.59-78. But when the *Lex Salica* was first committed to writing seems to be still an open question.

[2] Cf. Liebermann, *Gesetze der Angelsachsen*, iii.1.

[3] Bede, *Historia Ecclesiastica*, lib. ii, c. 5 (Plummer, i.90).

[4] *Ibid.*, ii.87: and see below p. 158, n. 5.

[5] Liebermann, *loc. cit.* A facsimile of the manuscript is now available, ed. P. Sawyer.

language has suffered inevitable changes in the course of transcription and we could hardly expect the texts not to have suffered some distortion in transmission. But in substance the laws are consistent one with another and with the circumstances of the late sixth and early seventh centuries and, as we have seen, their existence early in the eighth century is corroborated by Bede and corroborated not only in general but in one singularity, which to our mind shows that, when the text of the laws of Æthelberht reached him, it had already been interpolated. What is this interpolation? It is the first purported article:

> God's property and the Church's shall [if stolen] be compensated for twelvefold; a bishop's property elevenfold; a priest's property ninefold; a clerk's property threefold; a breach of the Church's peace twofold; a breach of the peace of a meeting twofold.[1]

This may represent, in a distorted form, a genuine piece of Kentish legislation in the later seventh century, though no parallel can be found in any law that has come down to us; but it seems to us to have no place where we find it. Why do we say this? Let us turn to the later Kentish laws that have survived from the seventh century. We notice that they are prefaced with title and preamble:

> These are the dooms which Hlothere and Eadric, kings of the Kentish people, ordained.
>
> Hlothere and Eadric, kings of the Kentish people, added to those laws that their ancestors had made the dooms which are set out hereafter.[2]

The laws of Wihtred are similarly entitled:

> These are the dooms of Wihtred, king of the Kentish people.

A long preamble follows, giving the precise date and place where the legislation was promulgated and recording the assent of the archbishop of Canterbury and the bishop of Rochester, who were present together with other representatives of the clergy.[3] The titles of these laws may be, as has been supposed, additions, though it would be rash to conclude that they are later than the preambles or the date when the texts, as we have them, were committed to writing. But there seems no doubt that the title of Æthelberht's laws is a subsequent addition to the text:

> These are the dooms that King Æthelberht ordained in Augustine's days.

There follows no preamble, such as Bede's copy must have possessed[4] and such as we find in the later laws, which appear to have been modelled upon the precedent of Æthelberht's laws in their original form. Instead of giving a preamble, the *textus receptus* leads off abruptly

[1] Liebermann, *Gesetze*, i.3; Attenborough, *Laws of the Earliest English Kings*, p. 4.
[2] Liebermann, i.9; Attenborough, p. 18.
[3] Liebermann, i.12; Attenborough, p. 24.
[4] Liebermann, iii.3; below, p. 4, n. 1.

with the article we have designated as an interpolation; and let us remark, for the point seems to us significant, the article is in a different style from the body of the laws. Now this is the only article which in any way purports to affect the Roman mission or the band of uncertain and unstable Kentish converts, which, be it noted, did not in the days of Augustine include the son of the king's Christian wife nor, so far as we have any certain knowledge, the king himself.[1]

It has often been remarked with astonishment that the penalty prescribed for stealing ecclesiastical property or for thefts from a bishop should be greater than the penalty for stealing from the king, who, we must conclude, if we accept this extraordinary article, was placed on the same level as a priest. But is it credible that, even assuming the laws to have been promulgated after Æthelberht's baptism (if that ever took place), the king would be ranked lower than his own bishops and on an equality with a priest, a priest who, on the testimony of one of Wihtred's laws, might be quite disreputable, too drunk to baptise a dying man?[2] Mass-priests were not on the same level as nobles, let alone kings, in Kent or anywhere else. It is not indeed until the time of Wihtred that the Church is, in any sense, put upon an equality with the king. Then the protection, *mundbyrd*, given by the Church is made as inviolable as the protection given by the king, and the penalty for infringing it is the same.[3] The penalty for infringing the king's protection, it should be observed, is, however, of the same amount at the end of the century as it was at the beginning under Æthelberht, namely, fifty shillings.[4] But in his laws there is no mention of the *mundbyrd* of the Church, no mention of any penalty for infringing it, no mention even in the interpolation. Nor has it, we think, been sufficiently stressed that the whole scheme of penalties in the interpolated clause is in flat contradiction to the advice given to Augustine by Pope Gregory in answer to the question, 'in what manner should those things which are stolen from churches be restored?' 'God forbid', replies the pope, 'that the Church should receive again with interest what it may seem to have lost of worldly wealth and seek to profit from worthless things.'[5] We may think that Bede at times rated Augustine's virtues rather more highly than they deserved; but we should need much persuasion to believe that Augustine had departed from the pope's principles as drastically as the interpolator took for granted. The interpolator belonged to a later generation when the English Church had come to terms with the world.

It is, of course, possible that in the course of transmission the penalties in the interpolated clause were increased in amount to bring them into line with current conceptions. On that point Bede gives us

[1] Below, pp. 162-4.
[2] Wihtred, cap. 6 (Liebermann, i.12; Attenborough, p. 26).
[3] *Ibid.*, cap. 2 (Liebermann, i.12; Attenborough, p. 24).
[4] Æthelberht, cap. 8 (Liebermann, i.3; Attenborough, p. 4).
[5] Bede, *Hist. Eccl.*, lib. i, c. 27 (Plummer, i.50).

no help. For while his reference to Æthelberht's laws shows that this clause stood at the head of the text before him – though apparently before or after a preamble which the *Textus Roffensis* does not contain – he speaks in generalities of the penalties and not in detail. That he should remark that the clause stood where it did suggests that it occasioned him some surprise.[1] But even if we suppose the amount of the penalties to have been much more moderate when the clause was first introduced into the text, the other arguments against its inclusion in the original text remain. We submit that there are good reasons for excluding this dubious clause from the text of Æthelberht's laws. If we exclude it as the presumed offspring of later piety, there is not one syllable of Æthelberht's dooms, in all their eighty-nine articles, to suggest that they apply to a Christian community. Indeed, they suggest the very reverse. Thirteen articles towards the end of the laws deal with the position of women:[2] some of these articles are obscure, but it is at least clear that any of the conceptions of Christian marriage are foreign to the legislators. Marriage is a matter of purchase: even marriage by capture seems a distinct possibility. There is no thought of marriage as an indissoluble union. Separation – we can hardly call it divorce – is a matter for monetary compensation, and so is adultery.[3] It would be difficult to explain how these articles came to be promulgated by a king instructed in the elements of Christian morals or under the influence of Christian bishops. That Bede should have accepted them as such is so incredible that we must conclude either that he had not the full text of Æthelberht's laws before him or that he did not read them thoroughly. Let the reader contrast them with the dooms of Wihtred where the influence of the Church and the Church's privileges are plainly seen.[4] Freed from the interpolation, the text of Æthelberht's laws has a logical unity. The king stands, as we should expect, in the forefront of his own dooms. Those of his subjects who are on their way to his court are under his protection, as are the houses he visits. His property, his dwelling-place, his household have a high immunity. If there is manslaying in his presence, not only must the victim's relatives be compensated, but the king must be compensated too.[5] If a man robs another in the king's presence, he may forfeit all his property to the king and only if he is lucky will he get off with a fine.[6] The first eleven articles are concerned solely with upholding the king's majesty. Next, as we should expect, the nobles receive some notice and then the commoners. The clergy entirely escape mention.

[1] *Ibid.*, lib. ii, c. 5: In quibus primitus posuit qualiter emendare deberet qui aliquid rerum vel ecclesiae vel episcopi vel reliquorum ordinum furto auferret . . . (Plummer, i.90).

[2] Æthelberht, caps. 73-85 (Liebermann, i.7-8; Attenborough, p. 14).

[3] An adulterous wife was, moreover, replaced by the adulterer with another woman (Æthelberht, cap. 31).

[4] Wihtred, caps. 1-7, 9-24 (Liebermann, i.12-14; Attenborough, pp. 24-8).

[5] Æthelberht, caps. 5, 6, 21, 23 (Liebermann, i.3-4; Attenborough, pp. 4, 6).

[6] *Ibid.*, cap. 9 (Liebermann, i.3; Attenborough, p. 4).

We have spoken of Æthelberht's 'laws', but it is desirable to make it clear that these laws are not legislation in a wide sense. They do not enounce general principles or new principles, such as might have followed Æthelberht's conversion to Christianity, nor do they provide a code for every justiciable cause in the kingdom. They do not declare that specific wrongful acts shall in the future be treated as crimes. They describe many crimes clearly enough, but clearly also these acts are already recognised as crimes. The aim of the laws is quite evidently the simple and direct one of proclaiming the scale of pecuniary penalties henceforth to be paid for specific offences. We may reasonably suppose that one object is to substitute definite mulcts for arbitrary or uncertain mulcts, but, if so, the object seems equally to be financial. The more substantial payments will accrue to the king, by way of what we would call fines, where he is personally concerned,[1] and he may receive part of the compensation paid in other cases.[2] It is plain that there is already in existence the concept of what will later be known as the king's peace and that a breach of the peace entails a penalty that will accrue to the king. But though the king has a more exalted peace than any other, a noble too has his *mund*, as has also a ceorl, and the widows of nobles and ceorls.[3] Later the bishops and other clergy will have their *mund*[4]; but obviously there would be no reference to this in the laws of a pagan king, as we hold Æthelberht to have been. Penalties for breaches of the peace, whether of king, noble or ceorl, must be paid, as well as compensation for loss of life or personal injury and for loss of property. There is then a double series of mulcts and the laws establish a tariff in a great many cases.[5] And let us note that by far the greater number of mulcts are calculated in shillings and sceattas. The shillings appear to have been gold tremisses[6] and the sceattas (twenty to the shilling) silver coins of some sort, though, if silver coins were minted by the Kentings, no surviving specimen is known.[7] In any case the use of coins must have been widespread and money plentiful. Hence the need and possibility of a monetary tariff. This practical purpose of Æthelberht's laws we must emphasise. The king is not legislating because in this way he desires to assert his sovereignty or place himself on a level with other kings. We do not accept the belief that in legislating he is

[1] *Ibid.*, caps. 2-12 (Liebermann, i.3-4; Attenborough, pp. 4, 6).

[2] *Ibid.*, caps. 9, 84 (Liebermann, i.3, 8; Attenborough, pp. 4, 14). These may not have been the only instances in the original text: references to the king's dues at the end of chapters may have dropped out in transmission over five centuries.

[3] *Ibid.*, caps. 13, 14, 15, 75, 76 (Liebermann, i.4, 7; Attenborough, pp. 6, 14).

[4] Below, p. 12.

[5] The *bot* or the wergild is not always fixed nor can the *bot* be fixed when it is a question of forfeiture (e.g. caps. 2-4, 7, 9).

[6] That the gold tremis was the current coin of high value would seem to be unquestionable (Sutherland, *Anglo-Saxon Gold Coinage*; below, p. 158). There is no other coin in circulation that we can identify with the shilling.

[7] That silver was coined in the later seventh century is unquestioned: that it was coined in the sixth century remains to be proved. The alternative is to suppose that silver coins of the Later Empire were in circulation and were accepted in the absence of specially struck sceattas. The ratio of 20 : 1 in terms of gold indicates that the silver content of the sceatt was small, with whatever coins we are to identify it.

imitating contemporary continental rulers who are emerging from barbarism or that he is consciously following the *exempla Romanorum* as Bede supposed.[1] If he has models they were, we believe, for reasons we shall shortly give, provided by his ancestors. So far as we have knowledge, Kentish legislation is *sui generis*.

Now let us ask two questions. For what manner of people were Æthelberht's laws made and when were they promulgated? To begin with, we must emphasise that, in all probability, legislation of the Kentish kind was possible at this time only in that one small corner of England. Let us summarise what we set out at some length later by saying briefly that Kent was an exceptional kingdom in the closeness of its culture to such culture as the Merovingian Franks possessed, in its comparative wealth and skill in the arts, in its learning, perhaps in the continued existence of British Christians and British churches among English heathens and English idols.[2] We must not exaggerate. For all its eminence over the other petty English kingdoms, Kent was an agricultural and pastoral country, with few towns and town-dwellers, though these seem to have preserved, however feebly, more of Roman-British civilisation than was to be found elsewhere in England, except perhaps in London. If we would form some idea of conditions in other English kingdoms we might do worse than read Grimm's *Märchen*, those monuments of Germanic folklore which, overlaid as they may be by later accretions, reveal something of a pre-Christian past. An English kingdom in the sixth century was not very far removed from the little kingdoms of *Märchenland*, rude and pastoral, where a journey of a day or two or even less might take a traveller from the heart of one king's dominion to the heart of another.[3] Such a journey from Kent through one of such forests as are met with in the *Märchen*, a journey through the Andredasweald, would bring a man to the kingdom of the South Saxons, where there dwelt a primitive community of peasants, isolated by forest, marsh, waste and sea. Another short journey to the west or north would bring him to a like community, that of the Middle Saxons, surrounding but avoiding the city of London in their midst, a wasted spectre perhaps of its former self, but still animated by the Thames and the Roman roads, which made it in the sixth century, if we may believe Bede, a market place for many peoples coming by land and sea.[4] Of this city the king of the Kentings was lord, though in the time of King Æthelberht it was his nephew, the king of the East Saxons, who ruled there in his place.[5] But there the Kentish kings had a royal house and there later in the

[1] Above, p. 1.
[2] Below, pp. 161-2.
[3] There is a suggestive essay by Karl Pearson entitled 'Ashiepattle' in *The Chances of Death*, ii.51-91: we need not take too seriously his notions about a primitive Germanic matriarchy. For these small kingdoms in history see Chadwick, *The Heroic Age*, pp. 375-8, 380*n*.
[4] Below, p. 169.
[5] Below, p. 167.

seventh century they were represented by a reeve.[1] If, however, London preserved a separate identity, as it did throughout many centuries, politically and economically it formed, for much of the sixth and seventh centuries, a unit with Kent.

Kent doubtless is, in a sense, a barbarous land, but it does not differ in this respect from Frankland, though in some ways it may be nearer, as its laws suggest, to earlier Germanic social conditions and ideas of government. Yet, as in Frankland, there are a few centres – London, Canterbury, Rochester – with some pretence to culture and literacy, some reminiscences of a Roman past. If this culture is strengthened and extended by Latin Christianity in the course of the seventh and eighth centuries, in law, at least, the pagan element remains dominant. Such Christian elements as there are in early legislation are subordinate and are devised to protect the new religion,[2] which has a hard fight to overcome heathendom, for Christianity has but shallow roots, a religion imposed from above, with scanty influence upon the lives of the people.

Now let us endeavour to answer our second question: when were Æthelberht's laws promulgated? The date usually ascribed to them, 601-604, or more precisely 602-3, depends upon a number of assumptions: that Æthelberht was baptised in 597; that the title of the laws, though a later addition, correctly ascribes them to the period between the receipt of Pope Gregory's replies to Augustine's enquiries on matters of doubt (including restitution of thefts of ecclesiastical property), namely August 601, and Augustine's death, supposedly on 26 May 604; and that the first article formed part of the original text.[3] These three assumptions we reject: the first and third, because they both seem to be manifestly without foundation, and the second because there is no direct evidence to support it and it appears to be inherently improbable. It would make too great an interruption in our narrative to set out here the reasons why we question Æthelberht's alleged conversion to Christianity: they will be found in an appendix.[4] But if this pagan legislation was promulgated by a pagan king, uninfluenced by Christian conceptions or Christian teachers, then we cannot reject out of hand as the probable date any year in his long reign, which lasted until 616. The years from 601 to 604 might therefore be possible for the enactment of the laws, and certainly no earlier date could well be admitted if we accepted the view, which seems generally to be adopted, that writing was unknown to the Kentings before they learnt the art from the Roman mission.

There are, however, cogent reasons for taking a contrary view.

[1] Hlothere and Eadric, cap. 16 (Liebermann, i.11; Attenborough, p. 22); below, p. 10.
[2] Wihtred's laws, which are mainly of this character, supplement the earlier Kentish laws which are regarded as still in force (below, p. 12).
[3] Liebermann, iii.2-3. There is no certainty that Augustine died in 604: his death may not have taken place until 609.
[4] Below, pp. 162-4.

First let us face a chronological difficulty. The earliest date that has been suggested for Æthelberht's laws is 601, not much more than four years after the landing of Augustine and his mission. The Roman missionaries were admittedly ignorant of the English tongue to begin with, and Bede nowhere suggests that either Augustine or his companions became proficient in the language.[1] In any case the time would be very short for the acquisition by an Italian of a colloquial command of English, let alone its fitting to the Latin alphabet, supplemented by runic characters, a knowledge of which the inventors of the English script must have acquired. Nor should we sensibly modify the evident difficulties in the way of attributing the invention to the Roman missionaries if we imagine the laws to have been promulgated shortly before Augustine's death, whether we place it in 604 or in some later year. If, therefore, the missionaries were in any sense responsible for the reduction of English to writing, it would seem that this must have been through the agency either of the Frankish interpreters they employed or of English converts. The Frankish interpreters must clearly have had a reasonable knowledge of Latin and were presumably literate. They had, in fact, much the same qualifications as Bishop Liudhard, who took up residence in Canterbury thirty years before Augustine.[2] If we were faced with the necessity to choose between the Roman Augustine and the Frankish Liudhard as the more probable inventor of an English script, our choice might well fall upon the latter. He could have had little difficulty in mastering English as spoken in Kent and, like Queen Bertha, he would have very good reason for doing so. But we should be bound to reject Liudhard as the inventor for a number of reasons: the numismatic evidence points to a knowledge of the Latin alphabet in Kent before Bertha's marriage to Æthelberht;[3] when the Franks proposed to expand the Latin alphabet, then – if we accept the testimony of Gregory of Tours – they introduced what he calls 'Greek' characters which, if they were, as is perhaps possible, 'runes', were not the runes employed in England[4]; there had been diplomatic relations between the Kentish court and the Merovingian court as a preliminary to Bertha's marriage and these relations would imply written instruments and a knowledge of the Latin alphabet, whether the instruments were in Latin or in the vernacular. The evidence pointing to a knowledge of the Latin alphabet in Kent before the introduction of Christianity makes it unlikely that native converts played any part in the evolution of an English script, though it is to be presumed that those among them who were literate had, like many Kentings before them, a knowledge of runes. There is perhaps a more formidable difficulty. If the Roman mission, their Frankish inter-

[1] *Hist. Eccl.*, lib. 1, cc. 23, 25 (Plummer, i.42, 45).
[2] Below, p. 157.
[3] Below, pp. 158-60.
[4] *Historia Francorum*, lib. v, c. 44 (p. 199). For conjectures upon the nature of these characters, see below, p. 159.

preters or English converts invented or even made appreciable use of an English script, it would be extraordinary if they employed it, not, as Ulfilas and his disciples employed the Gothic script, to translate the Scriptures,[1] but to commit to writing pagan laws repugnant, in at least some respects, to Christian teaching. If we were to argue nevertheless that the laws might have been written by pagans who had been instructed in the art of writing by their Christian brethren, we should be merely adding supposition to supposition, improbability to improbability. Yet even this is not the least improbability, for Æthelberht's laws could not have been effective unless they were widespread and read by pagan nobles and pagan clerks – for on Augustine's death few nobles and few clerks could have been Christian – and so we should have to imagine the wide extension of the art of reading, as well as the invention of the art of writing, within the narrow space of years between 597 and, at latest, 609 – if we are not prepared to accept the year 604 for Augustine's death.[2] The time-scale is far too short to allow for the necessarily slow evolution of literacy. Whatever suppositions may be made, there is no escape from the chronological difficulty, even though we dismiss the independent evidence for a pagan origin of the English script. We need not elaborate the arguments further in this place, though later we point to still other evidence that the reader may ponder.[3]

If this view is accepted and if English was being written many years before 597, there is no necessary ground for ascribing the laws to the seventh century. They might perhaps come from any year after 565, the date of Æthelberht's accession. Since, however, he appears to have then been no more than thirteen years old, we might hesitate to suppose that he legislated until he had been some years on the throne and had attained manhood. Yet manhood came early in those days, and Clovis was king of the Franks and had begun his stupendous career at the age of fifteen. At all events there is no obvious reason why we should suppose a long interval to have taken place and ascribe the laws to a year late in Æthelberht's reign. They may well belong to the last quarter of the sixth century or even to some earlier year.

Now this legislation is written in a manner that does not look at all tentative, that has no air of novelty about it. There may have been a model for it. Some earlier Kentish king may have led the way. We can but speculate whether it was Eormenric or the shadowy Octa or the shadowy Oisc and whether laws were being written in Kent in the early sixth century, when, if legend be true, Clovis was legislating for the Salian Franks. Certainly we do not possess the whole body of Kentish legislation. We hear from Bede of legislation by Earconberht,

[1] There is a large German literature upon this subject: a convenient book for consultation is Joseph Wright, *Grammar of the Gothic Language*.

[2] There is no certainty about the year, but, as we have indicated, 604 is generally accepted.

[3] Below, pp. 158-60.

Æthelberht's grandson, in the interest of the new religion, requiring the abandonment of the old religion and the destruction of idols and prescribing the observance of Lent, all subject to penalties for disobedience.[1] Piety, it might be thought, would have preserved these laws, but they have not come down to us. That there have been other losses is suggested by the preamble to the laws of Hlothere and Eadric which we have already cited. 'The laws of their ancestors' suggests more than those of Æthelberht and the limited legislation of Earconberht of which Bede speaks. But we have no reason to suppose that the specimens of legislation that have survived are not representative.

Kentish legislation is concerned almost exclusively with criminal law, law which for the most part conceives of crime as a wrongdoing to be redeemed with money, though in the most serious of cases, robbery (but not apparently manslaying) in the king's presence, for example, the penalty may be forfeiture.[2] The establishment of Christianity introduces a new series of delicts and a new series of penalties, some ecclesiastical, like excommunication for adultery, but, even so, carrying monetary penalties which accrue to the king.[3] Towards the end of the seventh century, under Wihtred, and with the concurrence of the Church, sterner penalties were introduced. Theft from the king may be punished by death or slavery. An open thief may be slain without trial, and so may a thieving slave.[4] The unfree (*esne*) and the slave are liable to be beaten for what may seem to us trifling offences, for travelling on Sunday, for heathen practices, for breaking a religious fast.[5] It is a cruel age and it seems to grow crueller.

Of purely civil law there is little in this legislation. The future of orphans of freemen is safeguarded by providing that the mother shall have their custody and that a guardian shall be appointed from the father's kin.[6] The only notice of trade in the Kentish laws is a provision for protecting a Kentish man who has dealings in London, where, it will be remembered, the Kentish king has jurisdiction. Such dealings must be open and aboveboard, apparently in the king's market where his reeve exercises authority.[7] It has been supposed that this law relates to dealings in cattle,[8] but why men should journey from Kent to London for this purpose has not been explained. There was surely a

[1] *Hist. Eccl.*, lib. iii, c. 8 (Plummer, i.142).

[2] Æthelberht, cap. 9: this must be read with cap. 8 (Liebermann, i.3; Attenborough, p. 4).

[3] Hlothere and Eadric, cap. 5 (Liebermann, i.9-10; Attenborough, p. 24).

[4] Wihtred, caps. 26-28 (Liebermann, i.14; Attenborough, pp. 28-30).

[5] Wihtred, caps. 10, 13, 15 (Liebermann, i.13; Attenborough, p. 26).

[6] Hlothere and Eadric, cap. 6 (Liebermann, i.10; Attenborough, p. 18).

[7] Hlothere and Eadric, cap. 16 (Liebermann, i.11; Attenborough, p. 22). In later centuries there was a cyning-ceap in the king's soke, north of the present Poultry (*Pipe Roll, 4 Richard 1*, p. 306; Page, *London*, pp. 140-3; Richardson, *English Jewry*, pp. 7, 48*n*). The later corruption 'Conyhope' has led to an erroneous, if amusing, explanation in Ekwall, *London Street Names*, pp. 150-2.

[8] *Feoh*, the word used, does not necessarily mean cattle, though it is so translated by, among others, Pollock and Maitland (*History of English Law*, i.59) and Liebermann (*Gesetze*, iii.23), who, however, gives *Fahrhabe* as a possible alternative (*ibid.*, ii.69).

more diversified trade than this in a city to which men from all quarters resorted by sea as well as by land, resorted, we venture to believe, to buy and sell articles of value as well as agricultural produce. Doubtless the countryman would bring his produce to the city markets rather than carry money with him; but would he not take back with him something for use or adornment? The economy of south-eastern England may have been primitive in the seventh century, but it was a money economy.

Then of procedural law there is a good deal in Kentish legislation, chiefly in the nice regulation of oaths.[1] Of other forms of proof in Kentish courts there is no suggestion and, though we hear of the judges of the Kentish people, their function seems to be to prescribe penalties rather than to pass judgement.[2] Of land law, which provides so much of the content of legislation after the Norman Conquest, there is nothing. Unwritten custom regulates succession and transactions in land. On military service, and on police work which is so closely akin to it in later centuries, the Kentish laws are equally silent.

We have, we think, said enough of this legislation to give an adequate idea of its content and we must now say something of its inception and enforcement. The king does not legislate of his sole authority. Æthelberht, Bede tells us, promulgated his laws *cum consilio sapientium.*[3] There is no preamble to this effect in the single surviving text of the laws, but we must presume that Bede found in his copy a preamble similar to those in the laws of Hlothere and Eadric and of Wihtred which we have already noticed. He could have had no other basis for his statement. The Kentish king had therefore his witan in the sixth century as he had in the seventh. It precedes the introduction of Christianity. As the Church grows in influence, leading churchmen will be consulted, especially when ecclesiastical matters are to be discussed.[4] Ultimately this will lead to the inclusion of bishops and abbots as a necessary element in the witan; but in the seventh century this position has not been reached.[5] We are not told of the manner in which laws were prepared for submission to the witan. We can but guess; although we believe we can make an instructed guess, and the preamble to Alfred's laws is suggestive.[6] The texts themselves indicate careful drafting. In the background there must be skilled royal clerks, even in the sixth century. Æthelberht's laws are not the bungling efforts of inexperienced and illiterate beginners. With a draft before them the king's council will discuss, will suggest amendments or

[1] Hlothere and Eadric, cap. 10; Wihtred, caps. 16, 19-24. There is even more of this in Ine, caps. 14-17, 19, 21, 25, 28, 30, 35, 45, 46, 48, 49, 52-54, 57, 71.

[2] Hlothere and Eadric, cap. 8 (Liebermann, i.10; Attenborough, p.20).

[3] *Hist. Eccl.*, lib. ii, c. 5 (Plummer, i.90).

[4] See especially the preamble to Wihtred's laws (above, p. 2). The preamble to Ine's laws, of much the same date, records the presence of two bishops and a large number of clergy, as well as the whole body of ealdormen and other laymen (Liebermann, i.89; Attenborough, p. 36).

[5] Liebermann, *National Assembly*, pp. 3-4, 30-3.

[6] Below, p. 15.

additions. If this were not the case, it could hardly be said that the laws were promulgated *cum consilio sapientium.* At the end of the meeting, which may perhaps last for more than one day, the clerks will have the draft, with excisions and amendments, and will be left, we must presume, to prepare several copies of the final version, which, if later procedure is any guide, will be read in the local courts of the kingdom.[1] It is clear that copies were carefully preserved, otherwise there would be no meaning in the preamble to the laws of Hlothere and Eadric which says distinctly that – to use a modern phrase – these new laws are to be read with the laws of earlier kings. But here we come to a difficulty. Eadric was Hlothere's nephew and the two had been at enmity. Indeed Hlothere died of wounds received in battle with the South Saxons who supported Eadric and Eadric lived only a year and a half to enjoy his victory.[2] It may be that at one time he had been associated with his uncle in the government of Kent. It may be that he re-enacted his uncle's laws. It may be that – and this seems perhaps the more probable explanation – the text we have is a conflation of two or more original texts. The final long paragraph of these laws certainly looks like a quite separate piece of legislation, dealing only with the trading transactions of Kentish men in London.[3] It seems to have been merely joined on to the preceding enactments because it came from one or other of the two kings. Conflation of this kind is by no means unknown in later centuries. Even in the thirteenth century a famous piece of legislation, the Statute of Merton, is made up of several pieces coming from several occasions.[4] Modern ideas on textual integrity had no place in earlier centuries.

The laws of Wihtred, on the other hand, appear for the most part[5] to be what they declare themselves to be, the laws agreed by the witan in an assembly which is precisely dated and placed. They are definitely stated to be an addition to the laws of the Kentish people and must have been drafted with earlier legislation in view.[6] The second article, declaring that the *mundbyrd* of the Church shall be fifty shillings like the king's, seems evidently to refer to the article numbered 8 in the *textus receptus* of Æthelberht's laws, where the king's *mundbyrd* is declared to be of this amount. But the greater part of the legislation, which is devised to give a privileged position to the clergy, has no counterpart in any extant laws of earlier date.[7]

In principle there could have been no difficulty in enforcing these Kentish laws or at least in exacting the prescribed penalties. Even if the offender fled, his kin were responsible for him, and they could not all flee.[8] The kingdom had very narrow limits. The king, who was always

1 Below, pp. 17-27.
2 Bede, *Hist. Eccl.*, lib. iv, c. 24 (Plummer, i.268).
3 Above, p. 10.
4 Richardson and Sayles, *The Early Statutes*, pp. 4, 18-19.
5 As we suggest later, p. 13, the final article may well be an addition.
6 Liebermann, i.12; Attenborough, p. 24.
7 Wihtred, caps. 1, 2, 16-19, 21-2, 24 (Liebermann, i.12-14; Attenborough, pp. 24-8).
8 Æthelberht, cap. 23 (Liebermann, i.4; Attenborough, p. 6).

journeying up and down, could exercise direct authority, and he seems to have had many reeves. It was political instability, political rivalries and ambitions, which brought so much promise to an end. In the eighth century Kent passed under the domination of Mercia and in the ninth it was absorbed in Wessex. With Wihtred Kentish legislation ends.

We turn to the other English kingdoms. The kings of the West Saxons were the first to follow the example of the Kentish kings in committing their dooms to writing. Ine, who had come to the throne of Wessex a few years previously, seems to have promulgated his dooms, or certain of them, by 694,[1] at much about the same time as Wihtred was legislating in Kent. One article of Ine's dooms is written in terms so nearly identical to one of Wihtred's that borrowing is obvious. Both declare that a stranger, lurking near the highway, who neither shouts nor blows his horn, is to be treated as a thief. Ine's doom is more elaborate than Wihtred's and, if we can assume the existing texts to be faithful to their originals, it would be a natural inference that Ine borrowed from Wihtred.[2] But the preambles to the two sets of dooms, if we accept them as covering all that follows, indicate that Wihtred's dooms are a year or so later than Ine's.[3] The evidence is apparently conflicting. The explanation may, however, be that this article, which comes at the very end of Wihtred's dooms, is an addition drawn from some earlier law.[4] There are other resemblances between the legislation of Wessex and Kent, but none so striking as this. Some of the parallels that have been drawn seem indeed to be rather fanciful, that, for example, which Liebermann drew between the twelvefold payment of church-dues as a penalty for leaving them unpaid, to be found in Ine's dooms, and the twelvefold compensation to be paid for thefts of ecclesiastical and episcopal property, laid down in the first article in the *textus receptus* of Æthelberht's dooms.[5] It is immaterial whether we regard this latter article as interpolated or not; even though later than Æthelberht, it is still Kentish. The recurrence of the multiple of twelve in the case of different offences does not, however, seem to warrant any inference of borrowing. Nevertheless it seems certain that Wessex did follow the lead of Kent, and we have Alfred's word for it that two centuries later Æthelberht's dooms, and apparently other Kentish laws, were known to him.[6]

[1] Liebermann, iii.65.
[2] Wihtred, cap. 28; Ine, caps. 20, 21 (Liebermann, i.14, 98-9; Attenborough, pp. 30, 42).
[3] Liebermann, iii.24-5.
[4] Compare I Edgar, where chapters 8 and 9 are an obvious incongruous addition, due apparently to scribal errors in transcription (cf. Liebermann, iii.131).
[5] *Ibid.*, p. 65.
[6] See the preamble to Alfred's laws (Liebermann, i.46; Attenborough, p. 62). Alfred mentions specifically Æthelberht's, Ine's and Offa's laws as those from which he made a selection, but he speaks also of other laws which displeased him, and these could only be Kentish laws, which we know once existed and have been lost, whereas no other Mercian laws are known than Offa's and no other early West Saxon laws than Ine's.

Though some of Ine's dooms are laconic to the point of unintelligibility, a good many are more elaborate than any but a few of the Kentish laws that have come down to us. The articles in his dooms, it is true, number seventy-six, as compared with Æthelberht's eighty-nine, but in modern type they run to twice the length. Even so, it is possible that the text of Ine's dooms, as it is preserved in the form of an annex to Alfred's dooms, has been purged of articles of which Alfred disapproved, and it may be that other articles have been edited and shortened.[1] But taking Ine's dooms as they stand, there is an evident tendency towards elaboration and detail as contrasted with Æthelberht's dooms. But this same tendency is to be seen in the later Kentish laws, notably in the doom relating to trading in London, and if we had the whole body of Kentish legislation from Æthelberht to Wihtred we might find greater similarity between Kent and Wessex than the existing texts show. The legislator is coming to understand his task better. Ine's legislation strikes one as more mature, less experimental in some ways, than the surviving body of Kentish law. The proportion of criminal law in Ine's dooms is much less than in Æthelberht's; the dooms giving privileges to the clergy or promoting Christianity, though conspicuous enough, are less prominent than in Wihtred's. The amount of civil law, too, is by contrast notable. We may note an article for the protection of orphans, in purpose, if not in terms, similar to the parallel article in the dooms of Hlothere and Eadric.[2] On trade there is an article which serves as a complement to the doom regarding purchases by Kentish men in London. The Wessex article shows us travelling traders, who are assumed to be likely to deal in stolen goods and are required to conduct their transactions before witnesses. There is no reason to suppose that cattle-dealers are particularly envisaged, for cattle thefts are the subject of a quite different article, which seems to have in view the unsettled conditions on the Welsh border.[3] The presence and proximity of the Welsh is reflected in a number of articles[4] and is a feature naturally absent from the Kentish laws. Again, there are a good many articles concerned with agriculture[5] which have no parallel in any of the surviving Kentish laws. Another article we may remark, to which there is no parallel in any surviving Kentish law, is one laying down penalties for desertion on active service.[6] On the whole Ine's dooms cover more ground more

[1] This seems to be a reasonable interpretation of Alfred's preamble, but the language is perhaps ambiguous.

[2] Hlothere and Eadric, cap. 6; Ine, cap. 38 (Liebermann, i.10, 104-6; Attenborough, pp. 18, 48).

[3] Ine, caps. 25, 46 (Liebermann, i.100, 108-10; Attenborough, pp. 44, 50).

[4] Ine, caps. 23, 24, 32, 33, 54, 74 (Liebermann, i.100, 102, 114, 120; Attenborough, pp. 42-6, 54, 60).

[5] Ine, caps. 40, 42-4, 49, 55-60, 64-9 (Liebermann, i.106-10, 114-18; Attenborough, pp. 48-58).

[6] Ine, cap. 51 (Liebermann, i.112; Attenborough, p. 52). It is not perhaps superfluous to remark that *fyrd* does not mean 'militia', as the word is commonly rendered, but *expeditio* or *exercitus* as it is translated into Latin by contemporaries: see Attenborough's note at p. 190 and our *Governance of Mediaeval England*, pp. 47-55.

elaborately than the surviving Kentish laws and, as we have said, appear to be more mature. But this is not true of the whole text. A block of clauses in the last third of it consists of laconic and obscure notes.[1] Some prescribe penalties for delicts, of which the first may suffice for an example – 'Up to a fortnight after Easter a ewe and lamb are valued at a shilling'.[2] Others relate to leases or tenancies of land, the hiring of oxen or even the appropriate time for sheep-shearing.[3] The contrast in styles is so marked that the inference seems justified that there has been an amalgamation of two or more texts of different dates and perhaps of different origin. To take the surviving texts of early Kentish and West Saxon legislation for what they purport to be – a single legislative act on a particular occasion – would be highly incautious. The preambles are no guarantee of the date or authenticity of all that follows. There are many proved examples in later centuries of the conflation of texts[4] to serve as a warning to those who handle these imperfect renderings of legislation of an earlier age.

With Ine legislation in Wessex comes to an end for two hundred years. We know from the preamble of Alfred's laws that Offa of Mercia,[5] who reigned between 757 and 796, had left a body of laws behind him, but if any of them were re-enacted by Alfred we are unable to disentangle them from his other dooms. Presumably, however, Mercian legislation resembled in general that of Kent and Wessex. It seems clear that Ine's laws were regarded as still in force in Wessex and we have independent testimony that Æthelberht's laws were still in force in Kent,[6] and the natural inference is that Offa's laws were still in force in Mercia, or at least in that part of Mercia which remained English. Alfred's intention appears then to have been to supersede these provincial laws, if we may so describe them, by a code of general application for the whole of his dominions. He professes to have taken the best from existing legislation and to have added little of his own[7]; but Ine's laws, or a great part of them, were specially preserved and added as a kind of supplement to Alfred's code.[8]

Alfred's legislation testifies more to his good will than to the competence of the royal clerks. The disaster of the Danish invasions and the resultant decay in learning left their mark in legislation as they did everywhere. We should hardly expect perhaps to find any clear distinction between religion, morals and law, but here we have greater

[1] Ine, caps. 55-69: cap. 62, which is different in character, seems to be misplaced (Liebermann, pp. 114-18; Attenborough, pp. 54-8).

[2] Ine, cap. 55.

[3] Ine, caps. 60, 63-9.

[4] This is evident in the collection of laws ascribed to Ethelred (below, p. 24). We have already mentioned the Statute of Merton as an example from the thirteenth century.

[5] Alfred, Introduction, cap. 49.9 (Liebermann, i.46; Attenborough, p. 62).

[6] This is the implication of the Old English translation of the passage in Book ii, chapter 5, of Bede's *Ecclesiastical History*, where it says of Æthelberht's laws 'þa nu gena oð þis mid him hæfde 7 haldne syndon': see Plummer's note, *Hist. Eccl.*, ii.87. The translation is non-Alfredian and is quite independent of Alfred's own statement.

[7] Alfred, Introduction, cap. 49.9, *ut supra*.

[8] As printed by Liebermann, 1.88-123.

confusion than in any earlier legislation or, fortunately, than in any later. Alfred begins with much direct translation from the Bible and with a declaration of the duty of subjects towards their temporal lords.[1] This brings him to his preamble, in which he explains the sources of the laws he is promulgating. From this preamble he passes to an injunction to all men to abide by their pledged word, then to sanctuary, the violation of the protection given by king, archbishop, bishop and ealdorman, to treason and conspiracy and then again to sanctuary. And so the dooms continue to flit from brawling in the king's presence to the abduction of nuns, the slaying of pregnant women, sexual offences, the unlawful burning and felling of timber, accidental deaths and so on.[2] The concluding half of the code is mainly filled with rates of compensation for private wrongs and personal injuries,[3] though there are interspersed articles on burgbryce, the alienation of bookland, keeping the peace and public holidays.[4] In all these provisions there is, as indeed Alfred himself said, little that is new. Some have seen in them a spirit of moderation and aversion from violence which would accord with what we know of Alfred's character; but the legislation is still that of a barbarous land and its benevolence does not descend to the slave. The slave may be castrated when the freeman escapes with a pecuniary penalty.[5] The Church's holidays are not for the slave or the unfree (*esne*)[6] and the slave is still subject to the lash.[7] We must not idealise the English of the ninth century, not even Alfred, though we may reflect that the slave fared little better under Roman law, even when that was mollified by the influence of Stoic and Christian teaching.[8]

Alfred's code is most significant as marking the beginning of a continuous era of legislation which helps to make the tenth century the most notable in the history of the Old English polity. There has survived, though too often in a confused and incomplete state, legislation of Edward the Elder, Athelstan, Edmund and Edgar. The laws of Ethelred and Cnut, which bridge the tenth and eleventh centuries, stand apart and are best discussed by themselves. By the reign of Edward the Alfredian revival of learning had clearly begun to do its work. Two sets of laws of his have come down to us. We cannot assign them to any particular year, though one set is clearly later than the other. They may both come from comparatively late in the reign,

[1] Liebermann, i.26-46. All this is omitted in Attenborough's edition.

[2] *Ibid.*, i.46-68; Attenborough, pp. 62-78.

[3] Alfred, caps. 35-77 (Liebermann, i.68-88; Attenborough, pp. 78-92).

[4] Alfred, caps. 40-3.

[5] Alfred, cap. 25.

[6] Alfred, cap. 43.

[7] This follows since Ine's law was preserved which prescribed scourging for a slave who worked on Sunday (Ine, cap. 3). The unfree were subject to the same punishment for this offence in Kent (Wihtred, cap. 12). This is one of the points of resemblance between Kentish and West Saxon law.

[8] For the gradual amelioration of the legal position of the slave in Rome see Buckland, *Text-book of Roman Law*, pp. 61-86, and his *Roman Law of Slavery*, pp. 36-8.

which did not end until 924.[1] It will be borne in mind that Alfred's codification of the law, for such it may justifiably be called, was comparatively recent, whether we date it a few years before or after 890,[2] and a supplement to this *domboc*, as it is termed by Edward,[3] cannot have been regarded as a matter of urgency. When these supplements came, they were brief and were notably more skilfully drafted than earlier legislation. The first set of laws, after a general exhortation to reeves to do justice indifferently and in accordance with the *domboc*, and, in particular, to set down a precise date for the hearing of actions, deals with three matters only. First there are detailed regulations aimed at confining trading to towns in the presence of the portreeve: livestock, which were particularly liable to theft, are principally in view. The second law deals with what a later age will know as disseisin. Nothing is said regarding procedure except that, in the event of a successful action by the plaintiff and a refusal by the tenant to comply with the judgement of the court, he is to incur successive fines until he does. The third law is a brief provision that convicted perjurers shall not be able in future to clear themselves by oath, but must submit to the ordeal. It will be remarked that the new laws are concerned solely with procedure. The preamble shows that they were circulated to all the king's reeves, who were assumed to have already by them the Alfredian *domboc*. The second set of laws is also procedural. The preamble deplores that the previous laws had not been well observed. The further measures now taken require the holding of a court – the equivalent of the later hundred court – every four weeks and the fixing of precise dates for the hearing of actions. In cases of disseisin, if the reeve neglects to enforce a judgement in the plaintiff's favour, he is himself liable to a heavy fine. The remaining provisions elaborate the measures to be taken for combating the prevalent, and evidently organised, crime of cattle-stealing. These provisions are of particular interest because they are extended to East Anglia and Northumbria: this is the first step in making the laws of the king of Wessex cover the whole of England.

[1] For the texts of I Edward and II Edward, as they are known, see Liebermann, i.138-44, and Attenborough, pp. 114-20. Liebermann (iii.92-3) argued, on other grounds than ours, for a late date in the reign for II Edward: Attenborough (pp. 205-6) is inclined to demur.

[2] Liebermann (iii.34-5) argued for the years 892-3 as the date of promulgation; but Attenborough (p. 35) suggests that this is too late. The procedure described in the preamble (above, p. 15), involving the collection of copies of earlier laws and their collation, indicates that a considerable time elapsed, perhaps years, between the initiation of the scheme and its completion. The use of such a word as 'promulgation' may be misleading. There was probably no formal act, but the circulation of copies of the code to ealdormen, reeves and bishops with a covering epistle, very much as the Gregorian Decretals (intended to supersede earlier collections of decretals) were circulated to universities in the thirteenth century. In this case the covering epistle, *Rex pacificus*, has come down to us, and it is prefixed to the printed editions (ed. Friedberg, *Corpus Iuris Canonici*, ii.1-2). In speculating upon ninth-century procedure there must be a large element of conjecture; but we know something of the circulation of the Alfredian Chronicle and translations and also of the laws of other kings (below, pp. 18-27).

[3] I Edward, Preamble; II Edward, cap. 5 (Liebermann, i.138, 142; Attenborough, pp. 114, 120).

For Athelstan's short reign, 925 to 939, we have a remarkable amount of legislation, though what remains is but part of the whole.[1] Not only is it remarkable in extent but in its nature. It includes the first social legislation in England, providing for the relief of the poor, and, what is equally noteworthy in another way, two examples of subordinate legislation. The poor law, as we may justifiably call it, is in the form of a writ addressed to the king's reeves and requires them to provide, from the rents of the royal demesne, food and clothing for one destitute man and also to manumit every year one man who has been reduced to penal slavery. A reeve who fails in this duty is to find thirty shillings to be distributed among the poor under the bishop's supervision.[2] This is not general legislation, and there is not even an exhortation to noblemen to follow suit, but since royal estates were well distributed in southern England, it was at least a notable gesture. The subordinate legislation is in both cases the application of general legislation to localities, in the one case to the shire of Kent, in the other to the burghal district of London. Both pieces of legislation – perhaps by-laws or regulations would be a better word – are enacted by bishops and thegns in an assembly which prefigures the future county court, and both are subject to royal approval. They are concerned primarily with keeping the peace. The Kentish regulations are embodied in a letter to the king. They have some irrelevances, or what would appear so to us: the king is thanked for his legislation on tithes, while another article merely expresses agreement with his prohibition of the use of sheepskin for covering shields. The operative regulations begin with a general act of indemnity (as we may perhaps call it) for past crimes and then provide that no man shall leave one lord for another without permission, that every lord, by himself or his reeves, shall be responsible for bringing his own men to justice and that over-mighty subjects shall be exiled by the king.[3] The London regulations are more detailed and are upon another plan.[4] They begin with a statement of the law to be enforced, as the local legislators apprehend it, and then proceed to detailed provisions for an organisation to enforce the law. This organisation is the well-known 'frithgild' – or rather frithgilds, for the word is in the plural – devised as a means for policing the large area, covering Middlesex, Surrey east of the Wey and parts of the present counties of Essex and Kent, which seemingly constituted the burghal district.[5] For the purpose of administration the area was divided into shires; at the head of each was a reeve[6]; and within each shire there

[1] Liebermann, i.146-83; Attenborough, pp. 122-72. Liebermann endeavours to place the laws in chronological order. Attenborough follows the conventional numerical order.

[2] Liebermann, i.148; Attenborough, p. 126.

[3] III Athelstan: Liebermann, i.170; Attenborough, pp. 142-6.

[4] VI Athelstan: Liebermann, i.173-83; Attenborough, pp. 156-72.

[5] Richardson and Sayles, *Governance of Mediaeval England*, p. 24.

[6] This seems to be the necessary interpretation of the references to shire and reeve in VI Athelstan, cap. 8.2-4 and cap. 10. The shire in this sense may well be represented by the later hundred, but the hundred, *hynden*, in the present context (*ibid.*, cap. 3) appears to mean ten tithings, that is groups of ten men.

was constituted an association or 'gild', required to act in co-operation with the gilds in the neighbouring shires. The reeve was the executive head and the members of the association acted as the hue and cry did in later centuries. The object of the regulations was twofold, to repress the organised stealing of livestock – horses, cattle, pigs, sheep, even slaves – and to provide compensation for losses that could not be recovered. There is much that is obscure in the regulations as they have come down to us and we can but present in outline what seems a reasonable and consistent interpretation of them. However, for our present purpose, the importance of this subordinate legislation does not lie so much in its content as in the light it throws upon the structure of government and the administration of the law.

Despite its bulk, Athelstan's legislation is not impressive. The texts that have come down to us do not, it is true, adequately represent the originals and some are known to us only in an indifferent Latin translation. But the drafting is generally poor and the clauses are arranged awkwardly and inconsequently. Frequent councils seem to have been held. The laws themselves speak of councils at Grately (Hants), Exeter, Faversham, Thundersfield (Surrey) and Whittlebury (Northants),[1] but the legislation is repetitive and ill-considered. Trading outside a town or on Sunday is prohibited at one council and at another council these prohibitions are removed.[2] At one time any petty thief over twelve years old is liable to the death penalty, but, on mature consideration, the age limit is raised to fifteen.[3] The impression given by Athelstan's legislation as a whole is that of a well-meaning but rather irresolute and weak government, with an uncertain purpose, which cannot command the ready obedience of its officers and cannot command enough force to crush the disorder and lawlessness which is widespread over southern England. Want of governance is writ large in the texts. If this picture seems to contrast with the picture we might draw from other sources, of a victorious king who brought the Welsh, the Norsemen of York and Northumbria into subjection and quelled the king of Scots,[4] there is not, in fact, any incompatibility. Athelstan's necessary preoccupation with warfare on his western and northern borders must inevitably have diverted his energies and weakened the internal administration of his kingdom. There is, we may remark in passing, nothing to suggest that his legislation was intended to be effective beyond the Humber, and his hold upon the North soon proved to be insecure. Athelstan's impotence at home finds expression not only in his lamentations that the laws for keeping the peace that were promulgated at his first great council at Grately have not been observed,[5] but also in the savagery of the penalties he pre-

[1] For these five councils see *ibid.*, caps. 10, 12.
[2] II Athelstan, caps. 12, 13, 24.1; IV Athelstan, cap. 2.
[3] II Athelstan, cap. 1; VI Athelstan, caps. 1.1, 12.1.
[4] Stenton, *Anglo-Saxon England*, pp. 335-9.
[5] IV Athelstan, caps. 1, 2; V Athelstan, cap. 1.

scribed. The death penalty at twelve years of age is but one example. The more powerful protectors of criminals are threatened with exile to another part of the kingdom, together with their families, and the penalty for returning is death.[1] The harbourer of a criminal is to be slain, and if a free woman harbours a criminal she is to be cast down from a cliff or drowned. If a male slave steals he is to be stoned to death by eighty of his fellows, who are each to contribute threepence to make up the price of a replacement for the slain man. For a like offence a woman is to be put to death by burning: eighty female slaves are to make up the pile of logs and each is to contribute threepence for the purchase price of a substitute for the victim.[2] Here we have a grim reminder that Athelstan's wars brought many slaves to the slave-market. Southern England must have been copiously supplied in his day.

But withal there is another aspect to his legislation, and his poor law is not so much in contrast with his penal law as our description might suggest. Trade, as we have said, was regulated, if precipitately and unwisely in some respects. Precautions are laid down to prevent illicit cattle-dealing and to protect innocent transactions.[3] And in Athelstan's laws we have the earliest legislation governing coinage. No one is to mint money save with the king's authority, and mints are confined to boroughs. A fraudulent moneyer is to lose his right hand.[4] Other laws regulate the making of shields and the export of horses.[5] Attendance at the communal courts is made compulsory.[6] These provisions are very much of a jumble and some are obscure,[7] but they are, in their way, indicative that in spite of continual wars and disorder there is some progress in the ways of peace. Nor should we forget Athelstan's ecclesiastical legislation, which seems to have formed a prologue to the Grately ordinances.[8] Its main object is to compel the payment of tithes, churchscot and soulscot, not by ecclesiastical censures but by the civil power. Apart from this, Athelstan's legislation is secular. There is in the background Alfred's *domboc*, and that contains ecclesiastical legislation in plenty.

For the brief reign of Edmund, who followed his brother Athelstan to the throne in 939, three short series of laws have survived.[9] The first

[1] IV Athelstan, cap. 3; V Athelstan, caps. 1.1, 2.

[2] IV Athelstan, cap. 6.3-7.

[3] II Athelstan, caps. 9, 10, 24; V Athelstan, cap. 2. The local regulations in VI Athelstan have cattle largely, though not exclusively, in view (above, p. 19).

[4] II Athelstan, cap. 14.

[5] *Ibid.*, caps. 15, 18.

[6] *Ibid.*, cap. 20.

[7] We have particularly in view cap. 16, providing that two well-horsed men shall be furnished for each ploughland (or hide). This apparently refers to the common duty of following thieves (cf. VI Athelstan, cap. 5), though it has, erroneously we think, been taken as referring to service with a fyrd (Liebermann, *Gesetze*, ii.499, *s.v.* Heer, c. 3; Attenborough, p. 208).

[8] I Athelstan: see Liebermann's comments in *Gesetze*, iii.96-7.

[9] Liebermann, i.184-91; Robertson, *The Laws of the Kings of England from Edmund to Henry I*, pp. 6-14.

is purely ecclesiastical and need not detain us. The next in order of date appears to be that rated as the third. It is concerned solely with measures against theft. These measures have in them little that is new, but the savage punishment for thieving slaves decreed by Athelstan[1] seems tacitly to be abandoned. The only article that concerns them is one dealing with organised thefts by parties of slaves: the ringleader is to suffer death, but the others are to be punished with three floggings and are then to be branded as thieves by having part of the scalp removed.[2] The series rated the second, but apparently the latest, begins, not unexpectedly, by deploring the lawlessness of the country,[3] though a later article – which furnishes an indication of the relative date[4] – gives thanks to God and the whole people for the freedom from thefts now enjoyed by the country.[5] The inference clearly is that earlier laws against organised theft have been effective and have been resolutely enforced: the theme now is violence and the bloodfeud which must be repressed.[6] There is no record of any legislation by Edred or Edwy who succeeded Edmund. This does not necessarily mean that these kings did not issue laws but, if they were of no more significance than Edmund's, little regard might have been given to them. We must remember that we have no systematic corpus of laws after Alfred's *domboc* and that all that has come down to us is a number of imperfect and confused collections, all apparently of private origin, brought together upon no plan we can discern.

Of Edgar's legislation four series of laws have survived.[7] The second is ecclesiastical and contains nothing to our purpose. The others are of greater consequence, but more for the light they shed upon administration in the mid-tenth century than for any development of substantive law. It is doubtful whether there had been any marked development in the administration of the hundred since the time of Edmund, in one of whose laws there is a reference to the hundred that indicates a high degree of organisation. Fines could hardly have been paid to the hundred unless there had been a hundred moot and a hundred reeve.[8] And to judge from the earlier London regulations, there had been no drastic re-organisation since Athelstan's day: though the areas over which the reeves have jurisdiction are not there called hundreds or by any other specific name, their resemblance to the later hundreds is unmistakable.[9] In what seems to be his earliest

[1] Above, p. 20. [2] III Edmund, cap. 4. [3] II Edmund, Preamble.

[4] Liebermann (*Gesetze*, iii.128-9) leaves open the question of the priority of III Edmund, but does not notice the significance of this article. In the earlier recension of *Quadripartitus*, moreover, III comes between I and II (Liebermann, *Quadripartitus*, p. 66).

[5] II Edmund, cap. 5.

[6] *Ibid.*, caps. 1-4, 6-7.

[7] Liebermann, i.192-215; Robertson, *ut supra*, pp. 16-38.

[8] III Edmund, cap. 2.

[9] VI Athelstan, caps. 3, 8, 10. The reeves are at the head of 'shires', but not, of course, shires in the same sense as the shire of Kent or the shire of Edgar's law. It can hardly be supposed, however, that the *hyndenman* of VI Athelstan, cap. 8.1, differs greatly from the *hundredesman* of I Edgar, cap. 2. See also p. 18, n. 6, above.

legislation Edgar lays it down that the hundred moot is to assemble without fail every four weeks[1] and in a subsequent article a penalty is prescribed for failure to attend.[2] How far these prescriptions are new we do not know. It is probable that they do no more than give precision to what was already a loosely accepted rule,[3] and, apart from these two articles, the ordinance contains nothing more than variations upon the old theme of the pursuit and apprehension of cattle thieves.[4] It is a later law that introduces us to something apparently new when it speaks of the shiremoot which is to meet twice a year and is to be attended by the bishop of the diocese and the ealdorman[5]: the provision that this court is to have jurisdiction in both ecclesiastical and secular causes cannot, however, be exactly new, for earlier ecclesiastical legislation clearly envisages the intervention of royal reeves.[6] Nor can the shire moot be exactly new, for we hear of the shire of Kent under Athelstan and of a moot at which bishops and thegns are present.[7] But this ordinance does seem to mark the emergence of the shire, in the modern sense, from the burghal districts of southern England in the earlier tenth century. The borough is regarded as an administrative unit distinct from the shire; but the language of the law that requires the boroughmoot to meet three times a year carries with it the implication that such courts are already in existence.[8] They may now be regulated, but no more than the hundred courts are they new creations. As we have said, the shire moot is no new creation either, and its prior existence is implied in another law of Edgar's where he claims in every borough and in every shire the same royal rights as his father, Edmund.[9] So far as Edgar was an innovator, it was in administration and his innovations were confined to southern England. The Danes live very much under their own laws and their territorial division is not the hundred but the wapentake, which is equated with the borough for purposes of administration.[10] The Norsemen of York have perhaps a yet larger measure of independence under their own earl.[11] To a lesser degree this is true also of Mercia and East Anglia, to whose ealdormen copies of Edgar's legislation are sent in order that it may be made known generally in their provinces.[12] Edgar is not the direct lord of all England and he himself distinguishes between legislation applying only to the English and legislation applying to the whole nation,

[1] I Edgar, cap. 1. The moot is not expressly named here, but it is in cap. 7.
[2] I Edgar, cap. 7.
[3] Edgar repeats, in effect, II Edward, cap. 8: see p. 17 above.
[4] I Edgar, caps. 2-6. Caps. 8 and 9 are no part of the original text: see above, p. 13, n. 4.
[5] III Edgar, cap. 5.
[6] Above, p. 20.
[7] III Athelstan: see above, p. 18.
[8] The portreeve is mentioned in I Edward, cap. 1, and II Athelstan, cap. 12. This officer appears to be distinct from other royal reeves; but nothing is said of any court held by him.
[9] IV Edgar, cap. 2a.
[10] *Ibid.*, cap. 2a.1, 6, 12.
[11] *Ibid.*, cap. 15.
[12] *Ibid.*, cap. 15.1.

English, Danes and Britons, as he puts it.[1] English administration and English law have as yet proceeded only a few steps towards unification.

When we pass from the framework of administration to the law to be administered, the only notable item in Edgar's legislation is the provision for uniform standards of money, weights and measures throughout the kingdom,[2] though this was an ideal rather than a practical legislative act. The main theme of his laws is the old one of the repression of cattle-stealing and illicit cattle-dealing. Whether the elaborate provision of panels of 'witnesses', or local inspectors as we should call them, in boroughs and hundreds and all the other precautions enjoined[3] were in the least effective we can but speculate. Like uniform weights and measures, enforcement depended upon local initiative, and the good intentions of Edgar and his counsellors seem rather remote from practical application. If we take this pessimistic view, how then can we account for the esteem in which later generations held Edgar's laws? It was a condition of Cnut's peaceful acceptance as king of England that Edgar's laws should be observed, and Cnut more than once confirmed his undertaking.[4] It has been thought that this agreement meant no more than that the legal relationships between Danes and English that had obtained under Edgar should be observed,[5] but this seems to be too narrow an interpretation. It would appear rather that Englishmen under a foreign king looked back upon Edgar's reign as Englishmen under Henry I looked back upon the reign of Edward the Confessor, and that Cnut granted them Edgar's laws[6] as Henry granted them Edward's laws.[7] But Edward had been no legislator, nor is it likely that Edgar's administrative reforms, which seem to us the most noteworthy of his lawgiving, were remembered with gratitude fifty years later. But just as Edward's laws meant the whole body of pre-Conquest English law, so Edgar's laws surely meant the whole body of English law in force in his time, including in especial perhaps Alfred's *domboc*, which Edgar himself mentions in his laws as the great authority.[8] The miserable reign of Ethelred was ignored[9] very much as the miserable reign of Stephen was ignored by Henry II, who persistently looked back to the reign of Henry I for his

[1] *Ibid.*, cap. 2a.2.
[2] III Edgar, cap. 8.
[3] IV Edgar, caps. 3-11.
[4] Anglo-Saxon Chronicle D, *s.a.* 1018 (Thorpe, i.286; Plummer, i.154); Cnut's proclamation of 1020, cap. 13 (Liebermann, i.274; Robertson, p. 142); and the D version of I Cnut, cap. 1 (Liebermann, i.278: cf. *ibid.*, iii.198).
[5] Stenton, *Anglo-Saxon England*, p. 393.
[6] This has been the usual interpretation: see Plummer, ii.202, and Liebermann, iii.198.
[7] 'Lagam Eadwardi regis vobis reddo' (Liebermann, i.522; *Select Charters*, p. 119).
[8] II Edgar, caps. 3, 5.
[9] Cf. *Leges Edwardi Confessoris*, cap. 34.3: 'Sed postquam Eadwardus rex venit ad regnum, consilio baronum regni, legem dimissam, quia honesta videbatur eis et quia avus eam constituerat, fecit eam reparare et confirmare, et sic vocata est lex regis Ædwardi, que dimissa erat a morte Eadgari avi sui usque ad suum tempus' (Liebermann, i.663).

precedents.[1] There had never been a greater English king than Edgar – and the more we learn of him, the more we perceive the justice of contemporary opinion[2] – but it was not for his legislation that he was distinguished.

Edgar's death in 975, at the age of thirty-two, was an unmitigated calamity for England. Neither of the two sons who succeeded him was an effective ruler. Of any promise shown by the first of the two, Edward the Martyr, it is impossible to speak, for what we are told of him is largely hagiography. In 978, before he had reached manhood, he was murdered by the followers of his stepbrother Ethelred or maybe of his stepmother, Edgar's queen, Ælfthryth.[3] He left no legislation behind him and there is no reason to suppose that any was issued during his brief reign. On the other hand, his brother Ethelred, who was still a child when he succeeded, legislated more frequently in the thirty-seven or thirty-eight years of his reign than any previous king. The whole body of his legislation has not come down to us and what does survive is disordered and corrupt.[4] It is evident that, earlier than any legislation that has survived, Ethelred held an important council at an unidentified place (called Bromdun in his laws), where noteworthy decisions were taken[5]; but what these decisions were and what form they took are unknown. Then let us remark that the document numbered II Ethelred is a composite one. The first part is a treaty between Ethelred and Olaf Tryggvason, agreed late in 991, while the second part is an anonymous piece of legislation that might come from any time in the second half of the tenth century,[6] though we incline to believe it to be rightly attributed to Ethelred's reign. IV Ethelred, which survives only in a poor Latin rendering, is also a composite document. Of the first part, which consists of replies to an inquest in London, we shall speak later. The second part does not seem, as has

[1] Cf. Richardson and Sayles, *Governance of Mediaeval England*, pp. 89, 227. In his charters Henry invariably omits any reference to Stephen and, where it is necessary to refer to past grants, he mentions his grandfather. There was little enough law of his predecessors to which he found occasion to refer, but he finds it necessary to do so in the case of the law of the forest and then he refers to his grandfather (*ibid.*, p. 446).

[2] Edgar has been particularly unfortunate in the treatment accorded him by modern historians, who have misunderstood some part of the evidence and apparently overlooked another part (*ibid.*, pp. 42-5, 399-412). For contemporary or sub-contemporary opinion see the verses in Anglo-Saxon Chronicle E (Thorpe, i.227; Plummer, i.114-15), verses from which apparently Ælfric borrowed (Plummer, ii.152-3), though elsewhere, as in his story of the eight tributory kings, he had independent sources of information (Richardson and Sayles, *op cit.*, p. 43*n*). Plummer, *loc. cit.*, effectively disposes of the idea that Edgar's vices, deplored in the verses in Chronicle E, were moral failings: the poet objected, as many others did, to Edgar's admiration for foreign customs, especially foreign monasticism. See also VIII Ethelred, caps. 37, 43, and the *Vita Oswaldi*, p. 448. Other references to the same purport are given by Plummer, ii.164-5.

[3] Apart from the reticent Anglo-Saxon Chronicle, our most reliable source of information is the sub-contemporary *Vita Oswaldi* (pp. 448-52). It seems unlikely that Ælfthryth was an accessory to the murder. For ten years she had been Edgar's co-adjutrix in monastic reform and no evil is spoken of her by a contemporary: cf. Richardson and Sayles, *op. cit.*, pp. 401-4.

[4] Liebermann, i.216-70; Robertson, pp. 52-132.

[5] I Ethelred, cap. 1.2; III Ethelred, cap. 4.

[6] It is marked as an addition by Liebermann, i.224: for its date see *ibid.*, iii.155.

been supposed, to have any specific connexion with London but is a piece of general legislation.[1] So far as the legislative acts known as I-IV Ethelred can be dated, they appear to be all before the year 1000.[2] They constitute a recognisable group and they are all secular in character. The remaining legislative acts of Ethelred's reign, six in all – two being fragmentary – form a separate group. They are all pietistic and appear to fall between the years 1008 and 1014.[3] We need do no more than consider each group briefly in turn.

The first group is, as we have said, secular: I and III Ethelred are complementary, the former intended for those parts of England under English law and the latter for the Danelaw. They are concerned with keeping the peace and the prevention of crime, especially theft. In the legislation for the Danelaw there are, in addition, some articles regarding coining and transactions in land and there are the well-known articles providing for a court in each wapentake, with a body of twelve thegns to act as a jury both of presentment and trial.[4] Though there has been reluctance to admit any connexion between these latter articles and the English jury of post-Conquest times, the intention of the legislation for the Danelaw seems as a whole to be so plainly the extension to it of English institutions that there can hardly be room for the supposition that in this one particular the intention is to preserve a Norse custom and not to introduce an English institution. But the point in dispute need not be argued here.[5] The legislative portion of II Ethelred is concerned solely with what a later age will call vouching to warranty, and the procedure is detailed in a manner remarkable for the period from which it comes, whether the articles are rightly attributed to Ethelred or not. The drafting is elaborate and skilful and of a standard rarely met elsewhere. The legislative portion of IV Ethelred is also elaborate and may come from the same hand. A fair judgement is impossible since the translation into Latin, the only form in which it has come down to us, is careless and obscure.[6] The legislation is mainly concerned with maintaining the standard of the money in circulation and must be read in connexion with the brief articles regarding coinage in III Ethelred.[7] But in IV Ethelred the drafting was evidently very careful and detailed and the law applies to both Danes and English. The remaining articles are concerned with the payment of tolls, forcible entry and assault. Taking these two series of articles together –

[1] Below, p. 25.

[2] For a discussion of dates see Liebermann, iii.146, 150, 155-6, 162.

[3] *Ibid.*, pp. 167, 169, 178-9, 181, 185.

[4] III Ethelred, caps. 3.1, 13.2.

[5] Even though we call the twelve thegns of the Danelaw 'lawmen' (cf. Robertson, pp. 319-20), they are not for this reason distinct from the later jury (Richardson and Sayles, *op. cit.*, pp. 182-5, 207).

[6] Liebermann (iii.165-6) did his best to clarify and explain the text. He did not, however, take the view, as we have done, that caps. 3-9 were, in the original, a self-contained royal ordinance. By dividing the text in this way, we are, we think, enabled to arrive at a better interpretation, though not all the inconsistencies of the Latin can be resolved.

[7] III Ethelred, caps. 8, 16.

the legislative portions of II and IV Ethelred – it is fair to say that as mere exercises in legislative drafting nothing quite so competent had been known in England nor was to be known again until the thirteenth century.

Of the second group of Ethelredian enactments it is difficult for us, with our hindsight, to judge fairly. We know Ethelred to have been such a deplorable ruler, incompetent and treacherous, that the very pietistic tone of these later ordinances gives us the worst possible impression. But let us endeavour to be fair. The same pietistic tone will be found in one of Edgar's preambles: the plague which has afflicted and devastated the people has been merited because of their sin and their disobedience to God's commands.[1] We must remember that these ordinances of Ethelred's were meant to be read out at public assemblies, presumably the hundred courts, to a grievously tried people, who were withstanding as best they might – and it was not always a very good best – the horrors so graphically described by Wulfstan, who had no small hand in drafting these very ordinances.[2] If we are more than a little repelled by those churchmen who seize the occasion for the constant reiteration of the duty of all men to pay their church dues, all with the appropriate date – plough-alms a fortnight after Easter, tithes of livestock at Whitsun, tithes of crops at All Hallows, Peter's Pence by St Peter's Day, light dues thrice a year, soulscot before the grave is closed[3] – let us, in charity, concede that these dues are conceived as owing not only to those in God's service but to God Himself. In every way God is to be appeased, by fastings and prayers and the strictest of religious observances. The unquiet spirit of the martyred Edward is to be appeased too by giving him a day in the calendar of saints.[4] At the festivals of the Church there shall be peace and concord among all Christian men and all secular debts shall be paid.[5] Christians who have been enslaved are not to be sold overseas, especially to the heathen. . . .[6] We need not continue the homily. Affairs of State have no great place, but they do creep in. Ships for the great naval effort the king is making should be ready at Eastertide.[7] Desertion in face of the enemy may be punished with death,[8] and death is to be the reward for treason.[9] Legal trickery is to come to an end.[10]

The themes are invariable, though the wording and content of the ordinances vary. At one time the clergy are exhorted in many words to

[1] IV Edgar, Preamble, cap. I.

[2] For Wulfstan's part in Ethelred's legislation see Whitelock in *Trans. R. Hist. Soc.*, 4th Ser., xxiv. 35-8.

[3] V Ethelred, caps. 11, 12. It should be noted that VI Ethelred presents a parallel text to V Ethelred, both presumably derived from legislation on the same occasion, Whitsuntide 1008, at Knight's Enham (Liebermann, *Gesetze*, i.236, 247; iii.167).

[4] *Ibid.*, cap. 16. [5] *Ibid.*, caps. 19-20. [6] *Ibid.*, cap. 2.

[7] *Ibid.*, cap. 27. The inference must be that these are the ships mentioned in *Anglo-Saxon Chronicle*, s.a. 1008-9 (Plummer, p. 138).

[8] *Ibid.*, cap. 28. [9] *Ibid.*, cap. 30. [10] *Ibid.*, cap. 32.

practise celibacy[1]; the rules of Christian marriage are set forth[2]; Christian men are not to be condemned to death for trivial offences[3]; the standard of the coinage, weights and measures is to be maintained; national defence is to be safeguarded by the repair of fortresses and bridges, by military and naval preparations.[4] At other times masses against the heathen are ordered[5]; there is to be compulsory fasting and almsgiving[6]; theft is forbidden[7]; homicide is not to be committed in consecrated places[8]; tithes are apportioned between the fabric of the church, the clergy and the poor.[9] One can but pick and choose to illustrate the incoherence of these ordinances, their lack of practicability, the admixture of ecclesiastical discipline, charity and secular obligations. Legislation was never so loquacious, so vague or so futile.[10] The contrast between these ordinances and the high standard of the best of the legislation of the earlier years of Ethelred's reign is marked and painful.

As we have said, Cnut's acceptance as king of England was accompanied by his acceptance of Edgar's laws.[11] He did, however, issue a code of his own, which may have been intended as a clarification of the laws which he had accepted in general terms. It was promulgated at a council at Winchester at a Christmas feast in an uncertain year but not earlier than 1020.[12] There seems to be little, if anything, that is new in it, though some of the articles are not to be found in any earlier legislation that has come down to us. Unfortunately, although Cnut had implicitly set aside the legislation of Ethelred, the draftsmanship of his code bears a good many marks of the handiwork of his predecessor's draftsmen and borrows not a few articles from Ethelred's doleful ordinances. The first part of the code is ecclesiastical, the second secular, and it is the secular part that has the greater interest. We may notice the prohibition of heathen worship,[13] still rife and doubtless reinforced by the influx of Norsemen, the statement of the rights of the Crown in Wessex, Mercia and the Danelaw respectively[14] and the tariff for heriots.[15] There is little more that it would be profitable to say of Cnut's code in this place.[16] It is the last legislation of the Old English

1 vi Ethelred, caps. 1-5, 41.

2 *Ibid.*, cap. 12.

3 *Ibid.*, cap. 10. This is an elaboration of v Ethelred, cap. 5.

4 vi Ethelred, caps. 32-5: an elaboration of v Ethelred, caps. 26.1, 27, 28.

5 vii Ethelred (Latin), cap. 3.

6 *Ibid.*, caps. 1, 2.

7 *Ibid.*, cap. 6.

8 viii Ethelred, cap. 1. 9 *Ibid.*, cap. 6.

10 The language of this series of laws has a close parallel in the language of the royal charters coming from the same period: for these see Stenton, *Latin Charters of the Anglo-Saxon Period*, pp. 74-82.

11 Above, p. 23.

12 Liebermann, i.278-371; Robertson, pp. 154-218. The date is discussed by Liebermann (*Gesetze*, iii.194) and Whitelock (*Eng. Hist. Rev.*, lxiii.450-52).

13 ii Cnut, cap. 5.1.

14 *Ibid.*, caps. 12-15.

15 *Ibid.*, caps. 70-1. This is a good example of legislation merely declaratory of the existing law: cf. Richardson and Sayles, *Governance of Mediaeval England*, pp. 59, 128.

16 See below, pp. 45-6.

kings: it sums up all past laws. His few Danish and English successors will promulgate no new laws: perhaps it was thought that all that was required had been done. Certainly his legislation had great respect and great influence in the twelfth century.

Before, however, we take our leave of the Old English polity, there are some final words we would say. In our next chapter we shall have need to emphasise the continuity of English law, despite foreign conquest, and we would emphasise here that it was not only in the written law that we may see continuity, but in every aspect of government. We have remarked without comment the document which provides the first two articles of the fourth series of laws attributed to Ethelred. There is no unity, let us emphasise, in this series of so-called laws. We know them, as we have said, only in an unsatisfactory and obscure Latin translation, though this makes clear enough that these two first articles are not legislation at all and are quite distinct from what follows. These articles are, in fact, the replies to an inquest into the customs of London made about the year 1000.[1] The importance of this document for London history is well recognised: we believe it to be important for quite another reason. It shows the king directing an enquiry to be held very much like the enquiries held by the Domesday commissioners. It is clear that those commissioners must have enquired of many towns 'What are your customs?', and here we have a similar enquiry made of the Londoners by King Ethelred. In Domesday Book we have nothing from London; but if chance were to bring this missing section to light, we should not be surprised to find there entries such as these replies. Nor do we think that we ought to be surprised to find this fragment coming from ninety years or so earlier, though we may be surprised at the odd context in which it is found. We have here conclusive evidence that, as in other matters of public administration, the Old English kings anticipated their Norman successors and in a field which has been supposed to exhibit the singularity of Norman genius. True it is that the Domesday enquiries were on a vaster scale and that the results have, for the most part, been happily preserved. But it was an isolated and barren effort. There was not another such enquiry until 1170 when there was held the great but abortive Inquest of Sheriffs. It has left behind it but tantalising fragments,[2] and yet these fragments represent a nation-wide undertaking: with only the London fragment before us, we must not rashly conclude that King Ethelred's enquiries were confined to just one borough.

That is one lesson in continuity we would bring home. Another is that there is sufficient evidence to show that the legislation of the kings of the tenth and early eleventh centuries was commonly promulgated at councils held at the principal Church festivals. We have just seen

[1] For this date see Liebermann, iii.162.

[2] Richardson and Sayles, *Select Cases of Procedure without Writ*, pp. xxvi-xxviii.

Cnut issuing his great code one Christmastide at Winchester. Imperfect as our sources are, we may see his predecessors acting in like manner.[1] Now this evidence links up with the evidence recently brought to light that at these same festivals the English kings held solemn crown-wearings and that King William was no innovator in this matter, bringing in an outlandish custom from France.[2] William was no legislator. But we shall see his successors in the twelfth century legislating at great councils held on the occasion of solemn crown-wearings, exactly as the Old English kings had done.[3] We could suggest other lessons in continuity – in the shire and hundred courts, in the jury, in the king's revenue. But of these things we have said something elsewhere[4] and we need not add to this long chapter.

[1] There is direct evidence in the case of Ethelred, who legislated at Whitsuntide in 1008 (above, p. 26, n. 3); but the fact that the witan met regularly at Christmas, Easter and Whitsuntide carries the same implication (Liebermann, *National Assembly*, p. 49).

[2] Richardson and Sayles, *Governance of Mediaeval England*, pp. 405-11.

[3] Below, pp. 31, 33, 93.

[4] *Op. cit.*, pp. 156-250.

II

THE CONQUEST AND ITS CONSEQUENCES

By the inscrutable judgement of God the barbarian conquered on the field of Hastings. The Normans were without learning, without literature, without written law. Civilisation among them was represented by the Jews of Rouen and the Lombards and Lotharingians in the ranks of the higher clergy.[1] Had they known it, they had a long and toilsome climb before they reached the level of the law-making and legislation of the Old English kingdom. But they had no appreciation of such high matters: they were ignorant enough to despise the English.[2] Having, however, no alternative, they continued the system of administration they found in the conquered land and with it, inevitably, the English system of law, though not without some barbaric admixture of their own.

In the field of legislation the reigns of the first two Norman kings were – one might say, naturally enough – barren. The Conqueror has indeed been credited by modern scholars with three pieces of legislation.[3] One, however, is merely a writ addressed to the bishop and port-reeve of London – both, by the way, Normans. It is only by an abuse of language that this writ is categorised as a law or as legislation. It assures both the ecclesiastical and secular authorities that the Londoners will continue to live under the same laws as in King Edward's day, that no Londoner would be disinherited and that the king would protect them. Another writ, which perhaps has rather more claim to be ranked as legislation, though it is, in fact, an administrative decree, announces the withdrawal of ecclesiastical jurisdiction from the hundred courts and the exclusive jurisdiction of the bishop in ecclesiastical causes. The third piece of legislation, which also takes the form of a writ, deals with the procedure between an Englishman and a Frenchman. An Englishman is permitted to decline combat in criminal actions except in causes leading to outlawry, but even there the Frenchman may be forced to defend himself by compurgation. This is the only item of the three that was regarded as legislative in the twelfth century, when it was included in the legal collection known as *Quadri-*

[1] Richardson and Sayles, *Governance of Mediaeval England*, p. 27. Douglas, *William the Conqueror*, pp. 105-32, makes the best case he can for the Norman Church, but the basic facts are stated at pp. 118-19 and 130 *n.* 3.

[2] This prejudice continued until the reign of Henry II as shown by the well-known story of Richard de Lucy who, so the Battle Abbey chronicler alleged, protested at the indignity that disputes between Normans should be decided by the testimony of the English (*Chron. Mon. de Bello*, p. 89).

[3] Liebermann, i.483-6; Robertson, pp. 230-6.

partitus, the *Leges Henrici* and the *Ten Articles*.[1] The other pieces of legislation attributed to the Conqueror belong to that large class of apocrypha, of which we shall have much to say shortly. No legislative act has been attributed to William Rufus.

The obscurity of the reigns of the first two Norman kings in all matters that touch the law is due not so much to the paucity of our sources as to the brutal facts of history. England was an occupied and devastated land, and if not a place of perpetual warfare, always hovering on the verge of it. *Inter arma silent leges*. If the worst was over, the battle won, at the time of the Conqueror's death, the country was unhappy and unsettled, in the throes of a dynastic war little more than six months after King William had been laid in his tomb. Though the Old English institutions were inevitably hampered and frustrated, they still, as we have said, continued to function: there was nothing the Normans had to put in their place. Englishmen still wrote their charters and deeds in English.[2] The shire moot, the hundred moot, the husting, the borough moot, the English lawmen and jury continued in existence,[3] a necessarily chequered existence, although stimulated into a more active life by the Domesday enquiries, which English clerks must have rendered possible.[4] The Norman kings continued the crown-wearings of their English predecessors[5] and, like them, held their great councils on the great festivals of the Church. At these councils there was doubtless discussed the separation of ecclesiastical and secular tribunals, the procedure in actions between Normans and English, and other matters of general significance. The chroniclers, however, pay little attention to these meetings, for very little that was notable happened there. We learn most about the council at Gloucester at Christmastide 1085, when three bishops were appointed and when the decision was taken to make the survey that resulted in Domesday Book.[6] But no monuments of legislation emerged from these occasions.

With the accession of Henry I the political climate changed. The new king was much more intelligent than his immediate predecessor

[1] Below, pp. 42, 46. [2] Richardson and Sayles, *op. cit.*, pp. 26-7*n*.

[3] *Ibid.*, pp. 25-6, 94-5, 173-4, 182-4.

[4] The assumption that Norman clerks were employed rests upon little more than the myth of the Norman's transcendent ability. Whence these Norman clerks came has not been explained. Was Normandy superabundantly supplied? The burden upon such clerical skill as was available, locally and centrally, was immense, if only for a relatively short time (*ibid.*, p. 28). Some idea of the burden may be gained from V. H. Galbraith's study, *The Making of Domesday Book*, pp. 28-44, though we think it more probable that returns were made in the first instance by landowners, employing, of course, local clerks (*Governance of Mediaeval England*, p. 207*n*). It has been estimated, on the evidence of the surviving diplomata, that under Henry I – a far more advanced administrator than his father – probably not more than two scribes were employed in the chancery at his accession and that subsequently during his reign the number rose to 'at least' four (Bishop, *Scriptores Regis*, p. 30). Under Henry I there were other royal clerks employed in the exchequer, but this affords no parallel with the eleventh century, though doubtless a few clerks were then employed in the royal treasury (*Governance of Mediaeval England*, pp. 217-20). In any case, at least one English clerk must have been employed in the chancery under the Conqueror to write English writs.

[5] *Governance of Mediaeval England*, pp. 32, 38, 56, 142-6, 397-412.

[6] Anglo-Saxon Chronicle, *s.a.* 1085 (Thorpe, i.352; Plummer, i.216).

or his other brother, the duke of Normandy, and, by any rational standard, he was a good deal more intelligent than his father. He had moreover some tincture of learning.[1] His coronation charter – which since the twelfth century has been regarded as a legislative act – announces the rules by which he intended to be guided during his reign.[2] The charter is important, not only for its contents but because it set a precedent that was followed by later kings until coronation charters were, in effect, superseded by Magna Carta. They resemble the urban praetor's edicts of ancient Rome, which were declarations by the praetors, on taking up duty, of the rules to which they would adhere during their term of office. It cannot be supposed that twelfth-century kings had any knowledge of this parallel but it is a curious coincidence, and what is of particular interest is that the precedent set by Henry I should be followed by his successors.

Henry's charter was carefully conceived. If we should accept the date it bears as being the date of issue, we should find it difficult to suppose otherwise than that it had been prepared well before Henry's coronation at Westminster on 5 August 1200, three days after his brother's violent death. Happily the date of a charter cannot be construed strictly,[3] the date is the date of the intention, not the date of its detailed working out, though Henry may have meditated many a time what he would do if events should fall out as they did. The purport of his long charter can be briefly set down. The evil practices with which the country has been unlawfully oppressed will be ended – and the chief of these are indicated – and the law of King Edward will be restored, subject to the amendments introduced by the Conqueror with the barons' consent. What amendments these were we can only conjecture. Presumably they included the separation of ecclesiastical and secular courts; perhaps the rules of procedure governing actions between Englishmen and Frenchmen. Probably these words – saving something assumed to be good among the evil the Conqueror and his son had wrought – were a placatory gesture, intended to please all men, with nothing very definite in view: King Edward had left no code of law and no one could know what the amendments were. It is to be feared, however, that they included one law of the Conqueror's that was to vex men for many generations. 'As my father had them', says Henry, 'so, with the full agreement of my barons, I retain the forests in my hand.' If this was one of the Conqueror's amendments, it was the only one specifically mentioned.

[1] So far as we know, William I was unlearned. Henry apparently had some, but not an extensive, acquaintance with Latin. The legend of Henry I's learning was finally dissipated by C. W. David in *Haskin's Anniversary Essays*, pp. 45-56.

[2] The charter is incorporated in *Quadripartitus* and begins the *Leges Henrici* (Liebermann, i.544, 547). The text of the charter has often been printed: we may give references to Liebermann, i.521-3, whence Robertson, pp. 276-82, and (unannotated) *Select Charters*, pp. 117-19.

[3] The classical example is that of Magna Carta, dated 15 June 1215, but certainly not settled and sealed until the 19th (McKechnie, *Magna Carta*, pp. 36-41).

The reforms effected by Henry I have left their mark to the present day. The Queen's Bench Division of the High Court recalls – to those who know their history – the creation of the justiciar's court at the exchequer, rendered necessary by the king's conquest of Normandy. Eventually the justiciar's court in one of its aspects evolved as the Court of Common Pleas, which held its sessions in a fixed place, while the ambulatory court that accompanied the king received the name of the King's Bench. The Court of Common Pleas or Common Bench was swept away in the legal reforms of last century; but had it not existed for many centuries there would have been no separate court to require the distinctive name of the King's Bench. We should then have had today no Queen's Bench Division – an odd name it might seem to a foreigner, who did not know our curious precedents and our way of following them when they have lost all their meaning. Save for the contrivances of a king who died more than eight centuries ago, there would have been but one central court, as there was, for example, in France. There are around us many other reminiscences of the greatest of the Norman kings, if we but bethink ourselves. Except for his planning of the administration, there might have been no Chancellor of the Exchequer. . . . But we have described elsewhere how Henry and his coadjutor of genius, Bishop Roger of Salisbury, created an efficient judicature and an efficient financial organisation, without parallel in Western Europe[1]; and to what we have said so recently there is nothing we need add here. We do but recall these achievements of Henry's, which left such strong and permanent marks upon our institutions, in order to emphasise how great could be the changes, in the field of law as well as in administration, without a line of legislation.

Henry's surviving legislative acts are indeed few. We must discard one of those recognised by modern editors, the charter to the Londoners granting them the farm of London and Middlesex and granting them other privileges,[2] for which, of course, they paid. There remain only an ordinance for the protection of the currency, issued at Christmas 1100, and another of 1108 regulating the sessions of shire and hundred moots and the trial of pleas of land. Both are in the form of writs.[3] The former resembles, but is much less elaborate than, the corresponding law of Ethelred[4]: it is also more cruel. A forger or fraudulent moneyer is not only to lose his right hand but is to be emasculated. Henry's law may, however, in one respect be thought less drastic: under Ethelred moneyers working in secret places and traffickers in base coin might lose their lives. The other ordinance enforces, or perhaps re-establishes, the practice of King Edward's reign in regard to the places and times of meeting of the local courts, saving

[1] *Governance of Mediaeval England*, pp. 156-250.
[2] Liebermann, i.524-6; Robertson, pp. 288-92. For corrections to the text see *E.H.R.*, xlii.80-87.
[3] Liebermann, i.523-4; Robertson, pp. 284-6. For the dates see *Regesta*, nos. 501, 892.
[4] Above, p. 25.

to the king the right to summon them at other times for his own purposes. This ordinance further provides that real actions between tenants in chief shall be tried in the king's court, those between tenants of the same lord in the lord's court and those between tenants of different lords in the shire court. The law of the Conqueror regarding suits between Englishmen and Frenchmen[1] is implicitly amended, since it is now ruled that the trial in real actions is to be by battle unless the parties agree to some other method of proof.

The legislative output of the reign is not quite so meagre as these sole survivors might suggest. First let us note, however, that there were two other measures for protecting the coinage. In 1108 it was apparently ordered that all coins, halfpennies and farthings as well as pennies, should be circular – not as hitherto, in the case of halfpennies and farthings, sections of the round penny, broken at the cross – and the penalty prescribed in 1100 for currency offences was renewed.[2] In 1124 the king, who was then in Normandy, gave instructions to the justiciar, Roger of Salisbury, to take special measures to enforce the law. According to the chroniclers all the moneyers were assembled at Winchester at Christmas and summarily mutilated. The facts behind this incredible story are uncertain, but it may be that the statutory penalty had not been enforced locally and that those moneyers who had been found guilty were punished under the supervision of the king's justices.[3] The text of the instructions has survived in neither case, and in neither case is more implied than that administrative action was taken. We do but notice the incidents here as illustrating the difficulty of enforcing a statute, even with a strong administrative system such as had been evolved under Henry I. We have used the word 'statute', not because the word was commonly employed in this sense at the period, but because it actually occurs in a writ in favour of the archbishop of York, which grants to him the privilege of enforcing the law by his own justice in his own court. It may be well to have the words before us: 'et nova statuta mea de judiciis sive de placitis latronum et falsorum monetariorum exequatur et faciat per suam propriam justitiam in curia sua'.[4] Here then we have a reference to another 'statute' of 1100 or early 1101, beside that relating to the coinage, one dealing with the trial or punishment of thieves; but nothing more

[1] Above, p. 30. Englishmen as well as Frenchmen seem, however, to be offering battle at the time of the Domesday enquiries (D.B., i.377 b 2, ii.213; *Inquisitio Comitatus Cantabrigiensis*, p. 131).

[2] Florence of Worcester, *Chronicon*, ii.57; William of Malmesbury, *Gesta Regum*, ii.476; Eadmer, *Historia Novorum*, p. 193. No specimens of these round halfpennies and farthings appear to have survived: cf. Brooke, *English Coins*, pp. 81, 86-9.

[3] Anglo-Saxon Chronicle, *s.a.* 1125 (Thorpe, i.376; Plummer, i.255, ii.301); William of Malmesbury, *Gesta Pontificum*, p. 442; Simeon of Durham, *Historia Regum*, ii.281; Henry of Huntingdon, *Historia Anglorum*, p. 246. That some moneyers and their workmen succeeded in buying themselves off is clear (*Pipe Roll, 31 Henry I*, p. 42).

[4] *Historians of the Church of York*, iii.22-3. For date, Easter 1101, see *Regesta*, no. 518. The writ does not look like a product of the chancery, but one prepared by the beneficiary for sealing.

seems to be known of it.[1] The survival of this writ does, however, suggest that there may have been other minor legislation by Henry of which we know nothing.[2]

There was certainly one other 'edict' of very considerable interest which is recorded by a monastic chronicler because his house was particularly interested in it. This ordinance amended the law of wreck. The customary law had been that, if a ship was wrecked, the crew must repair it by a fixed time or else – if the ship was not yet seaworthy – both ship and cargo were forfeited. Henry I was shocked by this custom and decreed that, if only one man escaped from the wreck, he should retain the property in everything salvable. Since the right to wreck was a prerogative of the Crown, it might be thought that the king could exercise his discretion in the matter; but this was one of the rights that was sometimes granted out to subjects and it had in fact, been granted out by the Conqueror to Battle Abbey which possessed land bordering on the seashore. After Henry's death it was claimed that his ordinance had lapsed with him, and the abbey's men seized a wreck from which the crew had escaped. The abbot, who vouched the action of his men, was in consequence cited before the court of King Stephen, charged with trespass. The case was argued before the king's council and the abbot's plea was finally sustained that, since Henry had not acted with the common consent of his barons, his decree expired with him.[3] As we have seen, the principle that the king could legislate only with the consent of his barons had long been recognised, not only by the Norman kings but by their English predecessors.[4] Hence, of course, the practice of legislating at the great festivals when the king wore his crown and there was a great concourse of nobles.[5] The decision in the Battle Abbey case is nevertheless important because it shows that, after mature consideration by the king's council, the principle was held to extend to the rights of the Crown. We cannot be sure, however, that the case is adequately reported. Another principle, upon which there will be more to say, might be involved. Before many years were over it was regarded as established law that the king was bound to safeguard the rights of the Crown and to recover any which had been dispersed. Henry II swore at his coronation to do precisely this.[6] We are not told that this principle was advanced in the Battle Abbey case; but it is perhaps significant that Henry II did not seek to revive his grandfather's edict and that the customary law which Henry I had sought to abrogate continued in force until the reign of Edward I.[7]

The judicial reforms of Henry I led to the preparation of another

[1] Unless, as Florence of Worcester seems to indicate, it required the capital punishment of all convicted thieves (*Chronicon*, ii.57).

[2] That William of Malmesbury's general words summing up Henry's achievements imply any other considerable legislative acts seems very dubious (*Historia Regum*, ii.487).

[3] *Chronicon de Bello*, pp. 65-7.

[4] Above, p. 12. [5] Above, p. 31. [6] Below, pp. 56-7.

[7] Statute of Westminster I, c. 4 (*Statutes of the Realm*, i.28).

document which Edwardian lawyers included among the *Vetera Statuta*, namely the Chapters of the Eyre. Of course, by the end of the thirteenth century the Chapters of the Eyre had become preposterously swollen by successive accretions,[1] but the nucleus, the *vetera capitula*, is undoubtedly Henry's work.[2] To understand why the work was undertaken it is necessary to have before us an outline of the judicial system before Henry recast it. The administration of justice in pre-Conquest England had been essentially local, and the first two Norman kings had done little to modify the system. It is true that before the end of the eleventh century we find a royal justice resident in the counties who, as the texts of the twelfth century show, acts as a coadjutor or supervisor of the sheriff.[3] This seems to be no new departure, however, but a revival of an Old English office which had been allowed to lapse – whether by the Conqueror or by an earlier king in the eleventh century, the sources do not enable us to determine with any confidence. The Norman sheriff had been thus left free from control, a freedom he inevitably abused. But we anticipate.

So far as the practices in the Old English polity are concerned we must speak with some reserve, for our surviving sources of information are sparse, but nevertheless we believe that we can recover at least the outline, if we cannot supply the details, of the judicial system, and we can endeavour to fill in an exasperating blank space in the legal history of pre-Conquest England. To begin with, let us ask a question. What is meant by the word *judex*, which confronts us now and again in the legal texts of the tenth, eleventh and twelfth centuries? It is, of course, a vague general term; but it has also, it would appear, two specific meanings. Undoubtedly the lawmen in English boroughs, shires and hundreds were termed *judices* in Latin, and this usage continued well into the twelfth century. A *judex* of this sort might be a humble enough fellow, and another name for him was *judicator*, a term that lingered on for a very long time as the Latin name for a certain kind of suitor in the hundred court.[4] These suitors, as Maitland said, were the doomsmen of the court.[5] But there was an altogether more dignified minister called a *judex*, such a one as was expected to wait upon the king, in company with nobles and high-ranking thegns and clergy, at the crown-wearing ceremonies of the great festivals of the Church. Thus we have, for example, a list of those who attended upon King Edgar on such an occasion: it runs 'archiepiscopi et alii omnes sacerdotes praeclari et conspicui abbates et religiosae abbatisae ac cuncti duces, praefecti et judices'.[6] A *dux* is an ealdorman; a *praefectus* is a *gerefa*[7]; but what is the

[1] Cam, *Studies in the Hundred Rolls*, pp. 29-39.

[2] With our summaries in *Governance of Mediaeval England*, pp. 177-80, 203, compare the lists of early Chapters of the Eyre given by Miss Cam, *op. cit.*, p. 92.

[3] *Governance of Mediaeval England*, pp. 173-4.

[4] *Ibid.*, pp. 182-5.

[5] Pollock and Maitland, *History of English Law*, i.548.

[6] *Vita Oswaldi*, p. 436.

[7] Liebermann, *Gesetze*, ii.175.

English for *judex*? Perhaps we may get some light from a law of Edgar's which speaks of 'se dema þe oðrum woh deme' – the judge who judges another wrongly. What manner of man is this judge? He is a man who is capable of paying a heavy fine of 120 shillings – the equivalent of perhaps £1000 in terms of our money – and, over and above his fine, runs in danger of losing his thegnship if his erroneous judgement is corrupt. Moreover, though a royal thegn, he is not attached to the king's household. His office is a local one. If he incurs a fine for misconduct, it is for the bishop of the diocese – who sits in the shire moot – to levy the fine on the king's behalf.[1] The conclusion seems inevitable that in the *judex* of Edgar's day we must see a royal judge, who is the associate of bishop and sheriff in their judicial capacities. The parallel with the local justice of Norman times seems too close to be accidental.

The fact that a royal judge could be – to use a later word – attainted is important. Quite clearly the king's court will entertain complaints of a wrongful judgement in a local court: we think that the judgement is almost invariably one of the hundred moot. It seems, indeed, as if litigants are only too ready to appeal to the king. Not only Edgar, but Cnut also, has reason to legislate in the matter. No man, both say, shall appeal to the king unless he has failed to obtain justice locally; and the law of Cnut makes it quite clear that local justice is, at least as a rule, justice in the hundred moot.[2] The shire moot, we must remember, meets but infrequently.[3] Now, there are others, besides the judge, who are concerned in the judgement of the hundred moot: they are the lawmen. We know what may happen to the judge who gives a perverse judgement; but what happens to the lawmen? The pre-Conquest sources do not seem to help, but soon after the Conquest there was a noteworthy case which sheds light upon the past. There was certain land in Cambridgeshire, which the bishop of Rochester claimed but which had been treated by the sheriff as royal demesne. The dispute came before a special session of the shire moot over which Odo of Bayeux, the Conqueror's brother, presided. And we may perhaps give a reminder at this point that the office of local justice appears to have been in abeyance under the Conqueror and further that the sheriff could not act as judge in his own cause: hence, of course, the appointment of Odo to act as president of the court. The suitors gave judgement in favour of the sheriff, but Odo was suspicious and ordered a special jury of twelve to be elected and sworn. This jury confirmed the

[1] III Edgar, cap. 3: see Liebermann's note, iii.136.
[2] III Edgar, cap. 2; II Cnut, cap. 17.
[3] III Edgar, cap. 5; II Cnut, cap. 18. The limitation to two sessions a year in these laws had evidently been disregarded by the beginning of the twelfth century and perhaps under Edward the Confessor. This is the implication of Henry I's writ regarding the county and hundred courts (Liebermann, i.524, whence Robertson, p. 286, and *Select Charters*, p. 122). Henry reserved to himself the right to summon the county court at any time. Ultimately the sessions were held at four- or six-week intervals (J. J. Alexander in *B.I.H.R.*, iii.89-95): indeed, to hold sessions every four weeks seems to have been already the rule under Henry II (below, p. 88). For a good example of an action in the shire moot, a plea of land, under Cnut see Robertson, *Anglo-Saxon Charters*, pp. 150-2 (no. 78).

previous judgement. Suspicion, however, was in turn cast upon these jurymen, certain of whom were induced to admit that they had committed perjury. Proceedings now moved to London before a court consisting of barons, both French and English, with a fresh jury, which, again to use a later term, we may call a jury of attaint. In this court the suitors of the shire moot were found guilty of perjury and the shire was heavily amerced in the sum of £300.[1] We do not think there can be any reasonable doubt that these proceedings reproduce substantially the procedure under Old English kings. Both judge and lawmen were alike subject to attaint.

Legislative provisions and an action brought, with great difficulty, to a successful conclusion by an important personage like a bishop may give too favourable an impression of the judicial system of the Old English polity. A strong king like Edgar, as well as a weak one like Ethelred, is repeatedly complaining of the lawlessness of the country.[2] And we may be quite sure that the presence of a large band of aggressive and acquisitive foreigners under Norman kings did not make the situation any better. This state of affairs was abhorrent to the orderly minds of men like Henry I and Roger of Salisbury, and there was the further consideration that disorder meant the invasion of royal rights and the diminution of royal revenues. Henry and Roger determined to impose order and to increase the revenue. It is easy to take the lofty view and deplore that the administration of justice should be a source of profit, but in the twelfth century there was practical proof that Henry's justice, profitably administered, brought peace and security. We do not want for contemporary witness. 'No man durst misdo against another in his time. He made peace for man and beast. Whoso bare his burthen of gold and silver, no man durst say to him aught but good.'[3] Let us now tell how Henry and Roger set out upon their self-imposed task.

The crucial event is Henry's conquest of Normandy in 1106 and the consequent organisation of the English and Norman exchequers, which were the courts of the English and Norman justiciars.[4] This did not mean that the court *coram rege* ceased to function, but that in each country, whether the king was present or not, a central royal court was in session during the terms of the legal year. The royal judges who staffed these courts formed a single corps in each country and were available also for administering justice locally.[5] It would seem that already before 1109, when the two exchequers appear to have come

[1] *Textus Roffensis* (ed. Hearne), pp. 149-52; Facsimile (ed. Sawyer), ii.175v-176v: and see our commentary in *Governance of Mediaeval England*, pp. 207-8.

[2] Above, pp. 23, 26-7.

[3] Anglo-Saxon Chronicle, *s.a.* 1135: we give Thorpe's translation, ii.229.

[4] *Governance of Mediaeval England*, pp. 157-9. We do not, of course, suggest that the offices were created *ex nihilo* (Professor le Patourel in *History*, l.297*n*); but there is no evidence and, as it seems to us, no probability that Roger of Salisbury had any predecessor exercising like functions. We had thought that we have made our conclusions plain beyond the possibility of mistake (*op. cit.*, p. 159).

[5] *Ibid.*, pp. 175-6, 210-15.

into existence, royal justices had sometimes gone on eyre in England[1]: but the organisation of the exchequer provided a coherent and effective judicature for which there was no precedent. The judges, termed 'justices of all England' in contradistinction to the local royal justices, sat, as occasion required, in the court *coram rege* or in the justiciar's court or in the itinerant courts which held their sessions in the counties. If these justices were not professional – and at this stage they could not be said to be learned in the law – they were on their way to becoming professional.[2] Their principal purpose was doubtless to maintain the king's rights – that is, to try the pleas of the crown – but they sat also to ensure criminal justice and to try pleas of land.[3] They were acting as the king's justices were to act under Henry II and later, for example, under Henry III. Doubtless their law, procedural and substantive, was not so advanced as it was to become in the age of Glanville or the age of Bracton; but it was the same law in a less sophisticated form. Not the least of their functions was to review the local administration of justice and to exact heavy penalties for the failures of the suitors of hundred courts and county courts.[4] So harsh were their visitations that men fled before them, and so dreaded were they that under Henry III it was insisted that the king's justices should not visit a county more often than once in seven years.[5] Presumably the king's justices sometimes tilted the scales of justice to the king's advantage; but that they heightened the standards of justice everywhere is a truth that cannot be questioned. Let us not judge them by the standards of England today, but by the standards of the bitter, cruel England in which they lived, a land of lawless privilege and unrighteous unfreedom, a land where chattel and penal slavery was still a living memory.[6] It was for these justices that the chapters of the eyre were devised. The text of the chapters under Henry I has not survived – it may well have varied from eyre to eyre – but of its terms we can get a very good idea from the texts of 1194 and 1198.[7] For the rest, there was, as we have seen, very little legislation that could have guided the king's justices, even at the end of Henry I's reign. What the law was that they administered we must discuss. But before we do so we should say a few words about law and its administration under Henry I's successor, Stephen.

No legislative act is credited to King Stephen. If this is less than his due, it is because Henry II of set purpose consigned to oblivion all the acts of his predecessor, whom he ranked as no better than a usurper.[8]

[1] *Ibid.*, pp. 174-5.
[2] *Ibid.*, pp. 214-15.
[3] *Ibid.*, pp. 177-84.
[4] *Ibid.*, pp. 181-2.
[5] Pollock and Maitland, *History of English Law*, i.201-2; Cam, *Studies in the Hundred Rolls*, pp. 83-8, 103-13; Treharne, *Baronial Plan of Reform*, pp. 398-406; Richardson and Sayles, *Select Cases of Procedure without Writ*, pp. xxix-xxx; C. A. F. Meekings, *Crown Pleas of the Wiltshire Eyre*, pp. 3-5.
[6] *Governance of Mediaeval England*, pp. 121-2.
[7] Howden, *Chronica*, iii.263-4; iv.61-2; Cf. *Governance of Mediaeval England*, p. 180.
[8] Above, p. 24, n. 1.

And then, it seems clear, after the arrest of Roger of Salisbury and the break-up of the administration which Stephen had inherited from Henry I, the authority of the Crown was progressively weakened.[1] First there came Matilda to contest the throne and, though she failed ignominiously, the Angevins retained a considerable foothold in the country. And then in 1152 came Matilda's son Henry, who set up a rival administration in the West which Stephen was unable to dislodge. Stephen's fortunes varied, but he was never a beaten man, nor was Henry particularly successful in his ill-prepared and ill-equipped military enterprises.[2] What matters for our present purpose is that the firm and regular administration of the law became impossible[3] and that effective legislation, even if it had been contemplated, was impracticable. But in the first year of his reign Stephen did issue two charters which have as much right to be called legislation as the coronation charter of Henry I. The first of Stephen's charters seems, in fact, to have been in the strictest sense a coronation charter, issued perhaps at Christmastide 1135.[4] It is very brief and it has but one solitary witness, a *curialis*, William Martel – not the archbishop of Canterbury; not the justiciar, Roger of Salisbury, though he seems to have remained in office[5]; not any of King Henry's earls. The charter grants to the barons and all the men of England the liberties and good laws which King Henry had granted them and all the good laws and customs that they had in King Edward's day. Stephen had seized the throne and got himself crowned in, as it were, the twinkling of an eye – to quote a contemporary[6] – and it was not to be expected that many more than his personal adherents would be present at the Christmas festival that followed so soon after his coronation. It was no time for festivities or much law-making. But by Easter Stephen had made good his hold on the throne. His consecration had been confirmed by the pope, and the episcopate, both English and Norman, as well as the principal barons had now given him their support, albeit with qualifications. Stephen's position needed further definition and this was done in a second charter, plentifully witnessed, which emphasised in its opening protocols his consecration by the pope's legate (the archbishop of Canterbury) and its subsequent confirmation by the pope himself.[7] The first paragraphs give certain undertakings to the Church. We need not examine these paragraphs at length; their purport is to restore the Church to the position it had occupied under the Conqueror. We may add perhaps that we are unable to accept the view that in this charter Stephen made any fresh concessions to the clergy, a

[1] *Governance of Mediaeval England*, pp. 191-4, 226-7.
[2] *Ibid.*, pp. 252-4.
[3] *Ibid.*, pp. 192-3.
[4] *Select Charters*, p. 142.
[5] Richardson, Introduction to *Memoranda Roll, I John*, p. lxxxiii.
[6] Henry of Huntingdon, *Historia Anglorum*, p. 256.
[7] *Select Charters*, pp. 143-4. For the date and some of the circumstances of the charter see Round, *Geoffrey de Mandeville*, pp. 16-24.

view which does not seem to have sufficient regard to the events of his or the preceding reigns.[1] One concession he did, however, make in the following paragraph: he released from forest law the lands that had been newly afforested under Henry I. In the next paragraph Stephen appears to renounce any right he might have to profit by vacant bishoprics or abbacies, though there is no express renunciation and he was certainly charged later with exploiting his rights during vacancies.[2] He then promises to extirpate all wrongful exactions, injustices and miskennings[3] by sheriffs and others and finally to maintain good laws and the ancient and just customs in levying murder fines,[4] in legal actions and in other causes. In every article Stephen looks to the past, to the good old laws and customs and, as he says in his first charter, to the laws of King Edward's day.

What were these laws and customs, we may ask, or rather what did men in the reigns of Henry I and Stephen believe they were? These laws and customs, at least in principle, must have been administered in shire and hundred and perhaps – for we must speak cautiously – by the king's justices. It may sound paradoxical, but to find these laws and customs we have to look in the apocrypha of our law, in the early items of the series of anonymous and pseudonymous works which, beginning early in the twelfth century, extend to the end of the thirteenth, to *Fleta*, *Britton* and the *Mirror of Justices*, a long series of tracts and treatises of varying authority and dubious utility. England knew no twelfth-century Justinian to codify the laws of King Edward's day. The first and last codification had been the work of Alfred the Great.[5]

There were several attempts under Henry I to provide a digest of Old English law for those who could not read the original texts. The most considerable and the one we mention first was made in the second decade of the twelfth century by an anonymous author whose work was entitled *Quadripartitus*. The title is explained by the division of the treatise into four books. The first book was to contain English laws translated into Latin; the second book was to contain such recent written law as it was necessary to add; the third was to explain the nature of actions at law and the method of pleading them; the fourth was to treat of theft and its subdivisions.[6] We speak of the treatise as it had been planned, but only the first and second books have come down to us. The second book can hardly be said to fulfil the author's promise: it goes wonderfully awry and was perhaps never finished as

[1] *Governance of Mediaeval England*, pp. 288-9.

[2] William of Malmesbury, *Historia Novella*, p. 20.

[3] Penalties for mistakes in formal pleading.

[4] The hundred was penalised if a stranger was murdered and the perpetrator of the murder was not brought to justice. See further below, p. 52, and Pollock and Maitland, *History of English Law*, i.89.

[5] Above, p. 17.

[6] For the text as a whole see Liebermann, *Quadripartitus*, pp. 76-166, where, however, the texts of the Anglo-Saxon laws are given in outline only. The full texts of the latter are distributed over the *Gesetze der Angelsachsen*. The scheme of the book is set out in paragraph 32 of the *argumentum* (*Quadripartitus*, p. 89).

the author intended. The third book is represented by the *Leges Henrici*, which will next engage our attention: but it seems to be by another hand. The fourth book appears never to have been written.

Only the first book of *Quadripartitus* is of any great consequence as a law-book. There is, however, little that is in the least original in it, beyond the *dedicatio* and *argumentum*. The body of the book consists of a translation into Latin of practically the whole corpus of Old English legislation, from Alfred's compilation to Cnut's code, together with the various associated pieces: the tenth-century treaties with the Danes and a number of minor legal tracts.[1] Some of the legislation here translated we know only from the Latin renderings, and for this we owe the compiler a debt of gratitude, but for little else. He does not methodise his texts in any way and the order in which he presents them is more than a trifle odd. It looks as if the work of translation had been apportioned between a team and then put together just as the portions came to hand. It would be wearisome to detail the sequence of all the bits and pieces, which varies from manuscript to manuscript.[2] We can, however, give a good idea of the lack of method by taking as representative a text which seems to embody the compiler's intentions – if intention be not too complimentary a term.[3] We describe the contents of this text as briefly as possible. The preliminary matter we may pass over. First comes Cnut's code and then most of Alfred's compilation. The result is, of course, that Ine follows Alfred; but the order of the Alfred-Ine text is changed so that Alfred's scriptural introduction, still further expanded with passages from the Book of Exodus, follows Ine. There then comes a portion of Athelstan's laws, but the sequence of royal legislation is thereafter interrupted, as it continues to be at other points, by borrowings from minor tracts. These interruptions we need not specify as they occur. Royal legislation is resumed with Edgar and Athelstan, in that order. The Danish treaties are then interposed. There follow Edward the Elder, Edmund, Ethelred, divided by minor tracts from a further section of Ethelred, then Edgar again and more Edmund. King William's decree regarding procedure in actions between Englishmen and Frenchmen comes next, doubtless to represent the Conqueror's amendments to King Edward's law, and finally a further instalment of minor tracts, concluding with the *Rectitudines Singularum Personarum*.[4]

Thus ends the first book. The second book has a sufficiently long preface, over which we need not linger. The texts begin with Henry I's coronation charter and two letters of Henry's to Pope Paschal II. The second of these letters announces the forthcoming visit to Rome of

[1] *Ibid.*, pp. 89-146; *Gesetze*, i.535-42.
[2] *Quadripartitus*, pp. 65-6, 89-146.
[3] The order finally adopted by Liebermann in *Gesetze*, i.535-42.
[4] A pre-Conquest tract, probably of the eleventh century, describing the rights and duties of the several orders of society, particularly the unfree: Old English text and Latin translation in *Gesetze*, i.444-53.

Gerard, the newly elected archbishop of York, and upon this peg is hung a selection from Gerard's correspondence, intended, oddly enough, as a defence of his conduct. There follow the canons of the ecclesiastical council of 1108 and Henry I's ordinance regarding meetings of the county and hundred courts. With these documents the book, at least as it has come down to us, ends.[1]

After our description of them, it may be superfluous to comment that in these two books the author shows no trace of legal training or understanding of the requirements of the most humble of lawyers. What his third book would have been we cannot tell. We doubt whether it was ever written, but its place was supplied, as we have indicated, by the *Leges Henrici*. The language of the introduction corresponds too closely with what the *argumentum*, prefixed to the first book, tells us was to be the scope of the third book, for there to be any doubt that the *Leges* was written for that very purpose.[2] But we feel convinced that the author of the *Leges* was not the author of *Quadripartitus*, despite the many similarities in language and expression, similarities which led Liebermann to a contrary opinion.[3] The *Leges Henrici* is the work of a man familiar with the administration of justice in hundred courts and county courts and also, perhaps, to some extent conversant with the administration of justice before justices in eyre. His range of reading appears to be wider than that of the author of *Quadripartitus* – at least he utilises a few more books and books of a different sort. But, above all, he has some idea of the practical application of the law and the requirements of litigants. If he clings too closely to his sources, which, as far as substantive law is concerned, appear to be mainly the Old English laws as they appear in the first book of *Quadripartitus*,[4] he does his best to organise his matter on a plan which he tries – without great success perhaps – to make logical. His introductory pages on the duty of a judge, the nature of actions and so forth are not so distinctive. They are too vague, too homiletic, to be useful. But the author is living a generation before the re-discovery of Roman law came as a revelation to English lawyers and English administrators, before Justinian's Institutes became a common textbook, before the *ordines judiciarii* taught men the rules of methodical exposition and well before law-schools were organised in France or England.[5] He has, it is true, some foreign learning. He cites the *Liber Theodosiane legis*[6] and the *Lex Salica*[7] as well as Augustine[8] and Jerome[9] and

[1] *Quadripartitus*, pp. 146-66; *Gesetze*, i.542-6.

[2] The text is in *Gesetze*, i.547-611. After a proem and Henry I's coronation charter, the text begins with sections (3, 4, 5 and 9) professing to treat *de causarum pertractatione et diffinicione*, *de generibus causarum*, *de causarum proprietatibus* and *de qualitate causarum*. The author of *Quadripartitus* had stated that his third book was to treat *de statu et agendis causarum*.

[3] Liebermann, *Über . . . Leges Henrici*, pp. 53-9; *Gesetze*, iii.308.

[4] Some passages do not exactly correspond and it is possible (though we think, at least, doubtful) that he went back to the English texts: cf. Liebermann, *Über . . . Leges Henrici*, pp. 16-21.

[5] Below, pp. 72ff.

[6] *Leges Henrici*, cap. 33.4.

[7] *Ibid.*, caps. 87.10, 89.1.

[8] *Ibid.*, caps. 33.6, 72.1*b*.

[9] *Ibid.*, caps. 5.28, 33.6, 72.1*d*.

Gregorius in decretis.[1] He draws upon the *Lex Ribuaria*, upon Isidore and upon penitentials once attributed to Theodore and Egbert.[2] But he may have found all his citations in no more than one or two volumes[3] and it is unlikely that he had access to many books or ranged far afield. Above all we must not, as used at one time to be done, credit him with a knowledge of Roman law or see any such influence in his work.[4]

The law with which the author of the *Leges Henrici* is concerned is criminal law or, perhaps it would be better to say, delictual law, law of which breaches can be emended by a money payment, though he mentions, as his sources do, crimes against the king which are visited with loss of life or member. Of land law he says nothing, and this omission is significant. It has been claimed for the author that he was one of the king's justices,[5] but we think this claim to rest upon a misapprehension. We know a good deal about the justices of Henry I and especially what their business was when they went on eyre.[6] They went into the counties to try pleas of the Crown and pleas of land, and any one of them would, we suggest, have written a different kind of book, had he wished to be useful to his fellows or to those who would step into his place. It is true that the *Leges Henrici* says something of the pleas of the Crown,[7] but nothing that would be very useful to a justice taking an eyre or to a justice's clerk who accompanied him, nothing resembling the Chapters of the Eyre which both justice and clerk would have in their hands.[8] Nor does the book say anything of the summons of the eyre, of presentments and verdicts. In striking contrast, the author sets down the heads of the enquiries made by justices of the forest, which must have been based upon the articles of a forest eyre.[9] How he came by such a document we know not; but the manner in which he presents it reinforces the conclusion that he was no king's justice or justice's clerk.[10] And then he has no word to say of the growing volume of real actions begun by a royal writ. Moreover, it seems hardly possible that one of the king's justices could write a lawbook which did not betray some knowledge of the justiciar's court at the exchequer and the business done there, a court in which he himself would have had a seat. We would not press a comparison with Henry of Bratton a

[1] *Ibid.*, cap. 5.27.
[2] Liebermann, *Über . . . Leges Henrici*, pp. 22-3.
[3] *Ibid.*, pp. 22-5; *Gesetze*, iii.313.
[4] See below, p. 71, His citation of the Theodosian Code is a fraud: he betrays his ignorance of it.
[5] *Über . . . Leges Henrici*, pp. 44-5. This belief springs from the words of cap. 8.7: 'Et si quid professioni nostre congruum precedentium vel sequentium capitula docuerint.' There could hardly be said to be a *professio* of royal justices or indeed of lawyers at this period.
[6] *Governance of Mediaeval England*, pp. 174-81.
[7] *Leges Henrici*, caps. 10, 13, 19.
[8] Above, p. 36.
[9] *Leges Henrici*, cap. 17.
[10] Surely no royal justice would begin by saying 'Placitum quoque forestarum multiplici satis est incommoditate vallatum' or would speak of 'misera canum expeditacio'. The language of the Assize of the Forest is very different: see *Governance of Mediaeval England*, p. 446, and below, pp. 128-30.

hundred and thirty years or so later, when the common law had undergone many changes and minute specialisation, but the *De Legibus* does suggest the kind of book an experienced judge would write for the instruction of his younger brethren, a very different book from the *Leges Henrici*.

We may be reminded that a book which was perhaps written by a judge for the instruction of his fellows and their clerks, a book that served as one of Bracton's models, the lawbook that passes under the name of *Glanville*, says little of the king's courts, beyond a bare mention that the law it expounds is that practised in the court of the exchequer and in the courts of the justices in eyre. *Glanville*, however, is concerned with land law – except for a brief appendix on criminal law[1] – and it tells us a good deal in detail of the way in which real actions originated and were decided.[2] And then we must remember that criminal law was for the most part locally administered, and though the king's justices were occasionally called upon to take part in its administration, this seems to have been a somewhat rare occurrence under Henry I.[3] So for our part we conclude that the *Leges Henrici* was written with a view to the local courts, about which, indeed, it gives us a good deal of information, if we have the patience to look for it.[4] What manner of man it was who wrote it is a question easier to ask than to answer. If he was of the same class as the man who wrote *Quadripartitus* – and all we can learn suggests that the two were closely associated – then he may have been in the service of a bishop or perhaps of a great lay magnate. We doubt very much that he was a royal clerk or in the service of the king.

The *Leges Henrici* was a fairly expensive book to produce and a difficult book that required leisure to study, a book destined for men of much the same class as its author. Whether it was ever of great practical use is highly questionable. There was, in any case, room for cheaper, shorter books, books without philosophical introductions and with less, much less, detail, and these books duly made their appearance. Whether they appeared before, or some years after, the *Leges Henrici* is of little moment. They owed their genesis to the same impetus, the need to instruct men in the law of King Edward. The titles by which two such books – or rather tracts – are known, the *Instituta Cnuti* and the *Consiliatio Cnuti*, indicate sufficiently that they are, in the main, renderings of Cnut's code. We need spare them but few words. The former borrows largely from Cnut, but draws also on Alfred-Ine, Edgar and the minor tracts. An original contribution professes to set out 'the customary rights of kings among the English'. Since these rights are

[1] Why it is brief we explain below, pp. 107-8.

[2] For a discussion of *Glanville* see below, pp. 105-17.

[3] Apart from a case of treasure trove and the trial of a large batch of thieves, nothing seems to be recorded but the dubious case of the moneyers (*Governance of Mediaeval England*, p. 180; above, p. 34).

[4] Cf. *ibid.*, pp. 183-4.

sometimes shared with the king, the author mentions the third penny to which an earl is entitled, and he has a good deal to say of the privileges of the archbishop of Canterbury and other bishops. The purpose of the tract is obscure. It was evidently the work of a foreign ecclesiastic, with an imperfect knowledge of English, and he was presumably endeavouring to put his less gifted colleagues on terms with English law.[1] The *Consiliatio Cnuti* is a similar production, with less originality. It professes to set out the laws which Cnut decreed should be universally observed in England. A later hand heads the tract 'leges que vocantur Edwardi', thus testifying to the general, and scarcely incorrect, identification of Edward's laws with Cnut's laws. The purpose of this tract seems similarly to have been to put foreign ecclesiastics on terms with English law. To this end a later hand, so it would appear, has interpolated an elaborate explanation of 'tithing'.[2] Another brief tract associated with these attempts to expound in summary form the laws of King Edward is one which professes to set forth the laws of the Conqueror in ten articles. It has no short contemporary title, but is sometimes known as 'Hic intimatur' from the first words of the exordium, which explains that what follows is what King William, with his chief men, enacted after the conquest of England.[3] We must confess that, though high authorities have attributed considerable value to this tract and have believed it to summarise genuine legislative acts of the Conqueror that have been lost, we can find few merits in it and certainly not the signal merit of preserving legislation otherwise unknown.[4] As to the date of compilation, we can be reasonably sure that the tract was not before the compiler of the first book of *Quadripartitus*, and he, after all, cast his net widely enough. He incorporated the one piece of genuine legislation it is safe to ascribe to William and nothing else from his reign: it was not until much later that the *Ten Articles* were interpolated in one manuscript of *Quadripartitus*.[5] The main source of the *Ten Articles* is, without question, the *Instituta Cnuti*, and when we have added William's one genuine legislative act and Henry I's coronation charter[6] to the sources, there is but a trifle else that can come from some unknown source, and that unknown source can hardly have lain elsewhere than

[1] The text was printed by Liebermann in *Trans. R. Hist. Soc.*, N.S., vii.77-107. An abstract is printed in *Gesetze*, i.612-6, and the translations from the text of Cnut, *ibid.*, pp. 279-371. Liebermann dates the tract 1103-1120 (*ibid.*, iii.330).

[2] For the text see Liebermann's separate publication *Consiliatio Cnuti*. An abstract is printed in *Gesetze*, i.618-19, and the translations from the text of Cnut, *ibid.*, pp. 279-371. Liebermann dates this tract *c.* 1110-1130 (*Gesetze*, iii.333-4).

[3] Text in *Gesetze*, i.486-8, whence Robertson, pp. 238-42. We refer to it hereafter as the *Ten Articles*.

[4] Pollock and Maitland, *History of English Law*, i.88.

[5] Liebermann, *Quadripartitus*, p. 10.

[6] In this way we can account for all but articles 2, 3 and 4: cf. Liebermann, *Gesetze*, iii.278. As to art. 3 see p. 47, n. 2 below. Upon art. 2, which has been supposed to reflect the Salisbury oath, we comment later (below, p. 101). Art. 4 seems to be entirely apocryphal. The author claims that it proceeded from the council at Gloucester, the only council the chroniclers notice (above, p. 32) and doubtless the only one of which he had knowledge.

in the author's imagination. It seems idle to attribute to the Conqueror, on the strength of the *Ten Articles*, the prohibition of capital punishment.[1] And indeed it would have been strange if the Peterborough chronicler or some other of William's contemporary – or nearly contemporary–panegyrists had not remarked upon this stroke of uncharacteristic humanity. Nor, for other reasons, can we take more seriously an alleged law of *murdrum* which placed upon the slain man's lord the responsibility for the murder fine.[2] We can understand a benevolent man desiring the law to be as it is stated in the *Ten Articles* and we would not wish to call him by a harsh name. But a romancer he certainly was, a romancer who was not writing before the middle years of Henry I.[3] Perhaps we should have made no mention of him here, of so little importance is his work in itself; but, as we have said, it has been accorded undue merit in books of authority and it is as well that the error should be corrected. Nor should we devote many words here to another fictional work, the *Leis Willelme*, which has been ascribed, astonishingly enough, to the reign of Henry I or as early as William Rufus.[4] Its importance is undoubted, but it is for the reign of Henry II, and the *Leis Willelme*, as well as the *Ten Articles* in an expanded guise, will demand attention in a later chapter.

There remains to be noticed but one other lawbook, coming, it would seem, from the last years of Henry I, which, at least in its second edition, proclaimed itself to be the *Leges Edwardi Regis*.[5] It is now more familiarly known as the *Leges Edwardi Confessoris*. Hard things have been said of the writer who, though he had his struggles with the Latin tongue and sometimes forgot the fictional guise in which he intended to cast his work, did have a clearer mind and the power of organising his material far in advance of his predecessors. He has two themes, the privileges of the Church and the king's peace. He tells us some important things about sanctuary and the ordeal and perhaps he tells us some untruths about the trial of actions concerning Church lands in ecclesiastical courts and the rightful freedom of the Church from taxation,[6] though he admits that in practice churchmen paid danegeld just as laymen did. If he misleads us on such matters, in which he seems to have had a personal interest, it would be hard to say that he misleads us in the longer section of his work which treats of the king's peace, though we may wish for verification of some of his statements, for

[1] It is sufficient to say that art. 10 is derived from *Instituta Cnuti*, II, caps. 2.1 and 30.4 (*Gesetze*, i.309, 333).

[2] Art. 3. No parallel is to be found in any known source or in later practice.

[3] Liebermann's final conclusion was that the date was *c.* 1110 (*Gesetze*, iii.279). But the *Ten Articles* must be later than the *Instituta Cnuti*, which he thought might be as late as 1117 (*ibid.*, p. 310), and, again, the author of the *Quadripartitus* made no use of the tract. It cannot, however, be later than 1122, when the earliest manuscript to contain the tract, the *Textus Roffensis*, fol. 80-81v, appears to have been written: see Facsimile ed., i.18.

[4] Text in *Gesetze*, i.492-520; Robertson, pp. 252-74 (French only). For date see below, pp. 121-5, 171-5.

[5] Text in *Gesetze*, i.627-72.

[6] Caps. 4-11 (*Gesetze*, i.630-7).

example, that rural deans were entitled to one-tenth of the profits of justice.[1] It may be that in some county there was such a practice: our ignorance is too great to permit us to deny his assertion that such a practice did exist in his day. But though we may need to regard this and some other of his statements with caution, all in all he seems to be a guide of some worth to the local administration of justice under Henry I.[2] The symmetry of his little book was marred by the addition of a historical appendix and ill-assorted chapters dealing with the rehabilitation of those unjustly slain as thieves, with usurers, and with the sale of goods suspected of being stolen.[3] It is difficult to believe that these additions are the work of the original author: they certainly give the book a clumsy look, which it did not originally possess. In this state, however, it was taken over by an editor who improved the Latin, but occasionally failed to understand the author's meaning.[4] At an early date there was prefixed to this revision the *Ten Articles* attributed to William the Conqueror and there was appended to it a genealogy of the dukes of Normandy, ending with Stephen. Consequently the revised version of the *Leges Edwardi Confessoris* has these invariable companions in later manuscripts.[5] We mention these facts because they help to date the revision to some time about the end of Stephen's reign. There was a further revision of very considerable interest in the early years of the next reign, but on this we must defer our comments.

Our survey of the legal literature that was inspired by the reinstatement of the law of King Edward makes, we fear, dull reading, and dull, for the most part, the texts themselves are. Their popularity under Henry I and Stephen it is difficult to assess. The *Instituta Cnuti* was, to judge from the use made of it, well known to legal writers.[6] It survived to be used by Bracton,[7] who made use also of the *Leges Edwardi Confessoris*.[8] The latter was a successful book, as such books go, in later times and was read even in the fifteenth century,[9] while the *Ten Articles* enjoyed an adventitious success because it travelled down the centuries with this companion and it attained the crowning glory of inclusion in the *Select Charters* as the 'Statutes of William the Conqueror'.[10] Even Maitland had a good word to say for this imposture,[11]

[1] Cap. 27.2 (*Gesetze*, i.651).

[2] Cf. *Governance of Mediaeval England*, pp. 195-6.

[3] Caps. 34.1*b* – 39.2 (*Gesetze*, i.662-70). That these chapters are an addition is confirmed by the fact that one group of manuscripts ends at cap. 34.1*a* (Liebermann, *Über die Leges Edwardi Confessoris*, p. 9).

[4] *Ibid.*, pp. 2-9.

[5] *Ibid.*, p. 119.

[6] We have already mentioned its use by the compiler of the *Ten Articles*. It was used also for the *Leges Willelmi* and the Pseudo-Cnut *de Foresta* (below, pp. 173-9).

[7] Richardson, *Bracton*, pp. 132-5.

[8] *Ibid.*, pp. 112-15, 130-5.

[9] Liebermann, *Über die Leges Edwardi Confessoris*, p. 123. In the fifteenth century the fabricator of the spurious coronation oath drew upon the third edition of the *Leges Edwardi*. The relation between the two texts seems first to have been remarked by Liebermann (*Über die Leges Anglorum*, pp. 53-4), though he did not appreciate that the oath was a fifteenth-century fabrication, as to which see *B.I.H.R.*, xiii.144-5, and *Trans. R. Hist. Soc.*, 4th ser., xxiii.131, 155-6.

[10] *Select Charters*, pp. 97-100.

[11] *History of English Law*, i.88.

while of the *Leges Edwardi Confessoris* he could say no better than that 'it has gone on doing its bad work down to our own time'.[1] We would reverse both judgements. However, so far as concerns the *Leges Edwardi Confessoris* in the two editions we have noticed and the rest of the Henrician legal literature, we doubt whether it was of any great importance to contemporaries. It was doubtless a wise political gesture on Henry's part to give back to the people of England the law of King Edward, but what he gave back was something moribund. True, this moribund gift took a long time a-dying, but nothing could resuscitate it. The function it had once served was usurped by a new jurisprudence that owed little to the past and that entailed no legislation, at least legislation in the sense we now give to the word. The new jurisprudence was concerned primarily with the land law, and it was built up, writ by writ, into a loose series of related, if ill-defined, forms of action, which were reshaped by the assizes of Henry II and finally systematised by the anonymous lawyer of genius who gave us *Glanville*. We are here concerned with the commencement of the story.

The origin of the writ process must be traced to the Old English kingdom. Relatively few writs have survived, not a great many more than a hundred, mostly from the reign of Edward the Confessor, but sufficient is known to acquaint us with their nature and the efficiency of the Old English chancery. It is clear that standard formulas had been evolved by the time of the Confessor, though there are indications that the wishes of the impetrant were studied in settling the terms of the writ.[2] It is possible that in some instances the writ was prepared by the party concerned and was not drafted, though it was approved and sealed, in the royal chancery. Many more writs have survived from the reigns of William I and William II than from the reign of Edward, for the most part in not very trustworthy transcripts and nearly all in Latin.[3] Some may be translations or there may have been vernacular counterparts. In part they appear to have been drafted by the impetrants.[4] The brief laconic formulas of the past still appear; but in style the writs show a declension from pre-Conquest standards. It seems evident that English clerks disappeared or fell into a subordinate position in the chancery, which was, of course, no longer English, but a migratory office, moving to and fro across the Channel with the Norman king's household. The feature that interests us here is the survival of a fair number of writs dealing with legal process,[5] for which

[1] *Ibid.*, p. 104.

[2] Harmer, *Anglo-Saxon Writs*, pp. 57-61. Miss Harmer prints 121 documents, not all, however, royal writs (pp. 119-424).

[3] *Regesta*, vol. i, with addenda in vol. ii.390-412.

[4] Bishop and Chaplais, *English Royal Writs*, p. xv. We may note that the editors believe (p. xiii) that 'from about 1070' royal writs 'ceased almost completely to be written in the vernacular'. But *Regesta* nos. 208B and 506 suggest continuity (if on a diminished scale) into the twelfth century, as does the use of English for similar purposes outside the royal chancery (cf. *Governance of Mediaeval England*, p. 26*n*).

[5] Writs concerned with legal procedure have been collected by Van Caenegem, *Royal Writs in England*: lists at pp. 406-12; texts at pp. 413-515.

we have nothing exactly corresponding from before the Conquest.[1] This is not a matter for surprise since such writs are, for the most part, of fugitive interest to the parties. The survival of the Old English polity is, however, manifest. A writ may be addressed to the sheriff and all the thegns of Kent, French and English,[2] or to the sheriff and all the thegns in the bishopric of Rochester,[3] or again, to the sheriff and lawmen (*judicatores*).[4] Other writs direct that actions shall be tried in the hundred court[5] or the county court[6] or in a session of three and half hundreds.[7] There are no Norman inventions, though we may find evidence here, as elsewhere, of clumsy adaptation of English forms by men unskilled in English ways and the English tongue.

It is not until the reigns of Henry I and Stephen that surviving post-Conquest 'original' writs, as we may perhaps now call them, become at all numerous.[8] As in previous reigns the survivors can be no more than a small fraction of those that were issued. With their aid we can, in a measure, reconstruct the evolution of a new jurisprudence, and the writs are fortunately supplemented by a few reports of actions that have come down to us in monastic chronicles.[9] The writs seem gradually to be approaching a set form, the actions to be gradually assuming the likeness of the actions we find entered on the plea rolls of later reigns. But though there is now a corps of royal judges who are controlled by the justiciar and though the justiciar has a writing office where the greater part of the writs appear to be written and certainly are sealed,[10] procedure is not yet rigid. We notice this lack of formality in actions in which ecclesiastics are concerned, actions which lie in that debatable land where the jurisdiction of *regnum* and *sacerdotium* overlap, a field of acute controversy under Henry II. But for a long time there is co-operation between Church and State,[11] and this co-operation itself tends to fluidity, tends to make unnecessary that rigid definition which is the mark of the Age of Glanville. We shall need to say more of these matters. Here no more is necessary than to indicate that there is much that is vital to our understanding of the law of Norman England which the lawbooks of the period overlook.

But before we turn to the reign of Henry II there are some words we think it may be useful to say on a subject that fills rather too prominent a place in modern books – the customs or 'laws' of Wessex, Mercia and

[1] That such writs were issued before the Conquest is indicated by the references to appeals to the king for justice in the legislation of Edgar and Cnut (above, p. 37).

[2] Elmham, *Hist. S. Augustini Cant.*, p. 352.

[3] *Anglia Sacra*, i.338-9.

[4] *Chron. Abbatiae Rameseiensis*, p. 211. The printed text gives the meaningless corruption *justificatoribus*.

[5] *E.H.R.*, xxxv.392-3. This is a writ of Henry I, but it conveys the same lesson.

[6] *Cart. Mon. de Rameseia*, i.233-4.

[7] *Ibid.*, p. 236; *Chron. Abbatiae Rameseiensis*, p. 214.

[8] A selection will be found in Bigelow, *Placita Anglo-Normannica*, pp. 73-166, and a further selection in Van Caenegem, *Royal Writs in England, ut supra* (p. 49, n. 5).

[9] *Governance of Mediaeval England*, pp. 180, 192, 286-9.

[10] *Ibid.*, pp. 163, 168-9, 189.

[11] *Ibid.*, pp. 286-7, 315-17.

the Danelaw. Maitland, speaking of England under Norman kings, put the conventional view in these words: 'a text writer must still start with this, that England is divided between three laws, Wessex law, Mercian law, Danelaw'.[1] But this sentence hardly represents what the lawbooks do. Their origin is in Wessex and the outlook of the writers is provincial. True, they speak of these three laws, but they speak rather as antiquaries than as lawyers,[2] and as antiquaries who have looked into old-fashioned books and have never looked with any curiosity upon the England of their day. The earliest reference to the three laws occurs apparently in Cnut's Code, but solely with reference to royal rights.[3] The boundaries within which the three laws were recognised are set out in an Old English tract, which cannot be earlier than 1047 and in any case appears to come from the reign of the Confessor.[4] The fact that here Kent is included in Wessex and Middlesex in the Danelaw does not inspire confidence in its accuracy, at least in regard to the limits within which the customary laws of the West Saxons, Mercians and Danes were observed. It was upon such sources as these and some tracts of the tenth century that the later writers drew.[5] The county with the most strongly marked and the most tenaciously held customs was, however, Kent.[6] A generation or so ago, if any educated man had been asked to name one local English custom surviving from antiquity, he would almost certainly have answered 'gavelkind'. The feature which in the popular mind particularly distinguished gavelkind was that, under this form of tenure, land descended in the right line to all sons equally, but it had a number of other remarkable features. It was not abolished – and even then there were necessary exceptions – until 1925.[7] But the Cinque Ports and the Liberty of Romney Marsh remain to remind us that, of all the shires of England, it was the ancient kingdom of Kent that possessed the most distinctive customs.[8] Yet the law-

[1] *History of English Law*, i.106.

[2] They appear to have no originality, though their immediate source may not always be apparent.

[3] II Cnut, cc. 12-15 (Liebermann, *Gesetze*, i.316-20: above, p. 27).

[4] This appears to exist only in a Middle English version, printed by Morris, *Old English Miscellany*, pp. 145-6. There are borrowings in *Leges Henrici*, c. 6 (*Gesetze*, i.552). Later Latin versions, considerably altered, are printed in Simeon of Durham, *Opera*, ii.392-3, and Gale, *Scriptores XV*, pp. 560-2.

[5] The tenth-century tracts are Norðleoda laga and Mircna laga. Both were translated in *Quadripartitus* and the second in *Instituta Cnuti* (*Gesetze*, i.458-63).

[6] For a late thirteenth-century statement of Kentish customs, made in the eyre of 1293, see *Statutes of the Realm*, i.223-5. Since there was undoubtedly an eyre in that year, for which five rolls survive (Assize Rolls 373-7), there is no ground for questioning the fact or the substantial accuracy of the statement. The customs were certainly claimed in 1259 before the justiciar, Hugh le Bigod (Jacob, *Studies in the Period of Baronial Reform*, pp. 57-60, 349-52). For earlier evidence see Vinogradoff, *Villainage*, pp. 205-8.

[7] Administration of Estates Act, 1925, s. 45; Law of Property Act, 1925, s. 51.

[8] The continuity of the Confederation of the Cinque Ports was secured by the Local Government Act, 1958, s. 44: for its early history see Murray, *Constitutional History of the Cinque Ports*. The jurisdiction of the Lord Warden is still preserved, though it is now limited to the Court of Admiralty. The laws and customs of Romney Marsh, then of immemorial antiquity, were extended to all areas of England under Commissioners of Sewers in 1427 (*Rot. Parl.*, iv.333*b*; *Statutes of the Realm*, ii.236-8). For the history of the spontaneously organised body which ruled the Marsh see Derville, *Level and Liberty of Romney Marsh*.

books say no word about Kentish law. Nor do they say one word of the customs of London. Yet the two communities which, in the thirteenth and fourteenth centuries, insisted that the king's justices should respect their ancient customs were the Londoners[1] and the men of Kent[2] – not the Danes or the Mercians or the West Saxons, who had been absorbed into the uniform background of the counties they chanced to inhabit. Nor, when the lawbooks tell of *murdrum*, do they even hint that no murder fines were exacted in northern England.[3] And yet this is a significant, an important, distinction. To modern historians this distinction may suggest that the murder fine did not originate with William the Conqueror, as the *Ten Articles* pretend,[4] and that perhaps there is truth in the tradition that it was introduced by Cnut to protect his fellow-countrymen.[5] Protection may not have been necessary in lands where Danish kings had recently ruled. . . . But we must not be lured into this byway. Let us resume. We should not expect the lawbooks to tell us of Northumbrian tenures, for the land law seems to be beyond their purview, but the authors resolutely shut their eyes to any peculiarities of the delictual law beyond the three distinctive laws of which, with common accord, they say much. Even so, the latest of them, the author of the *Leges Edwardi*, draws no distinction between Wessex and Mercia, but merely between Danes and English.[6] We find the old distinctions again in the *Leges Willelmi*,[7] which we have yet to discuss, but for all the careful particularities of this tract, there are the same obvious omissions.

Now, in face of these omissions, it is evident that the lawbooks do not attempt to give us what we should regard as essential knowledge about the special laws of the different parts of England nor what any self-respecting lawyer would strive to tell his contemporaries, if these local laws were really of importance, other than, perhaps, to the localities. And we very much doubt whether *wer*, *wite* and *bot*, which had once been of vital significance to the law, continued even in the earliest years of the twelfth century to signify very much.[8] Certainly from the point of view of the kingdom at large, of the men who were fashioning a new judicature and a new jurisprudence, these things were no great matter. Justices on eyre may have to take note of local customs and local claims to special treatment; but the general pattern of administration will scarcely be affected. Judges will evolve an action of tres-

[1] *Trans. R. Hist. Soc.*, 4th ser., v.23-4; *Munimenta Gildhallae Londoniensis*, ii.289. These references relate to the eyre of 14 Edward II.

[2] See p. 51, n. 6 above. The customs were again claimed in the eyre of 1313 (*Eyre of Kent*, i. pp. xxxvi, 11, 18, 59).

[3] Freedom from the murder fine is disclosed in the pipe rolls: cf. *Governance of Mediaeval England*, p. 202.

[4] Cap. 3 (*Gesetze*, i.487); above, p. 47.

[5] *Leges Edwardi Confessoris*, cap. 16 (*Gesetze*, i.642). The coronation charter of Henry I, cap. 9, indicates that *murdrum* preceded the Conquest: 'Murdra . . . quae amodo facta fuerint iuste emendentur secundum lagam regis Eadwardi' (*ibid.*, p. 522).

[6] *Leges Edwardi Confessoris*, cap. 12.3, 4, 5, 18.3, 30, 31 (*Gesetze*, i.634-50).

[7] *Leges Willelmi*, cap. 1-3, 8, 16, 21.2 (*ibid.*, i.492-7).

[8] Cf. Pollock and Maitland, *History of English Law*, ii.448-51.

pass, itself a fertile mother of actions; but this action will have no links with the conceptions of a primitive Germanic past, of which the lawbooks provide an almost meaningless reminiscence. The judges will indeed, to begin with, call the action of trespass by a Roman name, *actio iniuriarum*, which is eloquent of the manner in which their conceptions took form.[1] Nor does the evolving law of tort take notice of *wer*, *wite* or *bot*. All such antiquities have disappeared from the real world by the second half of the twelfth century, and we doubt whether this change came with the 'marvellous suddenness' that struck Maitland.[2] We suspect that the antiquarianism of the lawbooks unwittingly conceals the changes that were in progress before the authors' unseeing eyes. These writers were, after all, engaged in reconstructing King Edward's law from books, and the most recent book they had came from the reign of Cnut: the oldest was as old as Ine. Some living law peeps out from time to time in the *Leges Henrici* and the *Leges Edwardi*[3]; but the authors are not careful to distinguish between the living and the dead, and the dead take up more space than the living, the living they so largely ignored.

[1] Richardson and Sayles, *Select Cases of Procedure without Writ*, p. cxii. See further below, pp. 83-4.
[2] Pollock and Maitland, *op. cit.*, ii.458.
[3] Above, pp. 44, 47-8.

III

PREROGATIVE AND PRIVILEGE

HENRY II, a Frenchman, an Angevin, who spent much less than half his reign in England, was the most considerable legislator since the reign of another foreign king of the English, Cnut. Apart from one minor measure, he seems, however, not to have begun to legislate until nine years after his accession. The texts of most of his later legislative acts have perished, while of those that survive some are uncertain or corrupt and some, claimed to be his, are blatantly false, foisted upon us by the carelessness of incurious editors. An unpromising basis, it might seem, upon which to construct a full or coherent story. We would we had better material, but we have, we think, enough to provide a satisfactory outline and sufficient detail to give a good idea of what Henry accomplished.

We have endeavoured elsewhere to replace by sober history some of the stories told in the textbooks of Henry's career and achievements,[1] but it may be convenient if we say something here of the antecedents and beginnings of his reign. To understand fully Henry's position when he was crowned on 19 December 1154, we must go back to the year 1120 when all his grandfather's hopes and plans were brought to nothing by the death of his heir in the tragedy of the White Ship. Henry I remarried in the following year, but his hopes were again disappointed, for his young wife gave him no male heir to replace the son he had lost. His attempt to secure the succession for his daughter Matilda was brought to nothing, not so much because of her personal failings – though these were sufficiently objectionable – but because to accept her as queen would mean the acceptance of her husband, Geoffrey, count of Anjou, as king of England and duke of Normandy.[2] The successful claimant, Stephen of Blois, who was as near of kin to the Conqueror as Matilda, had everything in his favour when he gained the approval of the pope to his coronation,[3] everything except the ruthless ability that had been his uncle's and the quality which was above all needed in a king who would control the feckless and reckless Norman baronage on both sides of the Channel. With an indisputable title to the throne Stephen might have ruled indifferently well, but Matilda could not forget or forgo her rival claim. Her husband

[1] *Governance of Mediaeval England*, pp. 251-64.
[2] Ramsay, *Foundations of England*, ii.309, sets out the position very clearly.
[3] Above, p. 40.

Geoffrey, prudent man, had no high ambitions,[1] and though, taking advantage of Stephen's weakness, he made himself master of Normandy, he had no desire to tempt fate by engaging in an unequal struggle with Stephen for the crown of England. Matilda did make the attempt and failed and then left the task to her son Henry. Henry was little, if any, more successful than his mother, but he was at least able, with his limited resources, to add to England's misery and to disrupt still further the administration of the country. His 'campaign' of 1153 might perhaps be more accurately described as a barbaric raid, with its trail of smoking ruins, and to describe its conclusion as a 'triumphal progress'[2] seems far removed from ascertainable fact. At best Henry had achieved a stalemate when, through the efforts of Archbishop Theobald, an accommodation was reached between him and Stephen's heir, William, count of Boulogne. This arrangement was elaborated at a meeting with Stephen at Winchester on 6 November 1153 and ratified in a treaty at Westminster in December, which formally recognised Henry's right of succession and put an end to overt hostilities. The treaty was, in fact, no more than a truce, and its very terms show that neither party, and Henry in particular, would feel himself bound by it. By retaining his hold on all he held by force of arms Henry showed quite openly that he intended to disregard his solemn obligation to permit the uniform administration of the country which the treaty prescribed. Providentially for England Stephen died unexpectedly within the year and Henry succeeded with no serious opposition.[3]

Henry's was a sorry inheritance and, despite all the advantages he enjoyed in the support of the Church and the most prominent of Stephen's adherents, it took eleven years before the country's administration was restored to the level it had attained under Henry I. There were other urgent problems beside administrative reform. Stephen had granted away much of the royal demesne and, in their bids for support, Matilda and Henry had granted away more. The treaty of Westminster, moreover, had not only confirmed Count William in all the possessions that fell to him by right of inheritance but also a considerable portion of the royal demesne. His marriage with the heiress of the earl of Surrey brought him a great deal more as well. Henry is said to have undertaken other obligations towards him that made him the second personage in the kingdom. But in any case the treaty ensured to a potential claimant to the throne resources that made him too powerful for Henry's comfort, if not for his safety. Nothing could show more convincingly how weak Henry's position had been than

[1] His attitude is well illustrated by the advice he is reputed to have given his son: Henrico heredi suo interdixit ne Normannie vel Anglie consuetudines in consulatus sui terram vel e converso varie vicissitudinis alternatione permuterat (*Chroniques des Comtes d'Anjou*, p. 224).

[2] A. L. Poole, *From Domesday Book to Magna Carta*, p. 164.

[3] *Governance of Mediaeval England*, pp. 260-1.

this hard bargain into which he had been driven in order to obtain recognition of his claims.[1] However, he had no intention of keeping to his bargain if he could possibly help it. The problem for him was that the treaty of Westminster had been put under the protection of the Church, and the solemn undertakings then given must in some way be overridden by an even more solemn undertaking. We may be wrong in giving credit to the astute Nigel, bishop of Ely, whom Henry made his finance minister, for suggesting a way out; but all we can learn points in his direction. Certainly it was some sufficiently learned ecclesiastic who thought of the parallel between a bishop who, at his consecration, found the possessions of his see dilapidated by his predecessors, and a king who, at his consecration, found the royal demesne dilapidated. As Nigel knew from recent personal experience, a bishop was required to recover what had been lost.[2] But the question was a burning one at the time, a problem every newly consecrated bishop had to face, both Gilbert Foliot, for example, and Thomas Becket. It was not an easy problem and every bishop faced it in his own characteristic manner. Nigel with guile,[3] Gilbert with anxiety,[4] Thomas with effrontery.[5] Now since episcopal and monastic land had come in dubious ways into the hands of many barons, everyone of importance must have known that this obligation was binding upon bishops, abbots and priors. Many must have known, or have been apprehensive, that the question would be posed in an awkward way for themselves. And if ecclesiastics lay under this obligation, should not a king, who was, in a sense, an ecclesiastical person, be subject to the same obligation? It had long been regarded as meritorious in a king that he had protected the rights of the Crown, though, to be sure, this was by physical force against an external enemy.[6] But might not the principle be extended to cover losses caused in other ways, by the action of a usurper of a throne or – though the question was perhaps delicate – by the action of the rightful claimant before he became king? Whatever the considerations that moved Henry and his advisers, he took an oath at his coronation to recover any rights of the Crown which had been lost and, in consequence, a series of inquests was held all over the country to discover what were the ancient possessions that had come into the hands of subjects.[7] In this way the treaty of Westminster was inevitably brought into question. The king resumed those portions of the royal demesne that had been solemnly guaranteed to Count William and the count appealed to the pope as the supreme guarantor of the treaty.[8] The

[1] *Ibid.*, p. 253.
[2] *Traditio*, xvi.151-2.
[3] We infer that he himself procured the papal letters that required him to resume the estates of the bishopric of Ely that had been dispersed.
[4] Foliot, *Epistolae*, no. 87 (i.113-14).
[5] *Becket Materials*, ii.371-2; iii.42-3, 250-2. Cf. *Thómas Saga*, i.118-21.
[6] So it is said of Edgar 'iura regni bellica potestate regaliter protegens' (*Vita Oswaldi*, p. 425).
[7] *Traditio*, xvi.153-6; *Governance of Mediaeval England*, pp. 149-50, 261-2.
[8] *Ibid.*, p. 260.

count, however, died before a decision could be given on the issue whether the coronation oath overrode a prior obligation secured by oath. That issue will never be decided; but subsequent kings, with the support of the papacy, were to find this coronation promise a very convenient protection against the consequences of any action of theirs that might be construed as dilapidating the royal demesne or against any demand upon them which might be construed as an invasion of the rights of the Crown.[1]

Though it stands by no means alone, one of the strongest pieces of evidence for reconstructing the course of events as we have done is a revised edition of the *Leges Edwardi Confessoris* which appeared in the early years of Henry's reign. The importance of this revision was not appreciated when it was attributed to the reign of John or, at latest, to a date round about the year 1200.[2] Indeed, it seemed to Maitland that the reviser was talking idle nonsense.[3] The seeming nonsense assumes significance when it is related to the circumstances in which it was written. But, in the first place, we must say something of its date. The reviser was clearly writing before the Assize of Arms, for he describes the institution, which was regulated by that assize, at an earlier stage of its development[4]: the conventional date for the Assize of Arms is 1181, but, as we hope to show, the true date is some years earlier.[5] Again, the reviser was writing before Henry's expedition to Ireland in 1171, for he does not include Ireland where we should expect to find it among the appurtenances of the Crown.[6] And, again, the reviser was writing before the Assize of Clarendon of 1165-66, for he leaves unaltered the law relating to the responsibility of a host for a guest as it stood before that assize was made.[7] Other reasons could be adduced for rejecting a later date for the revision, but those we have given seem conclusive for placing it within the first eleven years of Henry's reign, and we think that it must have been undertaken soon after his coronation. It is, at least in large part, a justification for Henry's action. We must remember, what is perhaps not always borne in mind, that the reviser had to fit his teaching into an artificial framework, the exposition, largely fictional, of the laws of the Confessor. He has in mind the facts of Stephen's reign and the circumstances of Henry's accession, but he must transfer them to the setting provided by the book he is revising or, rather, supplementing. So Stephen must be represented by the Danish kings of England and Henry must become Edward. But what Edward does in this imaginary historical setting provides a pre-

[1] Examples are Henry III's grants (see *E.H.R.*, lvi.529-39) and Edward I's frequent invocation of this clause to resist inconvenient concessions and to free himself from his undertakings regarding the charters (*Speculum*, xxiv.40-1).

[2] Text in Liebermann, *Gesetze*, i.627-72. For his speculations as to date see *Über die Leges Anglorum*, pp. 97-8, and *Gesetze*, iii.340.

[3] *History of English Law*, i.103-4.

[4] Cap. 32 A 9-15 (*Gesetze*, i.656).

[5] Below, pp. 99-100.

[6] Cap. 11, 1 A 3. 'Hibernia' is mentioned in cap. 32 E among the conquests of King Arthur but is placed in Scandinavia with Norway, Sweden and Gothland (*Gesetze*, i.635, 659).

[7] Cap. 23-23, 4 (*Gesetze*, i.648-9). For the amendment see below, p. 94.

cedent and justification for what Henry has done in actual fact. Thus the reviser says that these Danish kings had alienated and dilapidated much of the rights and dignities, lands and islands, belonging to the Crown of England and had given them to their Danish and Norwegian followers who infested the kingdom and destroyed it. Wherefore their grants and alienations should of right be completely revoked, reduced to nothing and entirely extirpated. And this is what the good King Edward did. He revoked their acts so far as he was able, although he could not revoke them all, for he had not sufficient power to reform and reduce the kingdom to its former state. He fulfilled his oath in so far as he was able, for he was not willing to be an oath-breaker, and he accomplished what he could.[1]

This justification for Henry's action, by providing an imaginary precedent, comes after the reviser had inserted into the text before him a dissertation on the kingly office, which includes an exegesis of the coronation oath. The first article of this oath, as the reviser gives it, is one that obliges the king to preserve and defend all the lands and honours, all the dignities, rights and liberties belonging to the Crown, with the corollary that he is to recall such as have been dispersed, dilapidated or lost.[2] As we have already suggested, we have here as conclusive evidence as we could wish for an intimate connexion between the revision of the *Leges Edwardi Confessoris* and the political situation which followed Henry II's coronation. But the reviser has a wider aim than to justify Henry's action. Evidently he has this in mind, but he wishes also to expound the nature of the kingly office and the limitations imposed upon the king through the necessity he is under to act with the advice of the baronage. If it would be an exaggeration to call him our first constitutional lawyer, yet, with all his shortcomings, he is the precursor of the whole line. His work is not to the modern taste. We do not like our law in fictional guise, nor do we value as authorities imaginary letters from imaginary popes to imaginary kings.[3] But in the Middle Ages it was otherwise. In its latest form the *Leges Edwardi Confessoris* became a popular lawbook, accepted as authoritative by Bracton[4] and the writer of *Fleta*[5]; and its authority was consecrated when in 1308 the king was required to swear at his coronation that he would observe, above all, the laws, customs and franchises granted to the clergy and people by the glorious king Saint Edward. There was no difficulty in finding the book where those laws were written out for all men to read.[6]

[1] Cap. 13, 1 A, according to Liebermann's notation (*Gesetze*, i.640*n*).
[2] Cap. 11, 1 A 2 (*Gesetze*, i.635).
[3] The reviser inserts a letter from Pope Eleutherius to King Lucius (cap. 11, 1 B; *Gesetze*, i.636-7). For the sources of this fabrication see Liebermann, *Über die Leges Anglorum*, pp. 40-1.
[4] Richardson, *Bracton*, pp. 112-15, 132-5.
[5] *Gesetze*, i.635, *n.c.*
[6] For the manuscripts of the third edition see Liebermann, *op. cit.*, pp. 101-5. To these add the Rylands Library MS. described by Liebermann in *E.H.R.*, xxviii.732-45. Though no surviving manuscripts other than those of the London collection contain this text, its use by Bracton and the author of *Fleta* shows that it existed elsewhere: cf. *Speculum*, xxiv.61-2.

In this way the doctrine of inalienability entered English law[1]: not by any legislative act; not, so far as we can tell, as the result of deliberation between the king and his barons; but rather by applying a recognised principle of ecclesiastical law to an analagous situation in secular affairs. The circumstances in which the coronation oath was taken prevented any challenge at the time, though some of those present might well have been moved to protest had they realised the consequences of the oath they heard pronounced. But the coronation oath is, as the earlier liturgies express it, a *promissio regis*, a unilateral declaration.[2] Intended to safeguard the rights of the subject, experience was to show that it could be used by kings as a double-edged weapon. If we take the long view, the doctrine of inalienability is a protection for prince and people alike; but in the circumstances of 1154 some of the people, and the more important among them, were bound to suffer. The resumption by Henry of former demesne of the Crown did excite the interest of chroniclers, even if they found it difficult to understand the reason, when they heard of the losses incurred by such great men as Count William, the king of Scots, the count of Aumale, William of Ypres; but great and small, laymen and churchmen, suffered alike. The principle once established, there was, however, nothing arbitrary in its application. The forms of the law were observed, and some of the cases – that of William of Ypres, for example – must have dragged on for years.[3] Yet once it was established that property had been demesne of the Crown, there could be no further question in the king's court, though the king himself might deal graciously with the sufferer.[4] True, there is one instance where the lawfulness of the king's action was challenged, by Count William of Boulogne in the court of Rome; but, as we have said, his was a very special case.[5]

The task of reinvesting the Crown with its former authority and resources was Henry's most pressing problem at his accession, but another, less tractable, problem was casting its shadow across his path, the problem of the privilege of the clergy.[6] Not long before his death Stephen had begun the hearing of one of the *causes célèbres* of the twelfth century, a charge of murder, the murder of the archbishop of York by one of his archdeacons, who, so it was alleged, had administered to him a poisoned chalice. The case was still pending when Henry became king. Stephen had insisted on his right to try the archdeacon on the ground, well established by custom, that an atrocious crime com-

[1] For a general historical survey see Riesenberg, *Inalienability of Sovereignty in Medieval Political Thought* and the essay by Professor Gaines Post in his *Studies in Medieval Legal Thought*, 415-33. For the history of the doctrine in England see Kantorowicz in *Speculum*, xxix.488-502, and *Traditio*, xvi.151-61.

[2] Bouman, *Sacring and Crowning*, pp. 141-7; *Traditio*, xvi.173-4.

[3] *Ibid.*, p. 155.

[4] *Ibid.*, p. 156.

[5] Above, pp. 56-7.

[6] For much of the following discussion, see *Governance of Mediaeval England*, pp. 285-320.

mitted by a clerk – and no crime could very well be worse – fell within the jurisdiction of the secular courts. Archbishop Theobald, on the contrary, claimed the case for the Church and, since Henry was under a deep obligation towards him, he got his way, though not without strong opposition from the king's council. Unluckily the archdeacon failed in his compurgation before an ecclesiastical court but was successful in his appeal to the Roman Curia. He returned to England to live the life of a knight, an open and notorious scandal. It is evident, we may remark in passing, that the archdeacon did not enjoy a good reputation – otherwise he should have found no difficulty in obtaining sufficient compurgators – but though public opinion was against him, we may well doubt whether he was guilty of this particular crime.[1] However, the case was not one to commend ecclesiastical justice to laymen, and subsequent events were to show that Henry came soon to question his own wisdom in conceding Theobald's claim, on behalf of the Church, to try flagrant clerical offenders against the king's peace. And then there followed in quick succession a number of similar cases, not all of equal gravity to be sure, in which the immunity of the clergy appeared to laymen to result in a miscarriage of justice. In fairness it must be said that such cases arose in Theobald's time as well as after Becket succeeded him and, so far as we can tell, Becket did not act unjudicially in any case with which he was concerned.[2] At bottom, it was the system – a new system in England – that was at fault, the privilege which withdrew criminous clerks from secular justice. To the school of thought to which Becket adhered the degradation of a clerk, followed by penance, was in itself sufficient penalty for any crime, even the most atrocious, he had committed: the criminal should not suffer a second penalty at the hands of a secular tribunal. *Nec enim Deus judicat bis in idipsum.*[3] To laymen this argument was derisory–capital crimes by whomsoever committed deserved capital punishment – and there was respectable canonist opinion that held Becket and his friends to be wrong.[4] And even the ecclesiastical author of the *Leges Henrici*, who had claimed that all those in holy orders were subject only to ecclesiastical discipline, had made no claim for clerks who were married and lived the lives of laymen: they should, he said, be treated as laymen.[5] Becket made no such distinction.

Inadequately punished felony stands in the forefront of the disagreement between *sacerdotium* and *regnum* which marked Henry's reign. But though there were some prominent clerical murderers – or so men

[1] Allegations of poisoning were commonly made to account for sudden illness followed by death, and quite sensible people, like Gilbert Foliot, who may well have secured the archdeacon's acquittal at Rome, disbelieved the accusation in this case (*Epistolae*, no. 114 (i.152-3)). For similar cases see *Governance of Mediaeval England*, p. 291*n*.

[2] *Governance of Mediaeval England*, pp. 304-5. It is only in the inferior ecclesiastical courts that corruption seems to be alleged (below, pp. 90-92).

[3] *Becket Materials*, iv.202; *ibid.*, i.28.

[4] Maitland, *Canon Law in England*, pp. 140-5; *Governance of Mediaeval England*, pp. 303-4, 312.

[5] *Leges Henrici*, cap. 57.9, 9a (*Gesetze*, i.577).

deemed them – they were quite exceptional, and the clergy, save perhaps in places where many congregated together, were not generally given to crimes of violence.[1] The basic fact is that there was a wide area of possible dispute, since the jurisdictions of Church and State overlapped at many points, and the increasing personal antagonism between Henry and Becket ensured that the area in dispute should widen, the conflicts deepen. Trivialities assumed the dimensions of tragedies. One of the matters that most aroused Henry's ire was the denial by his ecclesiastical counsellors that a corrupt ecclesiastical judge, sitting in a minor court, trying a case against a layman, was not amenable to an edict the king had recently promulgated which rendered corrupt judges, whether ecclesiastical or secular, liable to amercement. This was in Theobald's time.[2] Rigid attitudes were being adopted well before Becket had the opportunity to make bad worse. And yet it is undeniable that not a great many years earlier there had been a large measure of co-operation in the administration of justice, and it would be hard to tell from some recorded cases whether an action was regarded as civil or ecclesiastical. Co-operation appears to have been the rule ever since the two jurisdictions had been formally separated by the Conqueror.

To make the position clear it may be well to give an illustration: one example out of many should be sufficient. Early in Henry I's reign the abbot of St Augustine's, Canterbury, had claimed the right to be presented to a prebend in Dover Priory, a prebend which, he said, had been granted to previous abbots by the king's ancestors. This claim was disputed by the canons, and the case was heard before the king's court at Whitsuntide (apparently in 1108) when there would be a large gathering of barons and prelates. The writs notifying the result of the action, which was in the abbot's favour, are witnessed by two bishops, Roger of Salisbury and William (Warelwast) of Exeter, both of whom were doubtless members of the court. What is particularly significant is that, though a writ to this effect was addressed to Archbishop Anselm, the responsibility for enforcing the judgement, should the canons resist it, was placed upon the sheriff.[3] A considerable list of actions in the king's court dealing with what may perhaps be called borderline cases could be cited,[4] but by about the middle of the century the competence of the king's court was being disputed. We have seen how it came to be disputed in criminal cases. At much the same time a canonist of some distinction, Hilary, bishop of Chichester, was disputing the competence of the king's court to decide a claim by Battle

[1] The allegation that in nine years more than a hundred unpunished murders had been committed by clerks, beside other serious crimes, is an obvious fabrication and, like some other of William of Newburgh's stories told long after the event, quite unworthy of credit (*Historia*, i.140).

[2] *Becket Materials*, iii.43-5; *Governance of Mediaeval England*, pp. 305-6: We refer to this case again (below, p. 88).

[3] Elmham, *Hist. Mon. Sancti Augustini Cantuariensis*, pp. 357-8; *Regesta*, nos. 878-9.

[4] *Governance of Mediaeval England*, pp. 286-7, 315-16.

Abbey to exemption from episcopal jurisdiction.[1] Bishop Hilary failed on this occasion to gain the support of his brother bishops, but the tide was noticeably turning. The pope was beginning to assert his authority and to appoint judges delegate to hear actions of the kind.[2] A litigant who knew his business might have a choice of two tribunals, and his choice would depend not upon his cloth but upon his expectation of victory.[3] If we were to confine ourselves to the correspondence and commentary that accumulated round the Becket controversy, we might gain the impression that there was some high principle at stake that engaged the interest and honour of all churchmen. Most of them, however, were much nearer the earth. Whether it was a secular or ecclesiastical tribunal that decided any dispute in which they found themselves involved mattered very little, so long as they won.[4] Becket and his supporters do not represent the general opinion of the clergy, for whom the quarrel was well above their heads. Even Becket's fellow bishops were far from disposed to go all the way with him.[5] And when all the fury was spent and the dust of controversy had settled, it was discovered that there was very little to dispute about and that that little concerned only the most disreputable of the clergy who would have been a disgrace to any profession.

A wiser man than Becket – his antagonist Gilbert Foliot, for example – would have reached an accommodation with the king. There was no dispute that the clergy were entitled to privilege of some sort. This had been recognised as far back as the seventh century when Kentish kings were legislating for laymen and ecclesiastics alike.[6] Nor did the king's court claim cognisance of matters of doctrine or of matrimonial or testamentary causes[7] that touched the great body of laymen far more

[1] *Chron. Mon. de Bello*, pp. 84-103; *Governance of Mediaeval England*, pp. 290-1.

[2] *Ibid.*, pp. 293, 300.

[3] *Ibid.*, pp. 302-3.

[4] As the chronicler of Battle Abbey said in defence of the abbot's taking proceedings in the king's court, the only question to be determined was upon whose presentation the incumbent was instituted (*Chron. Mon. de Bello*, p. 125). This despite the insistence of the canonists that the *ius presentandi* was a spiritual matter and solely for an ecclesiastical tribunal.

[5] See Knowles, *Episcopal Colleagues of Thomas Becket*, ch. 4, pp. 91-139, 'The Conduct of the Bishops, 1164-70'. Unfortunately nearly all the sources come from Canterbury sympathisers of the archbishop, who cannot be expected to take a detached view of his opponents, notably of Gilbert Foliot: nor does Professor Knowles find him sympathetic.

[6] The purported legislation of Æthelberht regarding ecclesiastics is spurious (above, pp. 1-4). The earliest surviving legislation on the subject (695-6) is that of Wihtred, caps. 1-2, 16-19, 21-24 (*Gesetze*, i.12-14; Attenborough, pp. 24-28). The legislation of Earconberht (640-64) in favour of the Church is lost (above, pp. 9-10).

[7] It does not follow that the same conventions were observed locally in England or in the king's continental dominions. In London for example, testamentary causes went to the court of husting. To take an example from the king's continental dominions: the prohibition conveyed in 1163 to John of Canterbury or 'Bellemains', bishop of Poitiers, not to hear causes where landed property was in question or complaints of usury, can have no relevance to the Constitutions of Clarendon (*Becket Materials*, v.38-9). It is unfortunate that this should be suggested, for instance, by Sir James Ramsay (*Angevin Empire*, p. 41) and Mlle Foreville (*L'Église et la Royauté*, pp. 118-19). Although Richard de Lucy conveyed this prohibition to the bishop, it must have originated in a local complaint. The idea that there was a concerted attack upon ecclesiastical privileges throughout Henry's dominions has no basis. What the conventional division of jurisdiction between count and

intimately than any of the issues for which Becket fought. The real question at issue was what amount of privilege, what degree of immunity, was compatible with the integrity of the State and the maintenance of the king's peace. There were, of course, subordinate problems of reconciling the conflicting claims of *sacerdotium* and *regnum*. The *jus patronatus* is a good example, and of this we shall have more to say. Like other issues it could not be disentangled from its historical background, the background of the proprietary church, now no more than a memory. But to a layman, his advowson, his right to present an incumbent to a cure of souls, was still a piece of property, and it so remained until very recent years: as such, should not any conflicting claims to ownership be decided in the king's court? To a canonist this right was so closely bound up with spiritual things that only an ecclesiastical tribunal was deemed competent to decide the issue. A settlement which laymen would accept could but appear illogical to a canonist.[1] No sensible man would, however, quarrel violently over such a matter. But perhaps that reflexion is irrelevant: as Gilbert Foliot reminded him forcibly, Becket was not sensible.[2]

Whatever extraneous matters might be dragged in, the only acute issue was, and remained, the absurd one of the criminous clerk.[3] Absurd to us of the present day, wherever our religious sympathies may lie; but not absurd to that generation of churchmen nor to so wise a man as Bracton, the learned and faithful servant of secular justice.[4] Evidently, as we have said, Henry regretted his yielding to the insistence of Archbishop Theobald and his handing over the incriminated archdeacon to ecclesiastical justice. This had created an embarrassing precedent for the civil power, though we can hardly blame the clergy for ensuring that so notable a victory should be followed up. Partisans,

[1] For the proprietary church in the eleventh century see Boehmer, 'Das Eigenkirchentum in England' in *Festgabe für Felix Liebermann*, pp. 301-53. For the evolution of the *jus patronatus* see Thomas, *Le droit de propriété . . . et le patronage au moyen âge*, pp. 105-48.

[2] 'Semper fuit stultus et semper erit' (*Becket Materials*, iii.57). There is another version (*ibid.*, p. 305); but as Professor Knowles suggests, 'the bishop of London may well have felt that the words would bear repetition' (*Episcopal Colleagues of Thomas Becket*, p. 78*n*).

[3] Cf. Mr A. L. Poole's comment that Becket did not 'hand down a great legacy to the church; if anything he perpetuated an abuse – the immunity of clerks from secular punishment for their crimes' (*From Domesday Book to Magna Carta*, p. 199).

[4] Bracton indeed puts the Church's claims at the highest: 'Cum autem clericus sic de crimine convictus degradetur, non sequitur alia pena pro uno delicto vel pluribus ante degradationem perpetrata'. The only exception he will allow is in the case of apostasy, when the clerk is to be handed over to the lay power for burning (*De Legibus*, fol. 123*b*-124: Woodbine, ii.348-9). It is difficult to reconcile Bracton's statement here with what he says elsewhere or the practice of the courts in his day (*Governance of Mediaeval England*, pp. 510-11).

bishop had been in Poitou seems not to be known: presumably the bishop had endeavoured to encroach upon what were considered the count's privileges. M. Pouzet throws no light on the matter in his monograph on the bishop's career (*L'Anglais Jean dit Bellemains*, pp. 30-1). The bishop had been a close friend of Becket's in the household of Archbishop Theobald and continued to correspond with him. As treasurer of York he had been the mouthpiece of the ecclesiastical members of the court which had tried a rural dean charged with extortion, and he had clashed with Richard de Lucy by disputing the liability of the accused to a secular penalty (*Becket Materials*, iii.43-5; *Governance of Mediaeval England*, pp. 305-6).

in any age, do not look far beyond their noses. The number of cases was doubtless quite small where, to a layman's view, justice was not done or inadequate penalties were inflicted[1]; but in the atmosphere of growing antagonism, induced by Becket's arrogance and the king's resentment, the evil was inevitably magnified. To add to Henry's resentment complaints reached him of the denial of justice to laymen in archdeacons' courts and rural chapters, always unpopular tribunals.[2] At a council called for the purpose on 1 October 1163 Henry raised both these issues with the bishops. We are not told how the discussion went in regard to archdeacons' courts, though there is not likely to have been any dispute that laymen should be adequately safeguarded. But the trial of criminous clerks was a very different matter. Henry was endeavouring to withdraw the concession he had made to Archbishop Theobald and so to make clerks once more amenable to the criminal law of the land. To meet the objection that clerks should not be tried before a secular court, he proposed that the accused should first be tried in an ecclesiastical court, but in the presence of a royal justice,[3] and, if found guilty, should be delivered to the secular court.[4] That this proposal was in general agreement with what had been customary in England under Stephen and was still customary in Normandy does not seem open to question, nor that it was permissible under canon law as this had been understood by one school of canonists.[5] But Becket refused to consider the proposal, arguing that what was involved was a double penalty.[6]

No agreement having been reached at this council, the king resolved to bring the two questions before another council, but as items in a general survey of matters in dispute between Church and State. To reach agreement he proposed that there should be a return to the position as it had stood under his grandfather. As was his rule, Henry ignored all that had happened under Stephen. For him the law as it existed in 1135 was the law still. He paid no regard to the widening claims of the canonists to deal with matters that at one time had come without demur before the king's court. The text of the original document setting out the customary procedure under Henry I has not survived. According to Becket, who was in a position to know, it was prepared by Richard de Lucy, the more active and competent of the two justiciars, and Jocelyn of Bailleul, a prominent royal clerk.[7] We

[1] *Governance of Mediaeval England*, pp. 304-5. We have commented above (p. 61, n. 1) on Newburgh's exaggerated statement. [2] For these see below, p. 68.

[3] As we explain later, the justice intended must be the local justice (below, p. 90).

[4] So Diceto, *Imagines Historiarum*, i.313.

[5] Maitland, *Canon Law in England*, pp. 140-5; *Governance of Mediaeval England*, pp. 303-4, 312; above, p. 60.

[6] There is no satisfactory contemporary account of the proceedings at this council: cf. Knowles, *op. cit.*, pp. 56-8. But there is no doubt, on the evidence of Herbert of Bosham (*Becket Materials*, iii.266-75), that the issue of criminous clerks became, if not designedly, the principal subject of discussion. For other accounts of the council see *ibid.*, ii.376-9: iv.26-7, 95-7.

[7] This, at least, seems to be the interpretation of his description of them as 'pravitatum illarum auctores et fabricatores' (*Becket Materials*, v.395).

must suppose that the work was efficiently done, though naturally the result would represent the views current in the king's immediate circle. But all we have is what emerged after some days of discussion at Clarendon between disputants who did not meet in a spirit of sweet reasonableness,[1] and the Constitutions of Clarendon, as they stand, are not a creditable piece of draftsmanship. There are signs of concessions to the bishops: the article which denies civil rights to excommunicates until they have reconciled themselves with the Church[2]; another article which pledges the king to compel lay magnates to respect the judgements of ecclesiastical courts.[3] The inference must be that there was real discussion, and there seem to have been some pretty drastic amendments. The various versions of the text that have come down to us clearly derive from an official copy, presumably that handed to Becket, and a fairly satisfactory reconstruction of the original can be effected.[4] The articles are not in logical order. The important and the unimportant jostle one another; one subject may be dispersed over three articles[5]; and some articles are obscure to the point of unintelligibility.[6] We must not rashly blame the original draftsmen: their work may have been sadly mutilated, and circumstances were not propitious for re-drafting, which would be likely to restart the interminable wrangling. However, in this disorder, the amended draft, as we take it to be, was formally ratified by the bishops, earls and barons at a final meeting on 30 January 1164.[7] Three copies of the ratified document were made, one for each of the archbishops and one for the royal archives, doubtless to be multiplied for use by the courts.[8] Whether the Constitutions were ever published in the county courts, as other legislation was,[9] seems not to be recorded. However, the point to establish is that the legislative process was duly completed and the

[1] The discrepant accounts of the council present great difficulty. Miss Norgate's attempt at working out its chronology is probably as near as one can get (*England under Angevin Kings*, ii.44-5). However long the council lasted, it concluded on 30 January as the official record shows: Facta est autem . . . recordatio . . . quarto die ante Purificationem beate Marie Virginis (*Becket Materials*, v.79; *Select Charters*, p. 167). As each clause in the draft was read there was, it seems clear, discussion, although it may not have taken precisely the form that Herbert of Bosham alleges (*Becket Materials*, iii.280-5). So R. de Diceto speaks of 'immensos tractatus' (*Imagines Historiarum*, i.312).

[2] Art. no. 5.

[3] Art. no. 13.

[4] The text in *Select Charters*, pp. 163-7, removes some interpolations from the text given in *Becket Materials*, v.71-9. Other texts are defective. Some of the articles are guaranteed by Herbert of Bosham, who reproduces them from the original chirograph (*ibid.*, iii.280-4).

[5] Excommunication is the subject of articles 5, 7 and 10.

[6] Notably article 3 dealing with criminous clerks. While the interpretation proposed by Maitland is now generally accepted as against that previously adopted, Mlle Foreville argues that the intention was that clerks should be tried in secular courts (*L'Église et la Royauté*, pp. 138-9).

[7] The text of the Constitutions is quite explicit: see above, n. 1.

[8] We have the word of Herbert of Bosham for this (*Becket Materials*, iii.288).

[9] The earliest legislation for which we have detailed information regarding its publication is Magna Carta (Richardson in *B.J.R.L.*, xxviii.427-8); but the analogy of the publication of the Conqueror's decree separating secular and ecclesiastical courts (Liebermann, *Gesetze*, i.485) and of the coronation charters of Henry I and Stephen (Poole, 'The Publication of Great Charters', *Studies in Chronology*, pp. 313-14) suggests that publication in the county court was the normal course.

Constitutions became law, to be enforced in the usual way by the king's courts.

Let us give an illustration. The seventh article of the Constitutions prescribed that no tenant-in-chief was to be excommunicated or his lands put under interdict unless the king or, in his absence, the justiciar had been consulted. Some few years later, apparently in 1168, a papal mandate, directed to the bishops of London and Norwich, was obtained against Hugh Bigod, earl of Norfolk, with this consequence:

> The bishops of London and Norwich are to be in the king's mercy and are to be summoned by the sheriffs and beadles to appear before the king's justiciar because, contrary to the statutes of Clarendon, without the licence of the justiciar, in pursuance of the pope's mandate, they laid an interdict on the land of Earl Hugh and published in their dioceses the excommunication which the lord pope had pronounced against him.[1]

Whatever second thoughts Becket may have had after 30 January 1164, whatever might be the difficulties of bishops with their conflicting loyalties to king and pope, the statutes, duly promulgated, were there to be obeyed and law-breakers must take the consequences of their rash acts. The lord pope might express his disapproval of some of the statutes and his tolerance of others,[2] but these were scarcely more than academic contentions, tentative moves in the everlasting *Kriegspiel* between *regnum* and *sacerdotium*, until Becket's murder transformed bitter comedy into stark tragedy. The king's justices paid no regard to papal mandates, still less to papal opinions. For them the last word rested with the king. It is true that, confronted with the argument that the clergy were not bound by the Constitutions, Henry demanded from the bishops a sealed declaration of their acceptance, which all apparently gave, except Becket.[3] But with or without any such decla-

[1] We take the text from Lambeth Library MS. no. 1212, fo. 339, where it appears with the other items of the so-called *Novae Constitutiones*, but here headed 'Ista facta sunt post fugam sancti Thome in exilium'. We have corrected a few scribal errors.

> Londoniensis et Northwycensis episcopi sint in misericordia regis et summoneantur per vicecomites et bedellos ut sint coram iusticia regis ad rectum faciendum regi et iusticie eius de eo quod contra statuta de Clarendone interdixerunt ex mandato pape terram comitis Hugonis et excommunicacionem quam dominus papa in ipsum fecerat per suas parochias divulgaverunt sine licencia iusticie regis.

For the date see Stubbs's note to Howden's *Chronica*, i.232-3. It is evident that this is drawn from a judicial record, presumably a roll of the justiciar's court, for we know that about this time plea rolls had evolved from more primitive memoranda (*Governance of Mediaeval England*, p. 185). The proceedings arose out of a dispute between the earl and the canons of Pentney, which is one of the few cases of the kind in the twelfth century which is well documented (*Becket Materials*, vi.262, 543-60). Oddly enough, this legal record was added as a tenth article to that blatant Canterbury fabrication, the king's 'new constitutions', dated variously 1165 and 1169 (*Governance of Mediaeval England*, p. 308*n*; below p. 93). Lyttelton long ago stigmatised this article as an interpolation (*History of Henry II*, iv.498), although he accepted the other nine as genuine.

[2] *Becket Materials*, v.73-9.

[3] There can be no question of the sealing of the Constitutions by Becket or any other bishop. A glance at the text is sufficient to show that it was sealed by no one: there is no sealing clause nor is it in the form of a charter. The most specific statement is that of R. de Diceto: post immensos tractatus rex tandem ad hoc animos prelatorum inflexit ut regni consuetudines archiepiscoporum et episcoporum auctoritate firmarentur et scriptis (*Imagines Historiarum*, i.312). Separate sealed declarations were required from each bishop. The evidence is conveniently assembled by Mlle Foreville, *op. cit.*, p. 123.

ration the Constitutions were binding and, subject to the annulment, or rather amendment, of certain provisions in agreement with the pope, which we notice later, they became part of the common law. From the point of view of legal history – in contrast perhaps to political history – the interest of the Constitutions (or Statutes) of Clarendon lies in the fact that they are the first example of contested legislation of which we have certain knowledge and the first example for more than a century of any considerable legislative act.

The Constitutions of Clarendon are too well known to need any detailed description, but some observations may be useful on certain points. Inevitably in putting unwritten custom into writing there was a risk of giving it sharper definition than some might think warranted. Thus, in the first article it is laid down that, where a layman is a party, any dispute regarding advowsons or presentation to churches is to be determined in the king's court. But there is good reason for believing that the king's court had not had in the past exclusive jurisdiction in such matters, and in any case the status of many parish churches had changed since the beginning of the century. Then the churches had been largely proprietary, but where laymen were the proprietors their rights had gradually been reduced to the right of presenting the incumbent. There could be no close parallel between 1164 and forty or fifty years earlier.[1] And then as canon law developed, the *jus patronatus* was claimed to be the exclusive concern of ecclesiastical courts, and Alexander III not long afterwards took occasion to tell Henry this in no uncertain terms.[2] Nevertheless, the law in the Constitutions remained the law in England.[3] Here we have illustrated the cardinal fact that English law might be in direct conflict with canon law and that, while the clergy were in principle bound by canon law, in practice they had to accept the common law.

To this rule there was, of course, an outstanding exception. On certain points, and notably the principal point at issue, the provisions of the statutes had to be modified to meet papal objection. We must not, however, exaggerate the king's concessions. Let us emphasise that there is not in the Constitutions, as has often been supposed, any general limitation upon appeals to the Curia. There was, however, a limitation upon appeals from archdeacons' courts.[4] Under the eighth article, while there was no interference with appeals from an archdeacon's court to the bishop and archbishop, there could be no appeal from the archbishop's court to the pope, except with the king's licence. It is very difficult to believe, we may remark, that this was the custom under Henry I, or that there was any evidence to show that in those days appeals went all the way up from an archdeacon's court to Rome. Doubtless the alleged custom had no remote historical facts behind it,

[1] For references see above, p. 63, n. 1.
[2] X, 2.1.3; *Governance of Mediaeval England*, p. 314.
[3] *Ibid.*, pp. 314-15.
[4] *Ibid.*, pp. 306-9.

but some very recent events. The case of the archdeacon of York was still fresh in men's minds: there was to be no repetition of that. Connected with the eighth article is the sixth, designed to protect laymen appearing in archdeacons' courts. The bishop of the diocese is directed to supervise these courts and not to permit criminal actions against laymen unless the accusation is made by persons of repute, supported by reputable witnesses. If there was a notorious suspect against whom witnesses were unwilling to testify, then the bishop could call upon the sheriff to summon a jury to deliver a verdict in the bishop's court. Again recent cases are in mind and again there is nothing to lead us to suppose that this procedure or anything like it was the custom under Henry I. If archdeacons' courts had become scandalous, that was a present, not an ancient, evil.[1] But it is well to remember that their jurisdiction was limited: they could rarely have tried cases that were of any importance in themselves, such as would interest the king, and any restriction on appeals to Rome was therefore a very small matter. Important ecclesiastical causes went, and continued to go increasingly, to other tribunals, notably to judges delegate.[2]

These two articles, the sixth and the eighth, are, of course, intimately connected with the third, prescribing the procedure for dealing with criminous clerks. In the final settlement after Becket's murder this article was whittled down so that the only offences that would bring clerks before secular tribunals were breaches of the laws of the forest and such trespasses as disseisins on land in lay ownership,[3] which were soon to be covered by the assizes, of which we shall shortly have to speak. But once the sting in the third article had been drawn and clerical delinquents left to the mercies of the Church, there was little point in maintaining the eighth article, designed to prevent a recurrence of the archdeacon of York's case. So this specific restriction on appeals to Rome, never one of great consequence, was abandoned too. As for the sixth article, this lapsed. It had been misconceived. Who among the bishops would call in a lay jury to try a suspect against whom there was no evidence? And if there were no witnesses of credit against an accused layman in an archdeacon's court, he already had the right of appeal to the bishop's court and the article gave him nothing better. We hear no more, therefore, of royal interference with archdeacons' courts. They grieved almost exclusively people of little importance. Important people, if they were in trouble, could afford to find justice elsewhere, before judges delegate, who virtually mono-

[1] Below, pp. 90-2.

[2] Maitland, *Canon Law in England*, pp. 100-31. This procedure had begun well before the reign of Henry II. Maitland remarks that of seventeen suits in which St Frideswide's priory was engaged between 1150 and 1240, all of them seem to be begun before papal commissioners (*ibid.*, p. 107). Professor Knowles, from another standpoint, remarks upon 'the young men of English and Norman blood' in the reign of Stephen, who 'when they had become Ordinaries . . . might often find themselves employed as papal judge-delegates to administer the canon law and report to the Pope or ask for his guidance' (*Episcopal Colleagues of Becket*, p. 51.)

[3] R. de Diceto, *Imagines Historiarum*, i.410.

polised all but minor ecclesiastical litigation which, however great in volume, attracted as little attention as litigation in manorial courts. Nor were ecclesiastical reformers indifferent to the imperfections of minor ecclesiastical tribunals: in the thirteenth century the competence of the courts of rural deans was, for example, so restricted that they faded into insignificance.[1] It may seem curious that the Constitutions should say not a word of rural chapters, over which all the trouble seems to have started: the reason for this we will endeavour shortly to explain.[2]

Though after Becket's murder Henry found it prudent to give way on the secular punishment of criminous clerks, he conceded nothing else of moment. As we have said, the restriction on ultimate appeals to Rome in cases originating in archdeacons' courts meant very little. The really important article bearing upon appeals to Rome was the fourth, which required ecclesiastical dignitaries to obtain the king's licence before leaving the country and, even so, only on condition that, if demanded, they gave security to do nothing to the prejudice of king or kingdom. Since the pope's express agreement was obtained to this provision,[3] Henry gained as effective control as he could reasonably have expected. To round the story we should perhaps say a little more of the fate of the criminous clerk. It was all very well to agree with Cardinal Pierleoni in 1178 that clerks accused of secular crimes should not be tried in secular courts,[4] but this agreement evaded the first practical difficulty. How did one recognise a clerk or, rather, how did one recognise the clerk in a disreputable malefactor? Disreputable clerks were remarkably like disreputable laymen. The only course was to arraign a suspect and leave it to him to prove his clergy. This came to mean that the clerk was put on trial before the king's judges and verdict passed upon him before he was released to the bishop to be punished as the Church decided: and, if we are to believe ecclesiastical critics, clerks did not always manage to escape royal justice in this way.[5] Such was the ultimate consequence of Becket's intransigence.

Like other supreme examples of human folly, the affair of Cardinal de Rohan's diamond necklace, for example, the quarrel between the king and Becket will long attract much more interest than its historical importance warrants. The legal historian may reflect how much wiser Henry would have been if he had let the law take its course and had not allowed his emotions to get the better of his judgement and lure him into puerile retaliation, indecorous recrimination and futile negotiations. Much as the archbishop's friends, then as today, would resent the summary statement, nevertheless it is incontrovertible that Becket was a law-breaker who had gone into voluntary exile without the

[1] Below, p. 90.
[2] Below, p. 91.
[3] *Becket Materials*, vii.517, 522; *Governance of Mediaeval England*, pp. 308-9.
[4] R. de Diceto, *loc. cit.*
[5] *Governance of Mediaeval England*, pp. 510-11. Cf. Sayles, *King's Bench*, v. p. cxxxi.

king's licence – and the law against such an offender was sufficiently clear. As Henry had himself said some years earlier in Becket's presence, 'It is very true that a bishop cannot be deposed, but he could be expelled'.[1] Had Henry left the matter there, Becket might have lived out his life as an embarrassing guest, flitting from one French monastery to another, or as the pensioner of the French king[2] – or he might have submitted. How much more astute was King John in handling the not very dissimilar affair of Stephen Langton! John smothered his resentment and took his stand upon the established law, quite plainly stated in the twelfth article of the Constitutions of Clarendon, that vacant churches were to be filled with the king's assent and by the advice of those he should appoint for the purpose. As we have shown elsewhere, his insistence on the rule of law met with the success it deserved, though, it is true, victory was gained at a price.[3] But the law for which he contended, the law of 1164, is still the law eight centuries later. This, we suggest, is not an unimportant lesson of history.

The articles of the Constitutions upon which we have not yet commented deal for the most part with matters that are hardly justiciable. There are two exceptions, the ninth and the fifteenth, which were of permanent importance. The ninth article gives definite form to an action between ecclesiastics and laymen which before long will be known as the assize *utrum*, of which we must say more in a later chapter.[4] The fifteenth article lays down that pleas of debt are not to be drawn into ecclesiastical courts on the ground that they involve a breach of faith and so offend canon law. Attempts were repeatedly made over the centuries to evade this provision and were met by writs of prohibition, freely granted to defendants who wished for trial in the king's courts.[5] And it may be well to remark here that writs of prohibition were found to be an effective way of checking any encroachments of church courts and were a much more potent weapon than the misconceived method of interfering directly with the procedure of ecclesiastical tribunals.

[1] *Chron. Mon. de Bello*, p. 91.

[2] The facts of Becket's exile have been repeatedly set out. They may be found conveniently in Ramsay, *Angevin Empire*, pp. 65-125, and in much detail, not infrequently of doubtful authenticity, in the seven volumes of *Becket Materials*. How much would there have been to record if Henry had ignored the self-exiled archbishop and waited for Alexander III to move?

[3] *Governance of Mediaeval England*, pp. 337-58.

[4] Below, pp. 109-10.

[5] Pollock and Maitland, *History of English Law*, ii.198-202.

IV

THE IMPACT OF ROME

THE great revival of learning that marked the twelfth century inevitably brought to England some knowledge of the classical law of Rome. We must make it clear that there is no evidence that Roman law had any direct influence upon English law before the reign of Henry II. The leaven worked slowly. It is sometimes suggested that the *Leges Henrici* show traces of a knowledge of Roman law[1]; but it would hardly be possible for any lawbook to be less romanesque.[2] Such traces as there are betray merely the acquaintance of the compiler with books that were remotely influenced by the classical law or that drew at a distance from the Theodosian Code. The mention of the *Liber Theodosiane Legis* is a borrowed plume.[3] That there was some knowledge in Norman England of the *Breviarium Alaricanum* and of the collections of *Novellae* by Gregorius and Hermogenes, we have the testimony of William of Malmesbury; but there is nothing to show that in England they were studied as legal texts.[4] If the *Leges Willelmi* could be safely attributed to the early twelfth century we might have to admit the existence then in England of a solitary scholar who knew something of Justinian; but the early date attributed to the *Leges Willelmi*, or rather its derivative the *Leis Willelme*, rests upon a series of misunderstandings.[5] There is no evidence that Roman law was taught in England before Vacarius, who became a member of Archbishop Theobald's household not earlier than 1139 and probably some years later. It is true that he was an established teacher at Oxford by 1149 and he seems afterwards to have taught at Northampton and perhaps elsewhere; but it is not as a teacher that we must

[1] As Maitland pointed out, this idea rests upon a misapprehension (*History of English Law*, i.100*n*). His meaning does not seem to have been quite apprehended by later writers (cf. Saltman, *Archbishop Theobald*, p. 175).

[2] For a description see above, pp. 43-4.

[3] *Leges Henrici*, 33.4. The reference is, in any case, a mistake for the Epitome Ægidii (Liebermann, *Gesetze*, i.565; iii.313). However, the citation shows that the Theodosian Code was known to the author by name. The Theodosian Code (438) owes its title to Theodosius II, emperor of the East. It is a compilation of imperial constitutions from the time of Constantine I. It circulated widely in the West until Justinian's *Corpus* came to light.

[4] They were copied by Malmesbury 'as an appendix of historical interest to his chronological "deflorations" of the other works contained in the volume' (Stubbs, Introduction to *Gesta Regum*, i. cxxxix). There is nothing to suggest that the texts had any other interest for Malmesbury. The *Breviarium Alaricanum* owes its name to the Visigothic king Alaric II (484-507): it is a compilation of imperial constitutions, a simplified Gaius, etc. The *Codex Gregorianus* and the *Codex Hermogenianus* are collections of imperial constitutions made towards the end of the third and fourth centuries respectively. They afforded a model for the Theodosian Code. Further details will be found in Vinogradoff, *Roman Law in Medieval Europe*, ch. I.

[5] Below, pp. 121-5, 170-5.

think of him in Theobald's household. He was engaged as a man of affairs.[1] It may be true enough that he put other members of the household in the way of learning something of Roman law: any such suggestion can be but guesswork. As we shall see, there was at least one other member of the household with a higher contemporary reputation as a lawyer. That Vacarius delivered formal lectures at Canterbury seems to us to be of all suggestions the most improbable.[2] There is no hint that Canterbury was a centre of legal studies. A member of Theobald's household more celebrated than Vacarius, John of Salisbury seems to have acquired in France such knowledge of Roman law as he possessed.[3] He may have devoted a good deal of his time when in Theobald's service to legal business; but it would be a gross exaggeration to call him a lawyer, though he was evidently held in some repute as a canonist.[4] Not less celebrated a member of Theobald's household is Thomas Becket, who acquired some elementary knowledge of law, but at Bologna and Auxerre: none of his biographers suggests that he acquired it at Canterbury.[5]

It is probable that during Theobald's time and for long afterwards those anxious to equip themselves as *legisperiti* went abroad if they had the means to do so. And here we may perhaps enter a caveat against exaggerating the significance of Vacarius. He can have been no isolated phenomenon, even in Stephen's reign. From the life of Robert Gorham, abbot of St Albans, we learn that in the early 1160s master John of Tilbury acted for the abbot against the bishop of Lincoln with such effect that the *legis peritissimus* whom the bishop had engaged could but stammer a halting reply: 'indocte et incomposite locutus est'.[6] Who was this most learned *legisperitus*? Now it is to be remarked that this same description *legis peritissimus* is given to master Ambrose who in 1159-1160 was in the service of the abbot of St Albans. He is

[1] We can find no evidence to support the statement that 'Vacarius the jurist was brought to Theobald's household to teach Roman law' (Saltman, *op. cit.*, p. 166). But this statement is based upon de Zulueta's Introduction to the *Liber Pauperum*, and a good deal more has since been learned about Vacarius. It seems likely that he regarded himself primarily as a theologian in his later years. Two of his theological works have survived and he mentions others (*Traditio*, vii.287).

[2] Cf. Pollock and Maitland, *History of English Law*, i.118: 'That he taught in the archbishop's household, which was full of men who were to be illustrious in church and state, is highly probable'. A *non sequitur* seems to be lurking here. But the sentence appears to depend upon a speculation of Stubbs: 'the household of archbishop Theobald in the reign of Stephen to some extent satisfied the want which was afterwards met by the university system' (*Seventeen Lectures*, p. 163, and earlier, p. 150).

[3] In the scattered reminiscences of his career, John seems to make no reference to legal studies. A summary of what is to be gleaned of his course of study, extending over twelve years, is to be found in Webb, *John of Salisbury*, pp. 4-10: his student years were divided between Paris and Chartres. That John had read a great deal of law is evident from his citations (Van Caenegem, *Royal Writs*, p. 365 *n*); but it does not necessarily follow that he had attended formal lectures at Paris.

[4] He was one of those masters present whose services the abbot of Battle attempted to engage in 1176 (*Chron. de Bello*, p. 172: below, p. 75).

[5] He was a year at Bologna (FitzStephen in *Becket Materials*, iii.17): see further Radford, *Thomas of London*, pp. 34-8.

[6] Walsingham, *Gesta Abbatum*, i.142. Walsingham was, of course, a mere compiler, and the early lives of the abbots still await a critical editor.

described by the abbot's biographer as a native of Italy, the first in time of the *legisperiti* in England and the foremost in knowledge and morals.[1] If, therefore, the name of Vacarius was yet known at St Albans, he had had, so it was asserted, not only a predecessor in England but a superior in master Ambrose. But Ambrose seems to have gone over to the enemy, Bishop Robert Chesney of Lincoln, and he is found a few years later correcting and glossing for the bishop a copy of the Digest.[2] No wonder the monks of St Albans sneered at him in his discomfiture.

Let us go back to master Ambrose's successful adversary, John of Tilbury. John had been for some years in the service of Archbishop Theobald, and the surviving charter evidence suggests that he was a good deal more active in Theobald's service than was Vacarius.[3] In these documents, be it noted, there seems no trace of either of them before 1150, though this does not mean that neither was employed earlier; and we cannot be certain that, once engaged, they were employed continuously or for many years, though John's stay in the archiepiscopal household seems to have been the longer.[4] One document from late in Stephen's reign shows that the two legists were employed for some while simultaneously.[5] We must reject any idea that either Vacarius or John of Tilbury stood in anything like the same intimate relationship to Theobald as did Thomas Becket or John of Salisbury. John of Tilbury, however, was sufficiently long in Theobald's service to form a close personal friendship with John of Salisbury, whose literary tastes he shared. From the only known letter of John of Salisbury to John of Tilbury it appears that, after Becket went into exile in 1164 and John of Salisbury was whipping up all the support he could for the archbishop, John of Tilbury had pleaded that he was too old and infirm to join the band of exiles.[6] This may have been no more than an excuse; but the excuse itself indicates that John of Tilbury was some years older than John of Salisbury, and we are not likely to be far out if we put the birth of the elder of them about the year 1110.[7] It would follow that John of Tilbury learned his law in the 1130s and that he subsequently taught in schools where he was accorded the title of master. Where were these schools? Not in England certainly. Nor do we have much choice among schools in Europe. The place, we suggest, was in all probability Bologna. A fellow townsman of his, quite possibly a kinsman, was the more celebrated Gervase of Tilbury, the author of the *Otia Imperialia*. Born about 1152, Gervase spent his boy-

[1] *Ibid.*, pp. 136-7.
[2] Gilbert Foliot, *Epistolae*, no. 90 (ed. Giles, i.116).
[3] In the charters collected by Mr Saltman, John's name occurs eight times, that of Vacarius twice (*op. cit.*, pp. 242, 246, 273, 317, 347, 363, 453, 482, 496).
[4] This seems a fair inference from the more frequent occurrence of his name in Theobald's charters and from his close friendship with John of Salisbury.
[5] Saltman, *op. cit.*, p. 242.
[6] John of Salisbury, *Epistolae* (ed. Giles), no. 279.
[7] It has been deduced that John of Salisbury was born somewhere between 1115 and 1120 (Webb, *op. cit.*, p. 1).

hood in England but was in Italy in 1166 and became a doctor at Bologna where he taught canon law. Attached for a time to the court of Henry II and of the young king, he passed into the service of Archbishop William of Reims and then into that of King William II of Sicily, on whose death he went to Provence where he married and settled down and was appointed by the Emperor Otto IV marshal of the kingdom of Arles.[1] But it is not of Gervase's remarkable career that we would speak: what we would emphasise is that, when yet a child, he was sent to Italy for his professional training as a canonist. Is it not likely that he was following in the footsteps of John of Tilbury?

That Bologna continued to have the greatest attraction for scholars who could afford the expense we know from the careers of such men as Hubert Walter, Richard de Morins and Thomas of Marlborough. That Hubert Walter was ever a student at Bologna has been disputed, but the appearance of his name among those of other students in an obituary of S. Maria de Reno at Bologna is difficult to explain otherwise.[2] This does not mean that his studies were long or profound, but they may have helped to make him the efficient justiciar and archbishop that he proved to be. Peter of Blois was another notable figure who, for a time, studied at Bologna and had a long career in England.[3] Richard de Morins was a student of a different type who, later in the century, became a distinguished teacher and author at Bologna, where he was well known as *Ricardus Anglicus*. He too, like Peter, wearied of the law, and he returned to England to enter religion.[4] Bolognese teachers from England at the same period were Gilbert and Alan who made collections of decretals to serve as supplements to the *Compilatio Prima*, and their two collections were the basis of the *Compilatio Secunda*, the work of a Welshman named John.[5] Other English teachers at Bologna have not left their mark except in the obituary where Hubert Walter's name is also to be found.[6] Thomas of Marlborough is known from his own account of his career and his prolonged contest with Roger Norreis, the peccant abbot of Evesham. He tells us that he had lectured at Exeter and Oxford and he gives us the names of three of his Oxford teachers when he was a student there. That he later went to Bologna to

[1] For Gervase's career see *History*, xlvi. 102-14.

[2] Cheney, *From Becket to Langton*, p. 39*n*. But this seems rather like contradicting the evidence. Why Hubert should appear in the Bologna obituary (see further below, n. 6) except for the same reason as other Englishmen Professor Cheney does not explain, while the story told by Gerald of Wales, which he questions, seems undoubtedly to refer to Hubert and has been so interpreted for many years (cf. Pollock and Maitland, *History of English Law*, i.133 and references; *Traditio*, vii.323). The inference from this story is that Hubert appeared professionally before Alexander III (Introduction to *Memoranda Roll*, *1 John*, p. lxii).

[3] Peter of Blois, *Epistolae*, no. 26. For further details of his early life and studies see Armitage-Robinson, *Somerset Historical Essays*, p. 102.

[4] Walsingham, *Gesta Abbatum*, i.307; *Annales Monastici* (Dunstable), iii.28; *Traditio*, vii.329-32.

[5] For the *Quinque Compilationes* see below, p. 76.

[6] The obituary was first printed by Trombelli, *Memorie istoriche concernenti le due canoniche di S. Maria de Reno e di S. Salvatore*, pp. 329-55. Attention was drawn to it by A. Allaria in the *Dublin Review*, cxii (1893). The obituary was reprinted in Sarti and Fattorini, *De claris archigymnasii Bononiensis professoribus*, ii (1896), 287 *sqq*.

perfect his knowledge of law under Azzo does not suggest that the standard of teaching at Oxford was very high in the twelfth century.[1] And we should note that Richard de Morins had, like Thomas of Marlborough, seemingly taught at Oxford (as well as at Paris) before he began his distinguished career at Bologna.[2]

We have already remarked that John of Salisbury had acquired some legal knowledge in France, presumably at Paris,[3] but a better illustration of Parisian training is afforded by Gerard la Pucelle, who became bishop of Coventry in 1188. Late in his career he may have improved his knowledge at Cologne, but the basis of his learning was acquired in Paris.[4] We are fortunate in having a dramatic account of his advocacy in a notable trial at Westminster in 1176 before the papal legate, Cardinal Hugh Pierleoni. The defendant in the action was the abbot of Battle, who had great difficulty in obtaining the services of an advocate to represent him because his adversary was the son of the all-powerful justiciar, Richard de Lucy. An Italian lawyer had been retained, but he threw up his brief. At the last moment, when it seemed that the abbot might be forced to argue his case without professional aid, Gerard was persuaded to act. He was not, it is true, very successful, for the action ended in a compromise, but what is notable for our purpose is the chronicler's statement that Master Gerard 'proved his case by citations from the laws and decrees too long to insert here'.[5] Although he apparently spoke *extempore*, he had his authorities from Justinian and the Decretum at his finger tips. We doubt whether any parallel could be found in any English-trained lawyer before the time of William of Drogheda half a century or more later.[6]

Doubtless, as the twelfth century wore on, a more or less satisfactory professional training became possible at Oxford or Northampton and perhaps elsewhere. As we have suggested, the standard appears to have been lower than that at Paris, but students were given some acquaintance with the Digest and Code and, inevitably, with the Institutes, which was quite evidently the recognised textbook employed for elementary instruction in the reign of Henry II.[7] But there was no career for the civilian in England where the civil law was never more than the handmaid of the canon law. It may be that Vacarius com-

[1] *Chron. Abbatiae de Evesham*, pp. 126, 147, 158, 168, 267. The three masters he names, Honorius, John of Tynemouth and Simon of Sywell (rather than 'Southwell'), seem undoubtedly to have taught at Oxford (*Traditio*, vii.321-7).

[2] In the *Gesta Abbatum* (above, p. 74, n. 4) it is said that he had been a regent master (*rexerat*) at Bologna *et alibi*. It seems certain that he taught at Paris when young and the inference from his writings is that thereafter he taught at Oxford (*Traditio*, vii.334-7).

[3] Above, p. 72.

[4] *Traditio*, vii.296-303.

[5] *Chron. de Bello*, p. 178.

[6] Maitland's account of Drogheda and his *Summa Aurea* in *Roman Canon Law in the Church of England*, pp. 100-31, is still the best introduction in English. It is supplemented by de Zulueta in *Mélanges Cornil*, ii.641-57.

[7] We need look no further than the Introductions to the *Dialogus de Scaccario* and *Glanville* for evidence. That the Institutes of Gaius had been used in this way in the early twelfth century (presumably upon the Continent) is suggested by the reference to them in the legal collection copied by William of Malmesbury (*Gesta Regum*, i. p. cxxxviii).

piled his *Liber Pauperum* – consisting of select texts, suitably glossed, from the Digest and the Code – in order to meet the needs of poor students at a time when the full texts were impossibly expensive for them, but other students than the poorest were content to rely upon this compendium, and *pauperistae* became a term of abuse levelled by fellow students who plumed themselves upon their acquaintance with the full texts of Justinian.[1] Justinian's authority was not only unquestioned but acquired ever-increasing weight, and his books became increasingly the foundation for arguments in ecclesiastical causes. They were of equal potency with any arguments drawn from canon law in the stricter sense. One example will suffice. In the last years of Henry II's reign the dispute between Archbishop Baldwin and the monks of Christ Church, Canterbury, came to a head. The case prepared for the monks has survived: it contains ninety-three citations of the Decretum, forty-four of the Digest, thirty-nine of the Code, five of the Institutes and one of the Authenticum, in all eighty-nine from the *Corpus Juris Civilis*.[2] Before very long the Decretum became old-fashioned and the decretals of the popes became principal authorities and were collected by many hands until the *Quinque Compilationes* replaced the earlier and lesser collections,[3] to be superseded in turn by the authoritative collection of Gregory IX, given to Latin Christendom in 1234.[4] Justinian was never outdated.

But this is to look a long way ahead. Let us return to the reign of Henry II. There is good reason to believe that the administrative reforms which mark the reign of Henry I were almost completely undone in the disorder of Stephen's reign.[5] Henry II resumed the work of his grandfather in organising the judiciary and systematising the procedure of the courts. When we say that Henry II did this, we do not seek to attribute to him any larger part than an urgent desire for good government and the approval of proposals made by his ministers. It is possible that he was responsible for some details; but the respective parts played by the king and his ministers will always remain obscure to us. The task of restoring order was, however, so great that nothing very effective could be accomplished before 1166 and no ordered judiciary was set up before 1168.[6] In what was done it seems that the justiciar Richard de Lucy played a great part, but two other men of different background and training appear also to have had a large

[1] *Traditio*, vii.323.
[2] *Epistolae Cantuarienses*, pp. 320-30; Richardson and Sayles, *Governance of Mediaeval England*, p. 319.
[3] We have already mentioned the first two of the *Compilationes* (above, p. 74): there were eventually five, all arranged systematically under the same titles. They were absorbed into the Gregorian Decretals, compiled by Raymond of Peñafort under papal authority. The relationship between the *Compilationes* and the Gregorian Decretals is shown in the tables prefixed to Friedberg's edition of the latter.
[4] The Decretals were transmitted to the universities by Gregory IX with the bull *Rex Pacificus*, which is prefixed to the printed editions.
[5] *Governance of Mediaeval England*, pp. 191-4.
[6] *Ibid.*, pp. 194-204.

measure of responsibility. These men were Richard of Ilchester and Geoffrey Ridel, both archdeacons, who became bishops in 1173 but continued in the king's service.[1] Of their early training we know nothing for certain, although we must presume that to fit them for archidiaconal office they had acquired some knowledge of Roman law. We may take these three men, the justiciar and the two archdeacons, as typifying the influences which gave England the common law as it is expounded in our earliest textbook, the book that has come down to us under the name of *Glanville*, that is Ranulf Glanville, the justiciar in office at the time or not long before the book was written.[2] Essentially it is a treatise on procedure by writ; and though the Latin writ of Glanville's time had undergone a long evolution, it is directly descended from the English writ of the pre-Conquest kings.[3] The Old English writ was devised for English administration and it must be remembered that English administrative institutions remained for long unchanged under foreign kings, though by the last third of the twelfth century a new judicial system had been imposed upon them.[4]

We have already indicated that it was early in the twelfth century that a new office had been devised, the office of justiciar. The creation of this office was of great significance, not only in the evolution of English administration, but also in the evolution of the writ system, for it was the justiciar who was responsible for the issue of writs, whether in his own name or the king's name. The convention was that, when the king was present in the kingdom, his name came at the beginning of the writ: it was his command. When the king was absent, the justiciar's name headed the writ: it was his command. The substance and effect of the writ in either form was the same.[5] The justiciar is the embodiment of Norman justice: not the justice of the first two Norman kings, but the justice of Henry I and his great minister, Roger of Salisbury. This was justice of a new pattern, for which there are no known precedents. It centred upon a new court over which the justiciar presided, the king's court at the Exchequer, and it was staffed by 'barons' – hence the 'barons of the Exchequer' – who are called alternatively *justiciarii totius Anglie* and who went on eyre throughout the land.[6] This remarkably efficient organisation went to pieces under Stephen and was not revived until after Henry II had been more than twelve years on the throne.[7] Inevitably the revival was not an exact

[1] *Ibid.*, p. 212.

[2] This is clear from the *Incipit* which, however, appears to be an addition by another hand. Both Woodbine (p. 183) and Hall (p. xxxi) regard the *Incipit* as of doubtful authorship (see below, p. 105, n. 6).

[3] Above, pp. 49-50.

[4] *Governance of Mediaeval England*, pp. 173-215.

[5] *Ibid.*, pp. 162-4, 169. In the text we ignore the complications, almost purely formal, when the queen or the heir to the throne acts nominally as regent in the king's absence, for which see the references cited. Further details of procedure are given in the Introduction to *Memoranda Roll, 1 John*, pp. lxxv-lxxxvii.

[6] *Governance of Mediaeval England*, pp. 174-6, 188-90.

[7] *Ibid.*, pp. 191-204; above, p. 39.

counterpart of the original. New influences were at work. But the judicial organisation of England under Henry II was, in essentials, what it had been under his grandfather. The point, however, we wish to make here is that the justiciar represents in his functions the contributions of the English and the Normans to the common law.

Now for the third contribution, the Roman. Many lawbooks had been written in England in the twelfth century. It is probable that only a minority of them has survived: these we describe in other chapters.[1] Harsh words have been said of them, and harsh words most of them deserve. But in the last years of Henry II or soon after his death a lawbook of a kind entirely new to England appeared, *Glanville*, the remarkable book we have already called to mind.[2] The arrangement of *Glanville*, the exposition of the procedure of the courts, owes nothing to any book written in England. Nor, so far as we know, was there available to the author any precise model written on the Continent; but that he was strongly influenced by Roman manuals of procedure – *ordines judiciarii* as they are called – can, we believe, hardly be doubted.[3] These *ordines* were essential to the orderly conduct of actions in ecclesiastical courts and consequently were familiar to archdeacons and judges delegate – or at least the better among them – even though their knowledge of Roman law, civil or ecclesiastical, might be neither deep nor wide. And though, as we have said, we cannot point to any particular *ordo judiciarius* in circulation in England in the twelfth century that offers a parallel to *Glanville*, no one, we think, can look at the most popular of *ordines* in the following century, that of Tancred, and fail to be struck by the similarity of method.[4] There is, of course, one striking difference, for the procedure under Roman law was initiated by a libel, prepared and put forward on behalf of the plaintiff,[5] whereas the procedure in *Glanville* takes as its basis the writ devised for the form of action appropriate to the particular case. The writ is, as we have said, in the form of a command from the king or the justiciar, but the choice of any particular writ rested with the plaintiff. But this difference admitted, the problems of conducting an action were similar, so much so that when Bracton came to write his treatise on English law in the middle of the thirteenth century, he relied extensively on Tancred's guidance in matters of

[1] Below, pp. 41-9, 57-8, 120-31.

[2] Below, pp. 105-17. There are now modern editions of both the *alpha* text, by G. D. G. Hall, and of the *beta* text, by G. E. Woodbine.

[3] Professor van Caenegem, *Royal Writs*, p. 377*n*., suggests some *ordines* to which the author of Glanville might have had access. Mr Hall, however, questions the influence of the *ordines judiciarii* in his Introduction, pp. xxviii-xxix.

[4] For the early *ordines judiciarii* of the Anglo-Norman school see *Traditio*, vii.290-2. There is a serviceable edition of Tancred's *Ordo* by F. Bergmann, but it is more than a century old. For some indication of the influence of Tancred see Richardson, *Bracton*, pp. 5-8.

[5] The libel was a bill or petition to the court containing brief particulars of the plaintiff's case. This was in use in classical times, and the *libellus conventionis* is mentioned in Inst. 4.6.24. The written plaint in English courts closely resembled the contemporary libel as it had evolved in ecclesiastical courts (Richardson and Sayles, *Procedure without Writ*, pp. lvii-lxviii). For the plaint in early actions of trespass see below, pp. 83-4.

procedure and borrowed a number of passages from Tancred's *Ordo*.[1] The author of *Glanville* does not incorporate passages from any *ordo* of his time: he is not a direct borrower like Bracton. The influence of the *ordines* is shown in the methodical arrangement of the book, so greatly in contrast to the books on English law hitherto written.

The first and foremost lesson that the Romanists taught was, then, the characteristic Roman virtue of order. The spirit of order harmonised and reduced to a system a mass of writs, casually and sporadically invented or modified, that had accumulated over many years.[2] This system had, however, to be accommodated to traditional English or Norman institutions, to the county court, the seignorial court, trial by battle, ordeal, compurgation, the jury in its diverse forms. In the result the system may seem at times arbitrary or illogical; but we are dealing with a living organism that can be improved only by adjustments, not by drastic surgery and replacement. It was no small achievement to have produced *Glanville* and the earlier registers of writs.[3] Looking, however, at Bracton's treatise in our printed editions, we might think perhaps that by the 1250s the spirit of order was already preparing to fly. But though Bracton's treatise is far from the orderly *summa* of the law he first planned on the model of Justinian's Institutes, we must remember that, as we have it, the treatise is a vast, unfinished, abandoned draft,[4] and that its disorder was reduced to order by the master's disciple who used the treatise as the basis for the orderly *Fleta*.[5] After that, we may indeed think that the twilight descended upon English law once more. *Fleta* had but scant success and the later Middle Ages produced no monument of English legal science. The spirit of order was spent. . . . But we must not digress.

If the study of Roman law taught men first and foremost the virtue of order, what else did it teach them? And here let us stress that the Roman law they learnt was mediaeval Roman law. Of the classical background of Justinian's *Corpus* they had no knowledge, and everything they read there was related to their own daily life. Justinian's law was living law in ecclesiastical courts, as living as the *Decretum* and the more nearly contemporary decretals of the popes. The *ordines judiciarii*, which so greatly influenced the author of *Glanville*, were productions of the twelfth century: they had no classical counterpart

[1] Richardson, *Bracton*, pp. 92-147 *passim*.

[2] Above, pp. 49-50. The early post-Conquest writs have been classified by Van Caenegem. *Royal Writs*, pp. 405-515. Until, however, the courts were themselves systematised the writs themselves could hardly have been systematised. The two processes went hand in hand.

[3] There can hardly be room for doubt that behind *Glanville* there lies a primitive register: it is difficult to imagine how the justiciar's clerks could have done their work without formularies, regarded perhaps as their personal possessions. The earliest registers of which copies survive appear to have been compiled in the early years of Henry III. The opening paragraphs of two will be found in *L.Q.R.*, liv. 396-9. It will be seen that they are independent compilations, though their substance is the same. Cf. Mr Hall's remarks in his Introduction to *Glanville*, pp. xxxiii-xxxiv.

[4] Richardson, *Bracton*, pp. 53-71.

[5] A new edition of *Fleta* by the present writers is in progress for the Selden Society. The relation of the text to Bracton's treatise is indicated in the margin.

and were written especially to guide judges and practising lawyers in the rapidly evolving ecclesiastical courts with their increasingly professional atmosphere.[1] Any member of the king's court at the Exchequer or any justice itinerant who had had experience in administering ecclesiastical law[1a] – and there must have been a good proportion who at some time or other served in both capacities – was inevitably familiar with the language and some of the principles of Roman law. The author of *Glanville* assumes that his readers – and his first readers were as professional as himself – will be familiar with the practice of ecclesiastical courts.[2] If we cannot confirm this assumption by particular instances, we can point to bishops and royal clerks who went to considerable pains to equip themselves with a knowledge of Roman law. We have already mentioned Robert Chesney, bishop of Lincoln from 1148 to 1166, who had the Digest copied and glossed for his use.[3] A brother bishop, Gilbert Foliot – who, having been elected to Hereford in 1148, was translated to London in 1163 where he remained until his death in 1187 – shows in his letters that his vocabulary was tinged with Roman legal terms.[4] And Peter of Blois, writing to his friends among the king's clerks, deplores that they should give themselves up to the study of Roman law.[5] We have other evidence that the study of the liberal arts declined in face of a new enthusiasm for, as Daniel of Morley puts it, Ticius and Seius.[6]

Inevitably therefore the vocabulary of *Glanville*, like the vocabulary of the records of the king's courts, bears here and there a romanesque imprint. It has often been said that no man can write of law in Latin without using the terminology of Roman law, but beyond this inevitable use of the language common to all legal writings in Latin from the twelfth century onwards, technical terms borrowed from Justinian began to be applied to English law where there was, or appeared to be, a close similarity to Roman law. There is no more typical English action than the action of trespass, but the usual term for it, when it begins to appear in the plea rolls, is the *actio iniuriarum*. Of this action, oddly enough, there is no mention in *Glanville*, presumably because at this period and well into the thirteenth century it was begun by plaint, and of the plaint the author, rather inexplicably, does not speak. Of

[1] Kantorowicz, *Studies in the Glossators*, p. 72. [1a] For Richard of Ilchester, see Duggan in *T.R.H.S.*, 5th Ser., xvi. 18-20.

[2] So in lib. ii, c. 12: Excipi autem possunt iuratores ipsi eisdem modis quibus testes in curia christianitatis iuste repelluntur (Woodbine, p. 66; Hall, p. 32). Woodbine remarks (p. 204) that Bracton uses almost the same words at fol. 185 (ed. Woodbine, iii.71-2). But this is misleading, for Bracton gives a long list of the grounds upon which jurors may be challenged and adds that these are *exempli causa*. He says no word of witnesses in courts Christian, and these are the instructive words in *Glanville*: the king's courts had not yet developed rules of their own.

[3] Above, p. 73.

[4] Van Caenegem, *Royal Writs*, p. 365*n*. He may have had some acquaintance with the Code and Digest, but isolated citations may have been supplied by others.

[5] *Epistolae*, no. 140 (ed. Giles, ii.37).

[6] His reason for going to the studium at Northampton was that in other places 'discipline liberales silentium haberent et pro Ticio et Seio penitus Aristoteles et Plato oblivioni darentur' (*Philosophia*, prologue). On this passage see *E.H.R.*, lvi.601-2.

the influence of Roman law on the form this action took we shall say something later. Here it may be well to remark that trespass and *iniuria* are by no means precise equivalents, though they cover common ground: but English lawyers could find no Latin word nearer in sense to the concept they wished to express. Ultimately the word *iniuria* fell into disuse, but *actio iniuriarum* is still found in Bracton's treatise.[1] Again, such terms as *emptio-venditio* – buying and selling – and *locatio-conductio* – letting and hiring – are found in *Glanville*, but they cannot be used in the precise sense given to them in Roman law.[2] Societies so remote from one another as ancient Rome and Angevin England could not share the same concepts: mediaeval lawyers were perforce content with an approximation. Distinctions, however, were sometimes recognised. To *dos* two quite different meanings are given in *Glanville*, the one Roman, the other English.[3] This may perhaps seem a little perverse, since a mediaeval Latin term *maritagium* was in common use for the so-called 'Roman' sense – a quite different sense from the English sense of 'dower' – and the author had no difficulty in using the two words, *dos* and *maritagium*, in their appropriate context.[4] We may be pardoned if we call this a mistaken, if venial, parade of learning: unfortunately it helped to get Bracton into the hopeless tangle in which he found himself when treating of gifts to and between husband and wife.[5] Again, there is an apparent confusion between the Roman *possessio* and the English *saisina*, though only in what is, in effect, a list of the titles of topics to be treated[6]: in the thirteenth book, which is the section in question, the word *possessio* does not occur.[7] When elsewhere the author has occasion to speak of *possessio* it is in reference to movables, not to land.[8] There may therefore have been a distinction in his mind; but, if so, the distinction was not observed by others, and in the thirteenth century and later *possessio* was treated by English lawyers as

[1] Fol. 103 *b*; Richardson and Sayles, *Procedure without Writ*, pp. cxi-cxii. *Iniuria* had a wider meaning than trespass, since it covered any intentional injury directed against a person or his reputation. *Iniuria* therefore included slander – *carmen famosum* or *libellus famosus* – which was not actionable at common law in the king's courts, though Bracton in one place appears so to regard it (Richardson, *Bracton*, pp. 50, 136).

[2] See Mr Hall's comment at p. xxxviii of his Introduction.

[3] The definition of *dos* is divided between lib. vi, c. 1 and lib. vii, c. 1. Originally it must have run thus: 'Dos duobus modis dicitur. Dicitur enim dos vulgariter id quod aliquis liber homo dat sponse sue ad hostium ecclesie tempore desponsationis sue. . . . In alia acceptatione accipitur dos secundum leges Romanas, secundum quod proprie appellatur dos id quod cum muliere datur viro, quod vulgariter dicitur maritagium' (Woodbine, pp. 87-8, 96; Hall, pp. 58-9, 69). In both *alpha* and *beta* texts fifteen chapters separate the two parts of the definition. Consequently there is an abrupt transition from the end of book six to the beginning of book seven. It is difficult to believe that the original draft was so ill-written. *Dos* in the classical Roman sense was a contribution, from the wife or someone on her behalf, towards the expenses of the married state. *Maritagium* was not strictly equivalent to *dos* but was the nearest equivalent term, having regard to the different economic conditions of the ancient world.

[4] Lib. vii, c. 1 and c. 18 (Woodbine, pp. 96, 114-16; Hall, pp. 69, 92-3).

[5] Richardson, *Bracton*, pp. 46-8, 104-9.

[6] Lib. i, c. 3, where *possessio* is applied apparently to land only (Woodbine, p. 42; Hall, p. 4).

[7] Woodbine, pp. 157-74; Hall, pp. 148-70.

[8] Lib. x, c. 8 (Woodbine, p. 138; Hall, p. 123).

virtually a synonym for *saisina*.[1] We must not try the reader's patience further with these technicalities. We have said enough to indicate that there were severe limitations upon the use that English lawyers could make of Latin legal terminology and that they sometimes used it unwisely. The author of *Glanville* was more prudent than some others: it should be accounted a merit that, when he discusses the status of the unfree, he does not, like Bracton, use the word *servus* or give us echoes of the Roman law of slavery.[2]

It will be clear from the preceding paragraph that there was nothing that can be called a 'reception' of Roman law in the courts of common law or by common lawyers. Their attitude is quite different from that of the canonists who did 'receive' Roman law as an adjunct to canon law: if they were compelled to discard some Roman conceptions on marriage and money-lending, they did not discard a great deal.[3] Of substantive law the common lawyers took little, and this little has sometimes been exaggerated. There are parallels between Roman and English law because like situations will produce like solutions[4]; and it is possible that a solution to a problem found in England may have been influenced or suggested by a knowledge of Justinian or some later Roman source, though it is rarely that we can be certain. Let us take as an example the assize of novel disseisin, for a century the most popular of the forms of action devised under Henry II. Until recently all exponents of English legal history – and the greatest among them, Maitland and Vinagradoff – had spoken with one voice on the evolution of the assize.[5] A single citation will serve for all. 'At least one of the most important of all the early actions, the assize of novel disseisin, was directly framed on the model of the canonical *actio spolii*, which in turn had been based on the Roman interdict *unde vi*.'[6] We may pass over the unfortunate and fatal anachronism that invoked the *actio spolii*, for this action had not emerged until Henry II and the author of *Glanville* had long been laid to rest. Let us, however, admit that the elementary rule was known to Roman law, civil and canon, that when property was in dispute and one contestant had been deprived of it, the party who took possession must first restore it before the court would hear his claim. This admission does not take us very far, for self-help is the antithesis of

[1] Woodbine gives references in his notes at pp. 281-3.

[2] Liber v (Woodbine, pp. 83-7; Hall, pp. 53-8). We discuss the general question of servitude later, pp. 138-40. Bracton is at his worst when he is nearest his Roman authorities (fols. 4 *b*-5, 100 *b*): cf. Richardson, *Bracton*, pp. 84-5, 110-11.

[3] Below, pp. 85-6.

[4] There is a striking parallel, for example, in the evolution of the *actio iniuriarum* and the evolution of trespass. As it is said in Inst. 4.4.7, by the law of the Twelve Tables the penalty was a limb for a limb, but this had passed into desuetude. This text was, of course, widely known by the twelfth century and may have had some influence on the common law. Bracton, however, has a curious adaptation of the text that begins, 'Pena autem iniuriarum quandoque erit corporalis quandoque pecuniaria' (Richardson, *Bracton*, pp. 136-7).

[5] Pollock and Maitland, *History of English Law*, ii.48; Vinogradoff, *Roman Law in Mediaeval Europe*, p. 99.

[6] Hazeltine, Introduction to Hengham, *Summae* (ed. Dunham), pp. xxxv-vi. See our criticism of this doctrine in *Proceedings without Writ*, pp. cxxviii-cxxxi, and the further arguments by Van Caenegem, *Royal Writs*, pp. 386-90.

the rule of law, and all systems of law must exclude self-help if there is to be any system at all. In England we need not look to Roman law for an early statement of the rule: we shall find it in several places in the *Leges Henrici*, written under Henry I.[1] And there is ample evidence that in his reign an unlawfully dispossessed tenant would be reseised by due process of law.[2] Nor is there any doubt regarding the political occasion which led to the formulation of the assize of novel disseisin. The occasion was the long delayed scheme devised at Clarendon in the winter of 1165-1166 for the righting of unrequited wrongs arising out of the anarchy of Stephen's reign.[3] This is not to deny that those who framed the writ – for they must have included Richard of Ilchester and Geoffrey Ridel – may already have known of the Roman interdict and the practice of ecclesiastical courts. But the 'recognition' by a jury, which was an essential element in the procedure under the assize, was no part of Roman practice.[4]

Let us turn to another action where the influence of Roman law seems more certain, the action of trespass or *actio iniuriarum*, which, as we have already remarked, is not noticed in *Glanville*.[5] When, in due course, a writ was devised for beginning this action in the king's court, it is always alleged that the trespass was committed *vi et armis*. These words became a mere formality, but originally they must have been meant literally. This fact and the phraseology used in some early records of the action indicate that at one time there was no distinction between an action of trespass and an appeal of felony, which was decided by battle. But with the progress of the spirit of humanity and the invention of stringent rules to govern appeals of felony, rules that excluded many potential appellors, the injured party in an action of trespass was given the alternative of a jury and monetary compensation, an alternative forced upon him even though he might have preferred to fight his adversary.[6] We have a parallel in the invention of the writ of right and the choice allowed the tenant to leave the issue to a jury rather than to the God of battles.[7] It is not then in the substitution of rational proof for battle, and money for blood or broken limbs, that we have any sure indication of the influence of Roman law,[8] but we do see an indication in the language used by the plaintiff in his plaint – and all early actions of trespass seem to have been begun by plaint –

[1] *Leges Henrici*, cc.29.2a, 53.3-6, 61.21. There is no evidence of canonist influence in these passages: see our note in *Proceedings without Writ*, p. cxxviii.
[2] Van Caenegem, *op. cit.*, pp. 199-204.
[3] Below, pp. 93-7.
[4] The recognition is also what distinguishes the procedure under the assize from the earlier procedure in England, though the employment of a jury for this purpose was not something apart but arose from the organisation of the judicature and the wide use of the jury to decide issues in civil causes: see below, pp. 117-19. Neither Professor Van Caenegem (*Royal Writs*, pp. 204-6) nor Lady Stenton (*English Justice*, pp. 33-36) seems to give sufficient weight to these factors.
[5] Above, p. 80.
[6] Richardson and Sayles, *Procedure without Writ*, pp. cviii-cxxiii.
[7] Below, pp. 111-13.
[8] See above, p. 82, n. 4.

language which is, we take it, the language also of his count. The plaintiff in the king's court asks for damages in words such as are found in libels in ecclesiastical courts. A good instance is provided by one of the earliest plea rolls now surviving, where the plaintiff, who has been assaulted, declares:

quod noluit habuisse peioramentum pro centum solidis.

We may compare these words with a clause in a libel put forward by an Oxford scholar who has been slandered:

quam [diffamationem] nollem sustinuisse pro centum marcis.

In the king's court the litigant whose words we have cited is said to 'appeal', for in 1198 the action of trespass had not yet shaken off all trace of its origin in the appeal of felony; but there can be no doubt that he entered a plaint in writing or that this writing was drafted professionally by an adviser skilled in canon law.[1] Such phraseology was in time dropped in the king's courts as the action of trespass evolved: men ceased to 'lay the damages' by asserting that they would not have suffered some injury, physical or moral, for some specific sum of money. But the phraseology is found in *Bracton* and it left some mark upon manorial courts.[2] Lest it may be thought that we are extending unduly the meaning of Roman law when we draw comparisons with libels in ecclesiastical courts, let us add a few sentences of explanation. There is no doubt that in framing libels of this kind the canonists had in mind a text of classical Roman law. Bracton himself makes this clear when he equates the libellary formula with a passage in the Institutes.[3] As we have said, Justinian's law was living law in ecclesiastical courts; but its language had sometimes to be adapted to a contemporary idiom. So, very much as the assize of novel disseisin was, not so very long ago, supposed to be linked, through the canonist *actio spolii*, to the classical interdict *unde vi*, it seems certain that we can find a link between the action of trespass and the classical *actio iniuriarum* by way of a modified form of the Norman appeal of felony.

On substantive law the influence of Roman law was, with rare exceptions, at best indirect. This is not to underrate the advantage of a ready-made terminology to fit a system of law which at the end of the twelfth century had become very different from what it had been at the end of the eleventh, so different indeed that we can regard it as distinctly new. The effect of terminology upon legal concepts is difficult to measure in any precise way and we are probably justified in thinking that, above all, the value of the study of Roman law to English lawyers of Henry II's reign lay in its action as a cathartic on men's minds, sweeping away much confused and archaic thinking. We have

[1] Richardson and Sayles, *op. cit.*, pp. cix-cx.

[2] *Ibid.*, pp. cxi-cxiv; below, p. 87.

[3] Inst. 4.4.7; Bracton, fol. 103 *b*. See Maitland, *Bracton and Azo*, pp. 183-4, and Richardson and Sayles, *op. cit.*, p. cxi.

already seen – and shall see still further in a later chapter – what a sorry business men made of it when, in response to a concession by Henry I, they tried to recover the laws of Edward the Confessor from such ancient written laws and traditions as had come down to them.[1] But no man who had any acquaintance with Justinian, were it no more than with his Institutes, could regard law as his uninstructed forbears had done. That the revival of Roman law should re-orient men's minds was indeed an achievement beyond praise.

This last sentence might seem a just and inevitable conclusion to all that precedes, and indeed it would be our final conclusion if we regarded nothing else but the common law as it had evolved in, let us say, the year 1200. But there were certain provinces of canon law that impinged upon the common law and that cannot be left without some mention, the provinces of money-lending and marriage. Here it is difficult to praise. The State could not be indifferent to the canon law in either province. Indeed, by the latter part of Henry II's reign the usurer had fallen under the criminal law, and while the king left the living usurer to the judgement of the Church, on the usurer's death the king claimed his chattels.[2] *Glanville* also has something to say on money-lending in relation to the gage of land, which may involve arrangements that the Church may regard as usurious; but in these matters the king's court will not intervene.[3] The ecclesiastical prohibition of usury was, however, remote from the practical conduct of affairs and, while it was maintained in principle, in practice it was largely evaded or ignored until, at last, the taking of interest was regulated by statute. The story, long and intricate, is sufficiently well known and could not, in any case, be suitably treated here: under the Angevin kings we are only at the beginning of the problem. The law of marriage, like the law against usury, was Roman in the sense that it was the law of the Church of Rome. It borrowed little from classical Roman law nor could it have taken very much, for whereas the classical law knew different forms of union,[4] the Church knew only one form of marriage, the lifelong union of man and woman, a concept known also to the classical law. No one indeed has expressed the Christian ideal better than Modestinus, a pagan jurist of the third century, whose words are embodied in the Digest: 'nuptiae sunt

[1] Above, pp. 41-9, below, pp. 123-5.

[2] Lib. vii, c. 16 (Woodbine, pp. 112-13; Hall, p. 89). See *E.H.R.*, xliii.333-6, for the origin of this rule and its enforcement in England.

[3] Lib. x, c. 8 (Woodbine, p. 139; Hall, p. 124). The gage as between Christians was normally the equivalent of a beneficial lease. If, however, there were a loan on the security of land and the payments were not applied to the extinction of the debt, the gage was a mortgage. This was the form that Jewish loans on the security of land normally took. For a commentary on this passage, which is by no means clear, see Richardson, *English Jewry under Angevin Kings*, pp. 84-5.

[4] Besides *iustae nuptiae* the law recognised *concubinatus*, where there was no *maritalis affectio*, though this state became little different in its legal consequences from marriage. Slavery was a necessary impediment to marriage – and it can hardly have been otherwise in England before the twelfth century – but the law recognised *contubernium* between two slaves or a slave and a free person (Buckland, *Roman Law of Slavery*, pp. 76-9).

coniunctio maris et feminae et consortium omnis vitae, divini et humani iuris communicatio'.[1] Unfortunately, under the influence of theological theorising, the mediaeval law of marriage had, before the end of the twelfth century, resolved itself into a disastrous tangle, repugnant to good sense and good morals – at least as sense and morals are now conceived. Witness King John's matrimonial adventures.[2] No unprejudiced person, sufficiently informed in canon law, can, we think, dissent from Maitland's judgement:

> these intricate rules . . . are the idle ingenuities of men who are amusing themselves by inventing a game of skill which is to be played with neatly drawn tables of affinity and doggerel hexameters . . . a marriage law which was a mass of flighty fancies and misapplied logic.[3]

Doubtless the law of marriage, the pagan law, of sixth-century Kent would be repellant to us[4]; but would the law of the mediaeval Church be less repellant? Since, however, men and women only exceptionally came into conflict with the law of the Church, most of them lived their married lives much as men and women do to-day and doubtless as they did under King Æthelberht. Still more rarely did the State come into conflict with the Church's law of marriage. There is one notorious occasion, however, when in 1236 the barons refused to admit as good law legitimation *per subsequens matrimonium*. They would not, they said, change the law of England, and the rule for which they contended seems indeed to have been the law from the time of Richard de Lucy.[5] Otherwise the Roman canon law of marriage remained the law of England until the sixteenth century.

Our survey of the effects of the impact of Roman law upon the common law has necessarily been somewhat cursory, though we trust that we have given a reasonably clear picture of what was happening in the twelfth century. But by 1200 we are hardly half-way through the story. Let us therefore add a brief postscript. The study of Roman law intensified throughout Western Europe with the development and extension of ecclesiastical tribunals; and since the judges of the king's courts continued to be drawn largely from the ranks of ecclesiastics, they were inevitably influenced by their reading in the current textbooks of the schools. Certain of even the lay judges equipped them-

[1] Dig. 23.2.1. This is paraphrased in Inst. 1.9.1 as 'Nuptiae autem sive matrimonium est viri et mulieris coniunctio, individuam consuetudinem vitae continens'.

[2] We have endeavoured to explain as clearly as possible the relations between John and (*a*) Isabelle of Gloucester and (*b*) Isabelle of Angoulême in *Governance of Mediaeval England*, pp. 322-5. Neglect to master the mediaeval law of marriage has led historians into some remarkable fantasies. By modern standards John's conduct towards the first Isabelle was doubtless disgraceful, but he kept the right side of the law, a law that showed very little consideration for women.

[3] Pollock and Maitland, *History of English Law*, ii.389.

[4] Liebermann, *Gesetze*, i.7-8; Attenborough, p. 14; above, p. 4. As Maitland said, Æthelberht's laws seem to imply recognition of marriage by capture; but he was mistaken in supposing that this was countenanced by the Church (*History of English Law*, ii.393).

[5] Makower, *Constitutional History of the Church of England*, pp. 422-3, where the texts are cited.

selves in the same way.[1] One result was an effort to supplement the common law, where it might seem to be defective, with matter drawn either directly from classical Roman law or, more especially, from the better known contemporary civilians and canonists, Azzo, Tancred and Raymond of Peñafort. When therefore *Glanville* was adapted for use in Scotland, chapters directly based upon these writers were introduced into the text.[2] Bracton also introduced into his treatise a good deal from these writers as well as from the Oxford canonist, William of Drogheda, and from the Institutes.[3] To what extent this admixture was assimilated by English law is a difficult question to which we need not attempt an answer. A byproduct, as it were, of the renewed study of Roman law, and therefore of contact with Bologna, was the study of the *dictamen* and related subjects. This had begun by the beginning of the thirteenth century, and the result was the rise of a class of teachers at Oxford known as *dictatores*, who provided instruction for young men in the conduct of affairs at what we may call the manorial level – presiding over manorial courts, keeping court rolls, writing their lords' letters, drafting deeds, keeping accounts and so forth, acting, in fact, not unlike solicitors until recently, when they held office as stewards of manors.[4] The contact of the *dictatores* with Roman law is curiously illustrated by the use in manorial courts of the formula for 'laying the damages', found in ecclesiastical courts, upon which we have already commented.[5] The *dictatores* continued to teach at Oxford until the fifteenth century. The contact between Roman law and the common law in England came practically to an end, however, when the judges were laymen, drawn from the ranks of lawyers trained in the common law. This development synchronised with, and was at least partly determined by, the growing rôle of statutes in modifying the common law. Ecclesiastical law and the common law then became things apart and Roman law so much foreign law in the king's courts.

[1] The outstanding example is John of Lexington, steward of the king's household, who for six years was Bracton's colleague on the King's Bench (Richardson, *Bracton*, p. 5).

[2] *Juridical Review*, lxvii.155-87.

[3] Richardson, *op. cit.*, pp. 5-6, 92-151.

[4] *Dictamen* is the art of composing formal instruments in Latin, and *dictatores* were those who practised or taught the art: the latter was the meaning given to the word in England and particularly at Oxford. For their history and activities see Richardson, *An Oxford Teacher of the Fifteenth Century*; *Business Training in Medieval Oxford*; and *Letters of the Oxford Dictatores*.

[5] Richardson and Sayles, *Procedure without Writ*, pp. cxiii-cxiv.

V

THE ASSIZES OF HENRY II

IN 1159, so it would seem, Henry II issued a 'constitution' seeking to regulate in some measure the local courts, both secular and ecclesiastical, in England and Normandy. Rural deans were to accuse no one except on the evidence of reputable witnesses from the neighbourhood. Similarly, at the monthly meetings of county courts no judgement was to be passed except on the evidence of neighbours; nothing was to be done to the injury or prejudice of anyone; the peace was to be kept; convicted thieves were to be punished forthwith; everyone was to hold his own property undisturbed; and churches were to possess their rights.[1] The chronicler who tells us this obscures rather than elucidates the law, called elsewhere *lex prohibitionis*,[2] of which the text has not come down to us. All that seems clear is that local ecclesiastical courts were required to act only upon reliable evidence, while the procedure of local secular courts was regulated in some detail. In the only case arising out of this constitution of which we have details, the rural dean took advantage of his office to extort money from a woman accused of adultery, against whom there was no real evidence. When, on the complaint of the woman's husband, the dean was summoned before the king's council, the sole issue raised was whether evidence had been given by reputable witnesses. The dean named two, but failed to produce them. He was therefore convicted of a breach of the constitution. In the view of the lay members of the council, the dean should then have been amerced for an offence against the secular law; but the ecclesiastical members held that there should be only an ecclesiastical penalty. The king rejected this argument as perverse and the case was adjourned, never to be determined but to be buried in the controversy over the Constitutions of Clarendon.[3] Unfortunately nothing is known of the application of the constitution to the county court and we do not therefore know whether the chronicler's *testimonium vicinorum* meant an 'accusing jury' or jury of presentment, as has been supposed,[4] for he uses the same words in speaking of ecclesiastical courts. What we do know is that, when general eyres were resumed under Henry II, the royal justices were punishing defects in the procedure of the local

[1] 'Continuatio Beccensis' in Robert of Torigni, *Chronica*, p. 327. The words we take as referring to county courts are 'cum judices singularum provinciarum singulis mensibus ad minus simul devenirent': *provincia* is, of course, an elegant synonym for *comitatus*, frequently employed. The term may have been chosen if the edict was intended to apply to Henry's possessions on both sides of the Channel.

[2] *Becket Materials*, iii.44.

[3] Richardson and Sayles, *Governance of Mediaeval England*, p. 306.

Haskins, *Norman Institutions*, pp. 219-20, 329.

courts as they had done under Henry I.[1] There were, however, as yet no general eyres in 1159 and were not to be until 1166. So far as secular courts in England were concerned, the constitution could have been only a transitory measure until a more effective control was imposed, and, as we have seen, any attempt to regulate the conduct of ecclesiastical courts was abandoned.[2]

At this point it may be useful, not only for the better understanding of this, but perhaps also of a preceding, chapter,[3] if we were to say something about the judges of both the secular and ecclesiastical local courts in the early years of Henry's reign. There seems to have been much confusion about them, which has led to a good many misapprehensions regarding, for example, the Constitutions of Clarendon and another enactment of equal celebrity, the Assize of Clarendon, which we shall shortly have to discuss.

We have already made mention of the local justice, whose origins go back before the Conquest.[4] Under Henry I the importance of this office was diminished by the creation of *justiciarii totius Anglie*, judges whose jurisdiction was not confined to a single county, who sat in the court at the Exchequer and who were sent on eyre throughout the country. But with the disorganisation of the central administration under Stephen, the local justice attained an unprecedented importance and earls and bishops were pleased to assume the office. The restoration of central control under Henry II made the office less attractive, but for eleven or twelve years there was no alternative except to rely upon local justices to keep the pleas of the crown and to try actions at common law.[5] The sheriff, it is true, was available to preside in the county court and to visit the hundreds twice a year on his tourn, but, particularly at this period, he had many other duties which must have occupied much of his time, and the part he played in the administration of justice is obscure. Probably it was not very great.[6] Some visitations to the counties were made by *curiales*; but we can name only one justice, William fitz John, who was at all regularly employed in this way, and after a few years he was diverted to missions connected with the royal household.[7] Not before 1166 was there even the beginning of an effective judiciary available for visiting the counties. At first its members were largely drawn from other employments,[8] but gradually they became more and more professional, and the local justice disappeared, not, it would seem, all at once, but at different times in different counties up to the end of the twelfth century.[9] Their end is obscure; but

[1] *Governance of Mediaeval England*, pp. 202-4.
[2] Above, p. 68.
[3] Above, pp. 59 ff., 76 ff.
[4] Above, p. 37 .
[5] *Governance of Mediaeval England*, pp. 174-7, 194-6.
[6] However, it seems clear that Simon fitz Peter, sheriff of Bedford, 1156-9, was presiding over the county court when he was insulted by Philip de Broi (*ibid.*, p. 304 and *n*).
[7] *Ibid.*, p. 197; Stenton, *English Justice*, pp. 69-70.
[8] *Governance of Mediaeval England*, p. 203.
[9] *Ibid.*, p. 196.

it seems certain that from about 1170 they were of little importance. They receive no mention in the Inquest of Sheriffs which provided in that year for a general enquiry into the corruption and misdeeds of all exercising authority locally, even archdeacons and rural deans.[1] When, however, we read of justices in connexion with the Constitution of Clarendon or the Assize of Clarendon, we must not think of the yet unknown justices who went out for the first time on the general eyre of 1168,[2] much less must we think of the two chief justiciars, as some have done.[3] We must think of these humbler local justices, whose course was nearly run, but whose existence in 1164 and 1166 gives intelligibility to some of the provisions of Henry's early legislation.

Let us now turn to the ecclesiastical courts. In principle, jurisdiction was vested in the bishop; but it would seem that before the Conquest laymen who had committed an ecclesiastical offence were being tried in the hundred court. That seems to be the only interpretation we can put upon the decree of the Conqueror, which forbade the hearing of any plea in the hundred court which concerned *leges episcopales* and the citation of laymen before a secular tribunal in spiritual causes. A bishop, however, could not have been expected to attend a hundred court with any frequency, if at all, and his place had been taken by an archdeacon, as the decree implies.[4] There is no suggestion that at the date of the decree – possibly 1072 – an archdeacon was anything but the bishop's deputy for specific purposes: he had no independent jurisdiction of his own. It was only gradually and at different periods in different dioceses that archdeaconries were created with delimited boundaries, and even so the extent of an archdeacon's jurisdiction depended upon agreement with the bishop.[5] Extremely little is known of the details of the arrangements in particular cases and no generalisation of any value can be made.[6] But if the early history of archdeacons is obscure, that of rural deans is even more obscure. When we get to know something of them, their jurisdiction seems not to have differed greatly in scope from that of an archdeacon. They appear to have shared the profits of justice with him[7] and, when their powers were restricted in the thirteenth century, the archdeacon assumed the jurisdiction they had relinquished.[8] The inference is that such criminal

[1] Text in *Select Charters*, pp. 175-8.

[2] *Governance of Mediaeval England*, p. 205; *E.H.R.*, xliii.167-8. Maitland renders 'iusticia regis' of the Constitutions of Clarendon, c. 3, by the vague 'temporal court' (*History of English Law*, i.448). Ramsay, *Angevin Empire*, p. 42, has 'one of the King's Justices'.

[3] Mlle Foreville translates 'le justicier du roi' (*L'Église et La Royauté*, p. 126).

[4] Liebermann, *Gesetze*, i.485.

[5] Makower, *Constitutional History*, pp. 317-18. It is clear that by 1127 archdeacons were employed generally in England, though their tenure of office may have been precarious and certain of them served in more than one diocese (John of Worcester, *Chronicle*, pp. 24-5).

[6] As, for example, in the Canterbury diocese: the limits of the archdeacon's jurisdiction were in dispute in the later twelfth century (Churchill, *Canterbury Administration*, i.43-4).

[7] In the Scarborough case, which excited Henry's ire (above, p. 88), the husband of the accused woman paid 22 shillings, of which twenty went to the archdeacon and two to the dean (*Becket Materials*, iii.44).

[8] Makower, *op. cit.*, pp. 318-20, 323.

jurisdiction as rural deans exercised – and we must emphasise the distinction between their judicial and administrative duties[1] – had been originally delegated to them by the archdeacon.[2] This will explain why deans are not mentioned in the Constitutions of Clarendon: only archidiaconal courts and the archdeacon's *jus*.[3] The archdeacon, we infer, exercised his right of jurisdiction as much in rural chapters as in a court over which he presided in person. The boundaries of a rural deanery corresponded as a rule to the boundaries of a hundred, and for ecclesiastical purposes the clergy of the deanery – or, in other words, the parochial clergy of the hundred – assembled in a rural chapter over which the dean presided.[4] These chapters appear to have been already in existence at the time of the Conqueror's decree[5], and it would be an obvious and natural course for an overworked archdeacon to delegate his jurisdiction, formerly exercised in the hundred court, to a local tribunal of this kind. Continental precedents presumably suggested that this was the appropriate course to follow, for in Normandy rural deans appear to have exercised a similar jurisdiction to that of their fellows in England.[6] There was this historical difference in England: for ecclesiastical purposes the chapter took the place of the hundred. And since the local justice sat in the hundred court,[7] we find a ready explanation of the provision in the third article of the Constitutions of Clarendon that criminous clerks were to appear in the court of the royal justice and that the royal justice was to send a representative to the ecclesiastical court to watch the proceedings there. The two courts were close neighbours.[8]

At the accession of Henry II the jurisdiction of both archdeacon's courts and rural chapters was clearly of comparatively recent growth: at the utmost it could not have had a history of more than eighty years and for some decades the exercise of jurisdiction must have been quite tentative. It was only gradually that bishops, and therefore archdeacons, disburdened themselves of part of their jurisdiction.[9] The scandals which arrested Henry's attention could not then have been of very long standing. They may have been promoted by lack of

[1] That in the twelfth century rural deans acted as agents for the bishop (cf. Makower, *op. cit.*, p. 322) is well illustrated by the employment of the deans of Lewes and Hastings by the bishop of Chichester in 1156 to deliver a papal mandate to the abbot of Battle and to summon him to appear before judges delegate (*Chron. de Bello*, p. 77).

[2] It is clear from the Constitutions of Otho, c. 20, that the presence of the archdeacon was often required at rural chapters early in the thirteenth century (Powicke and Cheney, *Councils and Synods*, i.254). In the twelfth century, in the Canterbury diocese, and presumably elsewhere, the archdeacon, after consultation with the bishop, instituted and deprived rural deans (Churchill, *op. cit.*, i.44).

[3] Constitutions of Clarendon, cc. 6, 8. On the other hand the unjust exactions of both archdeacons and deans are to be the subject of enquiry under the Inquest of Sheriffs (*Select Charters*, pp. 165, 177).

[4] So Stubbs, *Constitutional History*, i.121: no contemporary authority is cited. See also Makower, *op. cit.*, pp. 322-3, 383.

[5] *Ibid.*, pp. 322, 382.

[6] Besides the reference given by Haskins, *Norman Institutions*, p. 330 *n.* 6, see *Speculum*, vii.390.

[7] *Governance of Mediaeval England*, p. 195.

[8] Above, p. 64.

[9] Makower, *op. cit.*, pp. 317-18; Churchill, *Canterbury Administration*, pp. 43-4.

control during Stephen's reign: the times were not propitious for discipline in either Church or State. It was an age when the rural clergy had, as a rule, little learning and facilities for training were rare, and rural deans were unlikely to be well equipped for judicial office. Moreover, whatever supervision it was open to archdeacons to give they were often not in a position to exercise. It was, in a sense, fatal to their efficiency when archdeacons began to receive a serious training in law, a movement which Archbishop Theobald may have initiated.[1] They became too efficient for their proper office and were lured to other, largely secular, employments. The case of Thomas Becket is very much to the point. His office as archdeacon of Canterbury was to him a mere source of profit. Once in the service of the king, his archidiaconal duties could, of course, be performed only by deputy; but he drew the last penny he could from the office and was reluctant to forgo the abusive aid introduced by his predecessor, the exaction of which Archbishop Theobald had prohibited under pain of anathema.[2] Becket was not at all singular. Richard of Ilchester, the famous archdeacon of Poitiers, devoted his very considerable abilities to his duties in the English exchequer.[3] Richard was not above taking from those interested a handsome bribe for performing his secular duties.[4] There can be no doubt that he looked upon his archdeaconry in the same light, as a means of augmenting his income. Any student of the period could compile a considerable list of like cases.[5] It is perhaps otiose to remark that the whole conception of applying ecclesiastical emoluments to support royal servants was abusive, and the king must take his full share of blame for battening upon the system, for systematic it certainly and literally was. But Henry's reaction to the ills that sprang from it was to deal with the symptoms of corruption while ignoring the causes.

With the Constitutions of Clarendon ratified, Henry had completed the first stage of a programme of reform which was to occupy him for much of the rest of his life. It is in no spirit of irony that we speak of the ratification of the Constitutions and the completion of a task. All the noise and fury of the Becket controversy which echoes still cannot disguise the truth that the Constitutions became law on 30 January 1164 and that the subsequent modification of the third and eighth articles was a change equivalent in modern times to an amending act which

[1] This was Stubb's view (*Seventeen Lectures*, pp. 347-9). But as we have indicated in the previous chapter (above, pp. 71-2), Theobald's introduction of Vacarius into his *familia* had not the significance for the study of Roman law in England that was at one time thought.

[2] See the three letters brought together in *Becket Materials*, v.9-15, and in *Letters of John of Salisbury*, nos. 22, 128, 129, with which compare no. 28. Theobald was, of course, quite impotent to recall Becket to his duties or to take action against him in any way.

[3] *Dialogus de Scaccario*, pp. 17, 26-7.

[4] For the restoration of the church of Luton to St Alban's he insisted upon the grant to him of two-thirds of the revenues of the church (Walsingham, *Gesta Abbatum*, i.124).

[5] Among those prominent in the king's service, who became bishops, are Geoffrey Ridel, John of Oxford and Richard of Ely: while bishops, they all served as justices.

leaves the substance of the statute intact.[1] And it has to be remembered that the modified procedure for trying a criminous clerk meant, in practice, his trial and sentence in the king's court, though he escaped the extreme penalties of the criminal law. Nor, in course of time, did a convicted criminal need to be in orders to obtain benefit of clergy: he had but to be sufficiently literate to read the neck-verse.[2] The mollification of the law sprang not from any argument Becket put forward, but from his senseless murder. Without that no change is likely to have been made. *Sanguis martyrum semen Ecclesiae.*

At this point, however, lest we may be thought to have overlooked a document of importance, we should perhaps notice the 'New Constitutions', supposed to have been promulgated by Henry and attributed variously to 1165 or 1169. They purport to be aimed at further restricting ecclesiastical privileges and, in especial, appeals to the Curia, a supplement, as it were, to the Constitutions of Clarendon. Although these bogus constitutions have been accepted in very recent years as genuine legislation, they are, in fact, a characteristically clumsy fabrication by Becket's supporters at Canterbury,[3] who perpetrated even cruder and more blatant forgeries,[4] for they were as prolific as they were inept. But none of their achievements was so successful as this in misleading historians from Lord Lyttelton's time until our own.[5] We need not, however, dwell upon it, for the terms of the fabrication may easily be found elsewhere, and its interest is rather pathological than historical. Let us pass to serious matters.

Henry may have been diverted a little from his purpose by the Becket controversy, but by the end of 1165 he was prepared to resume the task of reforming the administration of the country. At a council which assembled at Clarendon at Christmas in that year or shortly afterwards[6] extensive changes were introduced in all branches of the

[1] The date, the fourth day before the Purification of the B.V.M., is that in the final clause. As to the legal effect of the Constitutions see above, pp. 65-6. We doubt whether Maitland was correct in saying that on this occasion 'Henry was not legislating' (*History of English Law*, i.137).

[2] Makower gives the principal texts (*op. cit.*, pp. 399-415). See also Gabel, *Benefit of Clergy*, pp. 62-87. The prisoner was frequently, though not necessarily, required to read the opening verse of the fiftieth (English fifty-first) Psalm *Miserere mei Deus* to prove his clergy: hence 'neck-verse'.

[3] *Governance of Mediæval England*, p. 308: above, p. 66, n. 1.

[4] We have in mind a fabrication purporting to be a charter of Henry II in favour of the monks of Christchurch, issued at Canterbury in the presence of the legates Albert and Theodinus (who were never there), entitled 'Revocacio articulorum quos rex Henricus secundus voluit ecclesiam anglicanam observasse'. Unfortunately the monks chose the wrong models for their forgery. So far as we are aware, this document is to be found, in a late fourteenth-century hand, only in Cambridge Univ. Lib. MS. Ee. 2.29, fol. 117. It is followed, appropriately enough, by the 'New Constitutions'. We are indebted to the Librarian for drawing our attention to this document and obliging us with a photostat.

[5] Lyttelton, *History of Henry II*, iv.266-74, 497-8. We may cite among recent works Foreville, *L'Église et la Royauté*, pp. 154-5 (where these *constitutiones* are translated in full), and Knowles, *Episcopal Colleagues of Thomas Becket*, pp. 131-4.

[6] The date is indicated by the entries on the Pipe Roll for 1166. The council is most likely to have been held at the Christmas festival 1165. There seem no grounds for supposing that it was preceded by a meeting at Oxford and that therefore the council at Clarendon was in the early months of 1166 (*Governance of Mediaeval England*, pp. 198-203, 443-4).

law. Great progress had been made since the beginning of the reign in the re-establishment of order, and the administration was gradually returning to the standard it had attained under Henry I, but over the years of recovery much had perforce been let slide, many wrongdoers had not been brought to justice. The intention now was to perform all that had been left unperformed since December 1154, to clear up the accumulated arrears. There were unpunished public wrongs: murder, theft, robbery, forgery, arson; there were unrequited private wrongs: the disseisins that inevitably happened in troublous times; there were offences against the king's forests. Three separate enactments dealt with the three classes of delict. But at this point we must anticipate a later discussion by making it clear that the document which has long passed as the 'Assize of Clarendon' is apocryphal, an ill-expressed, incoherent attempt at a commentary on the assize and written a good many years after 1166.[1] The actual assize bearing this name is a clear, succinct enactment of three articles: it is the first of the three enactments at this council.[2] The normal procedure by private appeal of felony, which obviously had been ineffective, is supplemented by a public process which brings to trial all those defamed of serious crime, including accessories. The suspects are to be brought before two juries, one consisting of twelve knights or other law-worthy men of the hundred, and the other of four men from each of the neighbouring townships.[3] If these juries find the suspicion to be justified, the accused has to undergo the ordeal by water. If he fails in the ordeal, he is to be mutilated by the loss of one foot. If he survives the ordeal, then, unless he is charged with murder or some other grave crime, he is, as a rule, allowed to remain unmolested upon giving sureties for good behaviour. Those who survive the ordeal, but are charged with exceptionally grave offences, have, however, to appear before the county court. If there the knights of the neighbourhood declare them to be guilty and the court confirms this verdict, the accused – or perhaps we should say the convicted – are to be given forty days in which to depart the realm with their belongings. There is only one other provision in the assize, directed against the harbouring of criminals. Hitherto the law had been that a host became responsible for anyone lodging with him when he had stayed three nights[4]: now the host is responsible if his lodger stays for more than one night.

The terms of the assize are, as we have said, succinct and it was found necessary to supplement them by more detailed instructions to those responsible for putting the assize into execution.[5] At this point, however, we do not propose to describe how the assize was supplemented,

[1] *Ibid.*, pp. 439-43.

[2] We have endeavoured to reconstruct the text (*ibid.*, p. 441).

[3] Despite the prescription of the Assize that four men were to be summoned from every township in the hundred, it became the practice to summon them from four townships only (Pollock and Maitland, *History of English Law*, ii.644).

[4] *Leges Edwardi Confessoris*, c. 23, 23.1 (*Gesetze*, i.648).

[5] Below, pp. 96-8.

but to draw attention to its form, short, succinct, sparing of detail. We should compare it with its companion enactment, the Assize of the Forest. This is drafted in a similar way, in five succinct articles, of which the first is no more than a preamble, stating the king's intention to reintroduce the law as it stood in his grandfather's day. Offenders are warned not to hope for mercy in consideration of a fine: they must expect mutilation. The other four articles, while preserving the king's rights, protect those whose estates lie within the bounds of a royal forest or who have licence to hunt there.[1] The text of the third assize – of novel disseisin, as it was later known – has not come down to us, though of its substance there is no doubt. Anyone who had been disseised since the king's coronation was given a speedy remedy. Whether he had a good title or not, he was reinstated while the disseisor was amerced for the trespass he had committed.[2] There was a tradition, recounted by Bracton, that this assize was devised only after long and anxious consideration.[3] While it may be true that, once the assize had gained its immense popularity and was widely applied to right many wrongs, its application in particular cases demanded much thought by the judges, we doubt whether, as it was first conceived, there was any intention of looking beyond the immediate situation. The principle behind the assize, by no means confined to English law, is the simple one of ensuring that a dispute over the possession of property shall be determined by the courts and that the violent ejection of one party by the other must be redressed before the better right can be legally decided.[4] The court will protect seisin irrespective of title: otherwise there is an end of law.[5] The primary object of the assize, when it was first instituted, was then the restoration of order and the relief of those who had been violently disseised since the king came to the throne but had been unable to obtain a remedy.[6]

We should perhaps notice one other important measure devised at this council, the assessment for taxation of land held by military tenure. Once more the king went back to the time of his grandfather. Landowners were required to state how many knights had been enfeoffed upon their estates at the time of Henry I's death, how many enfeoffments had since been made and for how many knight's fees was the landowner himself responsible or, in other words, how many

[1] *Gesta Henrici*, i.323-4.

[2] That the Assize originally covered disseisins since the coronation is to be inferred from the common form of writs given in *Glanville*, where this is the period of limitation (lib. ii, c. 3; lib. iv, c. 6; lib. xii, c. 11, lib. xiii, cc. 3, 4, 5, 6; Woodbine, pp. 57, 77-8, 153, 158-9; Hall, pp. 23, 46, 142, 150-1). Professor Van Caenegem favours this period of limitation on rather different grounds (*Royal Writs*, p. 286). By the time *Glanville* was written (*alpha* text), the period of limitation had been reduced to the king's last voyage to Normandy (lib. xiii, cc. 33, 35-37; Hall, pp. 167-9, 180).

[3] Bracton, fol. 164*b*: multis vigiliis excogitatam et inventam.

[4] Richardson and Sayles, *Procedure without Writ*, pp. cxxviii-cxxxi; above, p. 82.

[5] Cf. Pollock and Maitland, *History of English Law*, ii.52-3.

[6] Professor Van Caenegem (*Royal Writs*, pp. 283-7) and Lady Stenton (*English Justice*, pp. 35-42) have other – and conflicting – hypotheses about the origin and evolution of the assize. The views of the former more nearly approach our own.

knights did he maintain in his household. Provision was made for enquiry by jury. The questions, except the last, were not in most cases simple to answer. More than thirty years had gone by since the day when Henry I was alive and dead and in the natural order of events there would have been many changes, even apart from those brought about by the troubles of those thirty years. The ultimate result was widespread agreement on highly artificial assessments with little or no historical basis.[1]

All the measures devised at Clarendon succeeded in their object, except the Assize of Clarendon itself. This was a lamentable failure. The reason was that the available judicial machinery was quite inadequate for the enforcement of the assize. This is not the view taken by the textbooks and it is important to understand what actually happened. Let us therefore endeavour to reconstruct the procedure followed, so far as we are able to do so, from the information supplied by the pipe rolls and the document which goes under the name of the Assize of Clarendon, but which is, in fact, a private compilation reflecting, so it would seem, the practice in some counties.[2] We must bear in mind that before 1166 criminal justice was justice administered by local courts and that the king was represented in the counties, not by itinerant justices of high rank, but by the sheriff and the local justice whose duty it was to keep the pleas of the crown.[3] The crimes against which the assize was aimed were felonies, but not all felonies. There is, for example, no mention of rape. The reason for this omission is that felonies were, for the most part, prosecuted by way of appeal or, as we should say, by private prosecution. Any women who had been wronged had had their opportunity to obtain redress during the past eleven years. If they had failed to do so, the king was not greatly concerned: his justices took a lenient view of the offence in later years.[4] Nor does the assize mention mayhem or treason or treasure trove – for divers reasons, doubtless.[5] But the five crimes named[6] could not be left unpunished: murder, theft, robbery and arson were crimes of violence, and forgery – coining – had always been regarded as a heinous offence.[7] The normal procedure for bringing the criminals to book having largely lapsed for so many years, how was a prosecution now to be started? We take it that the assize was read in the county

[1] *Governance of Mediaeval England*, pp. 88-90.

[2] Below, pp. 125-7.

[3] *Governance of Mediaeval England*, pp. 194-6.

[4] Pollock and Maitland, *History of English Law*, ii.491.

[5] Mayhem was a matter of appeal, but seems to have been somewhat lightly regarded (*ibid*., ii.488-90). For *Glanville's* treatment of treason and treasure trove see below, p. 108: the author regarded them as difficult cases, and they were, in any case, not so frequent as to merit enquiry all over the country.

[6] The only authentic text of the Assize of Clarendon is the confirmation at Northampton in 1176 and the five crimes are there mentioned. The first three crimes only are mentioned in the pseudo-Assize of later date and in a writ of 1166, which we know only from a later copy (*Governance of Mediaeval England*, pp. 200*n*, 439-43). There is no evident reason why two crimes should be added after a lapse of ten years.

[7] Above, pp. 20, 25, 33.

court, and perhaps in the hundred court also, and that the opportunity was offered to informers to come forward or, more than probably, to delate evildoers secretly. There would be baseless suspicions and quite certainly, as we shall see, malicious accusations against people of good repute. Even if there had been gaols enough,[1] it would have been unjust to take such people into custody; and it is clear that a great many of those inculpated found sureties for their appearance in the hundred court, that many who found sureties did not appear and that those who did were allowed to make their law[2] – that is, to find compurgators who would swear to their innocence – though nothing of this is said in the assize. The number who, in any county, went to the ordeal was small; in some counties action was postponed; and in others no action seems to have been taken at all.[3]

These facts came to light when the justiciar Richard de Lucy and Earl Geoffrey de Mandeville set out on a general eyre in the spring of 1166. They seem to have had a little assistance in Staffordshire from Alan de Neville, but he was mainly engaged upon a forest eyre which, beginning in this year, was continued in 1167. Apart from such help as he gave, the justiciar and Earl Geoffrey acted alone in a visitation which took them rapidly from East Anglia and the home counties to Northumberland and across the Pennines to Carlisle, where on 21 October the earl died. Many counties were left unvisited.[4] It must be emphasised that the justices did not enforce the assize. It was one of their duties, but only one, to ascertain how the assize had been enforced locally. They amerced sureties who had failed to produce an accused man and inflicted fines where hitherto unreported murders had been disclosed – and of these there were a good many: but duties such as these would fall normally upon justices in eyre.[5] If, however, in this way the assize proved profitable to the Crown, it had not effected its purpose of punishing crime. The procedure had ensured that wrongdoers had received warning in good time and had, for the most part, made good their escape.[6] The lesson was not lost upon Richard de Lucy.

In little over a twelvemonth, another general eyre began, very much better staffed than that of 1166, an eyre that lasted for the best part of two years, and this was quickly followed by another.[7] Although these eyres were, in their turn, financially profitable, they must have disclosed very serious defects in the local administration of justice, and when Henry returned to England in the spring of 1170, the eyre then in progress was abruptly interrupted and instead the great investiga-

[1] It is clear from the Pipe Roll of 1166 that instructions had been given to sheriffs to build or repair gaols (*Pipe Roll, 12 Henry II*, pp. 11, 17, 36, 64 *et passim*).

[2] *Governance of Mediaeval England*, pp. 198-9, 202.

[3] *Ibid.*, p. 201.

[4] *Ibid.*, pp. 199-200.

[5] *Ibid.*, p. 202.

[6] *Ibid.*, p. 201.

[7] *Ibid.*, pp. 203-4; *E.H.R.* xliii.168.

tion known as the Inquest of Sheriffs was set on foot, an investigation that involved the despatch of judicial commissioners all over the country.[1] What, however, is of immediate interest is one of the articles of enquiry.[2]

> Concerning the chattels of fugitives from the Assize of Clarendon and the chattels of those who were found guilty by that assize, let it be enquired what was done and what issues arose therefrom in respect of every hundred and township and let it be written down in detail. And let it be enquired whether anyone was unjustly accused in that assize for reward or promise or hatred or any other wrongful cause and whether any of the accused were released or put on trial for reward or promise or friendship and who received a reward therefor. And let this be written down likewise.

Few fragments of the multitudinous documents arising out of the Inquest have survived and none of the answers to this article. We shall therefore never know how far astray the proceedings under the assize went; but the very terms of the article show why the assize failed and how unequal were the local ministers of justice to the task entrusted to them. Events prevented the early resumption of general eyres – Becket's murder, the expedition to Ireland, the rebellion of 1173-74. It was not until 1175 that there was another visitation by the justices; and later in that year the king, accompanied by three justices, made a special visitation of most of the country north of the Thames from Yorkshire to Gloucestershire.[3] It was presumably the experience gained in this way that prompted the reforms embodied in the Assize of Northampton.

It had become abundantly clear that no reform in the administration of justice could be effective which depended upon the competence or goodwill of local ministers. As a class these officers were both incompetent and corrupt.[4] The council that met at Northampton in January 1176 decided to place the entire responsibility for administering the Assize of Clarendon – now revised, amended and given permanence – upon the central judiciary, which over the last ten years had grown in numbers and efficiency. It is laid down specifically that the justices are to administer the assize in so far as the worst thieves and malefactors are concerned and it is to them that presentments are to be made by juries from the hundreds and townships. The justices are

[1] Richardson and Sayles, *Procedure without Writ*, pp. xxvi-xxvii.

[2] Inquest of Sheriffs, cap. 6 (*Select Charters*, pp. 176-7).

[3] *E.H.R.*, xliii.169.

[4] This is quite clear from the terms of the Inquest of Sheriffs itself. A singular illustration is provided by the story told by Roger of Howden of no less a person than Ranulf Glanville himself, who contrived the condemnation to death of a young man who had married (apparently somewhat irregularly) an heiress whom Ranulf had intended for his steward. The young man was, however, reprieved and, on the accession of Richard I and the dismissal of Ranulf from office, was released from prison (*Gesta*, i.314-16; *Chronica*, ii.286 – where the story is distorted on revision). The steward, Reiner of Waxham, who had acted as undersheriff for Ranulf in Yorkshire, was himself imprisoned and suffered confiscation (Introduction to *Memoranda Roll, 1 John*, p. xciii *n*).

required to try, in particular, the more serious cases of murder, treason (*prodicio*) and arson arising out of the late rebellion (*guerra*).[1] In this way the basis was prepared for the criminal jurisdiction of the justices in eyre as it was exercised for a century and more, and the change was little short of revolutionary.

The text of the assizes issued at Northampton, as it was preserved by Roger of Howden, appears to be corrupt or interpolated in places[2]; but the scheme and purport are quite clear. First, there is the revision of the Assize of Clarendon, as we have described it. Secondly, there is an extensive revision of the land law. The seisin of heirs of freeholders is protected and also the widow's dower: of this we shall have more to say. Another article changes the period of limitation in the assize of novel disseisin. In 1166 an action might be brought for disseisins that had been made at any time since the beginning of the reign, and presumably all the actions that could relate to this period had been determined.[3] The treaty of peace with the young king which terminated the rebellion had required that all those unlawfully disseised during the hostilities should be reinstated.[4] The new period of limitation goes back therefore no farther than the king's arrival in England after peace had been made. The third of the assizes issued at Northampton adds to the chapters of the eyre. One of the new articles of this assize, which we may remark, provides for an enquiry into escheats, churches, land and women in the king's gift: this was only an occasional addition to the chapters, the next occasion being in 1185, and the returns made then have survived.[5] Another article provides for a special oath of fealty to the king to be taken before the justices by all ranks from earls to villeins and for homage and allegiance to be performed by tenants-in-chief who had not yet done so.

This last article is of importance for determining the date of the Assize of Arms, which Howden inserts under the year 1181, but the date of which he clearly did not know.[6] This assize seems unquestionably to belong to 1176. Certainly 1181 cannot be the true date, for there was no general eyre in that year or the year following,[7] and the assize is expressly committed to the justices for its administration. But the consideration that to our minds fixes the date conclusively is that those covered by the assize are required individually to take an oath that they will put their arms at the service of the king at his command

[1] Assize of Northampton, cc. 1, 7 (*Select Charters*, pp. 179-80).

[2] *Gesta Henrici*, i.108-11; *Chronica*, ii.89-91. As we have stated elsewhere, paragraphs 10 and 12 seem obviously misplaced and may have had no place in the original text (*Governance of Mediaeval England*, p. 440).

[3] Above, p. 94.

[4] *Foedera*, i.30.

[5] *Rotuli de Dominabus* (ed. Round), pp. xviii-xix.

[6] *Gesta Henrici*, i.278; *Chronica*, iii.260. In neither case does Howden give a precise date. In the first instance his words are 'Interim rex Angliae fecit hanc assisam . . .': in the second instance he changes *Interim* to *Deinde*. Howden observes no precise chronological sequence in this part of his chronicle.

[7] *E.H.R.*, xliii.170.

and in fealty to him. This oath is parallel to the oath required under the third assize of Northampton and it is required for the same reason. Many of those concerned had been in arms against the king and had only recently been admitted to his peace. There was to be no question henceforth that their fealty to their immediate lord came before their fealty to the king. The general obligation to bear arms was now a direct obligation to the king: the link between man and lord was broken. We may add that, if we are right in our dating of the Assize of Arms, there can be no question of its being preceded by a similar measure applied by Henry to his continental dominions.[1] It was, however, a natural step at the time for him to extend an English institution to his other lands.

To make it clear that the English institution had priority and to stress how great the departure was from previous custom, we should say something more of the history of the obligation upon freemen to bear arms. The unfree, it may be remarked, are specifically excluded by the assize itself. This was no new departure: for many centuries the right to bear arms had been the exclusive privilege of freemen.[2] The position earlier in the reign is set out in some detail in the third edition of the *Leges Edwardi Confessoris*. The details correspond so closely to the assize that, though the language is very different – there is hardly a word in common – Liebermann believed that there was borrowing from the assize.[3] The significant difference is that, though in the *Leges* the armed forces are to be available at the king's command, the men are stated to be primarily at the service of their lords.[4] There is, of course, no mention in the *Leges* of the king's justices: enforcement of the law was, so it is said, in the hands of sheriffs, aldermen, hundred-reeves and other royal bailiffs. This law, we need hardly remark, is given a setting in the reign of King Edward, and it is to be supposed that the aldermen of the author's imagination are the Old English ealdormen, although they take precedence after the sheriffs. In his fiction, too, this institution is given a remote origin. Its existence, he tells us, enabled King Ethelred to contrive the slaughter of the Danes, though he does not tell us why, with this force at his command, Ethelred did not overcome the Danes without treachery. Let us not be misled by this claim for antiquity, nor by much more recent writers, who, though not consciously writing fiction, have claimed a pre-Conquest origin for the universal obligation upon freemen to bear arms: none of the supposed evidence will bear scrutiny.[5] And it is inherently improbable that the Conqueror would at any time have wished to arm all Englishmen who could claim to be free. He had good reason to suspect their loyalty.

[1] As Howden apparently supposed (*Gesta*, i.269; *Chronica*, iii.253).
[2] Below, p. 138. [3] *Gesetze*, i.656.
[4] *Leges Edwardi Confessoris*, cap. 32 A.9: arma habere et illa semper prompta conservare ad tuitionem regni et ad servitium dominorum suorum . . .
[5] *Governance of Mediaeval England*, pp. 48-55; below, p. 101.

The first hint we have that it was considered the duty of all freemen to fight for the king comes in a work of fiction of the reign of Henry I, the *Ten Articles* attributed to the Conqueror. Here King William is made to demand that all freemen shall defend the king's lands and honour, both in and out of England.[1] Such an obligation might indeed rest on those who held their lands by military tenure; but nowhere else does there seem to be any suggestion of a universal obligation,[2] and we can safely ascribe it to the author's imagination. Still, the idea was in the air, and at the Battle of the Standard we seem to see the idea in action. Even earlier there is an indication in a charter of Henry I that a duty lay upon burgesses to bear arms, an obligation that, in some form or other, was laid upon them in the Old English state; and the burgesses from the nearby Yorkshire towns were certainly present at the battle.[3] But while we may perhaps infer that there were, sometimes and in some places, local customs requiring freemen to bear arms in defence of their homes, and especially in districts uncomfortably near the perilous borders,[4] we cannot deduce that there was a general obligation in England or any nationally organised force, even in Stephen's reign. Except on this one occasion, there is nothing to suggest that the general body of freemen took up arms, nor does any contemporary tell us that they intervened at all between the two claimants to the throne. Knights and mercenaries there were in the rival armies: the freemen at large, apart from the townsmen here and there,[5] seem to have offered no organised defence, even against the savagery of the troops of Henry duke of Normandy.

We make no pretence to have elucidated the origin of the universal obligation to bear arms imposed in the twelfth century upon freemen. Some supposititious items in the genealogy we can, however, certainly discard – the mythical post-Conquest 'fyrd',[6] for example, and the oath-takers at Salisbury in 1086, an oath taken by a relatively small group of important landowners.[7] But the dispersal of error is no more than the first step towards truth. We should not ourselves be surprised to discover that Henry II was the originator and organiser, in the early years of his reign, of this universal obligation – doubtless using old materials – and that the reviser of the *Leges* was, here as elsewhere,

[1] Cap. 2. For this fabrication see above, pp. 46-7.

[2] It is to be noted that the *Rectitudines Singularum Personarum* assigns the duty of serving with an army (*expeditio*) only to the thegns and not to other freemen. It is a duty arising out of tenure (*Gesetze*, i.444-6). A clause in a well-known writ in favour of Ramsey Abbey (Harmer, *Anglo-Saxon Writs*, pp. 259-62, no. 61) has been interpreted as expressing a ceorl's obligations (Vinogradoff, *English Society*, p. 28); but it is neither said nor implied that the 'men' who are fyrd-worthy are ceorls. There is no reason to suppose that any but thegns – it may be lesser as well as greater thegns – were fyrd-worthy and mootworthy.

[3] *Governance of Mediaeval England*, p. 75. [4] Cf. Vinogradoff, *English Society*, pp. 32, 95.

[5] Bedford is a case in point: the burgesses were inflexibly opposed to Henry (*Governance of Mediaeval England*, p. 252*n*).

[6] *Ibid.*, pp. 53-5. We are unconvinced by Professor Hollister's arguments (*Military Organisation of Norman England*, pp. 216-67). His use of the word 'fyrd' as the name of a supposititious military organisation is unfortunate and surprising, for he knows that 'fyrd' means 'expedition'.

[7] Cf. Stenton, *Anglo-Saxon England*, p. 610: 'numbered in hundreds rather than thousands'.

engaged in finding a reputable precedent for his action. This, in our present state of knowledge, can be no more than a guess, perhaps an unlucky guess. Nevertheless, it seems more probable than the more positive assertions that pass current for the early history of the institution.

With the year 1176 we come nearly to the end of Henry's legislative activity. Only one major enactment are we able to credit to the rest of his reign, that which gave us the grand assize, seemingly devised at a council at Windsor in 1179.[1] 'The legislation of 1178 which established the court of Common Pleas'[2] – or, as others would have it, the court of King's Bench[3] – is an illusion, founded upon a misunderstood passage in Roger of Howden's chronicle which he expunged upon revision[4] and upon a complete misapprehension of the early history of the courts of common law.[5] The belief that the Assize of Arms belongs to 1181 we have already controverted. The belief that an Assize of the Forest belongs to 1184 rests upon a series of misunderstandings, primarily upon those of Roger of Howden but more largely, we fear, upon those of William Stubbs: but these misunderstandings may be more suitably indicated when we come to discuss the legal apocrypha of the period.[6] In *Glanville* there are references to certain 'assizes', the text of which has not come down to us. They are all procedural, dealing with record in inferior courts, *mort d'ancestor* in boroughs, the tenure of clerks presented to benefices in time of war, treasure trove, hue and cry.[7] Whether all these 'assizes' were what we should call legislation is uncertain: they cannot have been of major importance. But 'assize' is an ambiguous term, with many shades of meaning. The 'assize concerning essoiners', as the rubric runs in one manuscript, is an article in the Inquest of Sheriffs of 1170.[8] This, too, is procedural rather than legislative; but modern categories will not fit the circumstances of the twelfth century. Only one other 'assize' attributed to Henry II[9] need we mention, the Assize of Bread. This is not a royal ordinance, but, as the preamble states, an 'assisa . . . que probata est per pistores domini regis Henrici secundi'.[10] We do not know who these royal bakers were nor what authority they exercised. The assize may have originated in

[1] *E.H.R.*, xxxi.268-9.

[2] So Woodbine, *Glanville*, p. 226, following Adams, *Council and Courts*, pp. 214-47.

[3] This was Stubbs's view (*Constitutional History*, i.644-5), which was generally accepted until Maitland proposed a modification in *Select Pleas of the Crown*, pp. xi-xvii. In the *History of English Law*, i.153-4, he seems to have held that the King's Bench was established in 1178 and the Common Bench a little later, but the passage lacks his usual perspicuity. For further details of the various views expressed by other authors see Adams, *op. cit.*, pp. 215-17, and Sayles, *King's Bench*, i. pp. xii-xiv and also *Governance of Mediaeval England*, p. 213*n*.

[4] *Gesta Henrici*, i.207. On this see Sayles, *op. cit.*, i. pp. xx-xxii.

[5] For which see *Governance of Mediaeval England*, pp. 173-215.

[6] Below, pp. 127-30.

[7] The references are brought together in Mr Derek Hall's Introduction to *Glanville*, p. xxxv.

[8] Howden, *Chronica*, ii. pp. cv-cvi; D. M. Stenton, *Pleas before the King*, i.151-4, and the same author's *English Justice*, p. 48.

[9] So Maitland, *History of English Law*, i.138.

[10] Text in Cunningham, *Growth of English Industry*, pp. 568-9; Weinbaum, *London unter Eduard I und II*, ii.9-10.

the Verge and may have regulated the price of bread sold to the perambulating royal household and its troop of followers. The only justification for mentioning the assize here is that an 'assize' or 'constitutio' for regulating the price of bread at Winchester was made by King John in April 1204[1] and that a later Assize of Bread found a place in the Statute Book.[2] The assize of bread, like its invariable companion, the assize of ale, was, however, a matter of customary urban law of remote antiquity, widespread and locally enforced, and there are no grounds for crediting its origin to Henry II. A surviving London regulation may, in fact, be earlier.[3] But we must not blur the picture of Henry's legislation by dwelling upon supposititious enactments. Here we would emphasise that Henry's reign is marked by two great legislative occasions, the council of Clarendon in 1165-6 and that of Northampton in 1176. The first was devoted to a general settlement of the country after more than thirty years of disorder and ineffective central control. The second was devoted to a general settlement after the disorder created by the rebellion of Henry's sons, and the settlement included the correction of the mistake made at Clarendon in the measures taken for the repression of crime. The only council to be compared with these two is that at Clarendon in 1164, which resulted, as we have seen, in an enactment of greater permanent importance than has been generally recognised. The oft-repeated gibe at Henry II by Ralf Niger[4] – 'he abolished the ancient laws and every year issued new laws which he called assizes' – has therefore no substance. Nevertheless it is of assizes that we would now speak.

As we have said, there were few visitations of the counties by royal justices in the early years of Henry's reign, and of their proceedings we know little. But we do know that actions before local justices, and presumably before the occasional itinerant justices, fell into two categories: 'assizes' and *placita* by which we must understand pleas of the crown.[5] The 'assizes', then, were actions between subjects, or what came subsequently to be known as common pleas, relating for the most part to land; and it was this meaning that men gave to 'assize' when in later years they spoke of the grand assize and the petty assizes.[6] And before Henry's reign was over a book of considerable size was necessary as a guide to the procedure in these assizes and some related matters, although the legislative acts, the basis upon which this learning was mainly erected – themselves 'assizes' in another sense – could have been contained in few pages. . . . But before we proceed further we should, perhaps, pause and offer a few words of explanation. The

[1] *Rot. Litt. Pat.*, p. 41; below, pp. 148-9. [2] *Statutes of the Realm*, i.199.
[3] Cunningham, *op. cit.*, p. 567; Weinbaum, *op. cit.*, p. 69.
[4] R. Niger, *Chronicles*, p. 168: Nullo quaestu satiatus, abolitis antiquis legibus, singulis annis novas leges, quas assisas vocavit, edidit.
[5] A writ of the early years of Henry II addressed to the justices in whose bailiwicks the abbot of Abingdon holds lands speaks of the assizes and *placita* which will come before them (*Chronicon Mon. de Abingdon*, ii.222). See also *Governance of Mediaeval England*, pp. 194-5.
[6] Pollock and Maitland, *History of English Law*, i.147, 149.

many names under which an enactment could pass and the ambiguities in the use of the same word are apt to be confusing. There appears to be no difference in meaning between *constitutio* and *assisa* (in one of its meanings), as *Glanville* testifies in sundry places[1]; and, as we have already noticed, the Constitutions of Clarendon were described judicially as *statuta*.[2] So we get the equation, *assisa* = *constitutio* = *statutum*. At the same time 'assize' could mean merely the established law, as when men spoke of the Assize of the Jewry, well before there was any body of legislation specially affecting the Jews.[3] But for our immediate purpose 'assize' means an action concerning land decided in a particular manner. So much by way of clarification. . . . The question we have to consider is how it came about that simple enactments, such as those which laid the foundations for the assize *utrum*[4] or the assize of novel disseisin or the grand assize,[5] could be expanded in the detail given by the lawbooks, by *Glanville* and by Bracton. The answer is that very wide discretion was assumed by the courts to clothe the bare outline of the enactment with the appropriate forms, to apply ancient rules of procedure and, in particular, to frame the appropriate writs.

We must remember that in the twelfth century there was not, as there was for most of the thirteenth century, any differentiation between the chancery resident in England[6] and the courts of common law. There could be no complaint of the reluctance of chancery clerks to devise appropriate writs, no need for legislation to enable them to widen the scope of their writs to embrace cases *in consimili casu*.[7] Both the drafting of writs and their adjudication were controlled by the justiciar. Few or no writs 'of course' were issued by the chancellor, who accompanied the king in the wanderings that kept him out of England for more than half his time. It was the justiciar's writing office, the scriptorium attached to the Exchequer, that was responsible for 'original' – that is, originating – writs, and it was the justiciar who was head of the judiciary.[8] On some few matters he would not act without the authority of the king's council. As we are told in *Glanville*, any alteration in the period of limitation in the assize of novel disseisin

[1] See, in particular, lib. ii, c. 7, where the grand assize is termed successively *assisa, constitutio, assisa, constitutio, constitutio, assisa, assisa, assisa* (Woodbine, pp. 67-8; Hall, pp. 28-9). See also Woodbine's index, p. 301, *s.v.* constitutio.

[2] Above, p. 66.

[3] Cf. Richardson, *English Jewry under Angevin Kings*, 176-7.

[4] Constitutions of Clarendon, c. 9. The operative words are 'recognitione duodecim legalium hominum per capitalis iustitie regis considerationem terminabitur utrum tenementum sit pertinens ad elemosinam sive ad feudum laicum coram ipso iustitia regis'.

[5] There is nothing to suggest from the laconic references to these assizes in contemporary documents that the assizes themselves were of any length.

[6] That is, the staff of clerks attached to the justiciar, which, though not termed 'chancery', acted as the later chancery did in issuing writs (Richardson, Introduction to *Memoranda Roll, 1 John*, pp. lxxv-lxxvii).

[7] For the need for, and consequences of, the provision in Statute of Westminster II, c. 24, see Maitland, *Forms of Action*, pp. 50-2, and Sayles, *King's Bench*, v. pp. lxviii-lxx.

[8] Introduction to *Memoranda Roll, 1 John, loc. cit.*; *Governance of Mediaeval England*, pp. 159-64, 173-90. Note that in the examples of writs given by Glanville, the action is invariably triable before the king or the justices: lib. i, cc. 6, 13, 15, 19 etc. (Woodbine, pp. 43, 46-7 *et passim*; Hall, pp. 5, 9-11).

needed this authority[1] and, as we have seen, the period was altered at least once by legislation.[2] But when *Glanville* was being written the period had been again altered to the king's last crossing over to Normandy – a phrase that ensured frequent adjustments without change of formula.[3]

Now, all this would have been impracticable, and the assizes themselves would have given relief to few, but for the development of a centralised judiciary, a corps of justices who traversed the country on their eyres and at other times sat in the Exchequer at Westminster on the 'bench', as it came to be called.[4] The practical administration of the law taught them – and the justiciar among them – more than all the discussion in the king's council could have done. If the foundation of the law or much of it, as we find it in *Glanville*, is legislation, in its detail it is judge-made law. The book is not only a guide to procedure, as are other *ordines judiciarii*: it sums up the legislative achievement of Henry's reign. Without it, we should have very imperfect knowledge. It may be well, therefore, if we say more of it.

The name of the author of *Glanville* is unknown.[5] That the book was written by Ranulf Glanville, the justiciar, is a notion derived from its incipit.[6] We translate[7]:

> A treatise comprising the laws and customs of the kingdom of England in the time of King Henry II, when the head of the judiciary was the illustrious Ranulf de Glanville (at that period the man most learned in the law and ancient customs of the kingdom), wherein are contained only those laws and customs admitted in actions in the king's court at the Exchequer and before the justices in eyre.

Whatever these words may mean, they certainly do not mean that Ranulf was the author, but that, like some other legal treatises we shall have to notice, the book represents the practice of the courts while he was justiciar, that is in the years between 1180 and 1189; and the courts are those in which the justices sit, the Exchequer and the eyre courts.[8] If the author knows anything of the court *coram rege* as it functioned, for example, in Normandy or Anjou, Poitou or Guienne, he

[1] *Glanville*, lib. xiii, c. 32 (Woodbine, p. 172; Hall, p. 167). [2] Above, p. 99.

[3] *Glanville*, lib. xiii, c. 33 (Woodbine, p. 172; Hall, p. 167).

[4] *Glanville*, lib. ii, c. 6; lib. viii, c. 1; lib. xi, c. 1 (Woodbine, pp. 61, 117, 146; Hall, pp. 26, 94, 133). See also Introduction to *Memoranda Roll, 1 John*, pp. xiii-xiv; *Governance of Mediaeval England*, pp. 210-12.

[5] Hubert Walter and Geoffrey fitz Peter have both been suggested; but these are guesses with no evidence behind them (*ibid.*, p. 320*n*). Mr Derek Hall has tentatively suggested a third possibility, Geoffrey de Lucy, in preference to the other two: see his Introduction to *Glanville*, pp. xxx-xxxiii.

[6] The incipit is, of course, later than the text (cf. Woodbine, p. 183; Hall, pp.xlvii-xlviii). What the title given to the treatise was when it left the author's hand we do not know.

[7] The *alpha* text omits the words after 'kingdom' (Hall, p. 1).

[8] An error of punctuation has led to the supposition that the courts named were (1) *the* Curia Regis, (2) the Exchequer and (3) those of the justices in eyre (Plucknett, *Early English Legal Literature*, p. 35). But the court at the Exchequer was, of course, *a* Curia Regis, just as the courts of the justices in eyre were. The error arose through supposing that the Exchequer was separate from the Common Bench and that *the* Curia Regis was a distinct and separate court. Historians need to be reminded that Latin has no definite article: as Maitland stressed in another connexion.

ignores it. When, however, the king was in England, the court *coram rege* was staffed by the same corps of justices that staffed the Exchequer and the eyre courts, with which, in fact, it coalesced.[1] We must not read our history backwards and imagine a separate court of King's Bench in existence in the twelfth century. A court *coram rege* was then a court, an ordinary court, of common law in which the king presided. In honour of the occasion a good many magnates might be present,[2] but that did not make the court a court of a different species, any more than the presence of the king in the Exchequer[3] would, in some strange way, duplicate the Exchequer over which the justiciar presided. The justiciar is the king's *alter ego*: when the king is present his authority is subsumed in the king's. *Glanville* was written as a guide to all the superior courts in England without exception. We have said that the author is unknown, but we do know what kind of man he was. He had an intimate acquaintance with the practice of the courts and he had one characteristic, hardly discernible among previous writers on English law, a precise and orderly mind. We have already spoken of the influence of Roman law, but there are some facts it may be convenient to recall here. The author of the treatise had been trained, there can be no question, in the current practice of Roman law,[4] and he was familiar with the current guides to procedure under that law, the *ordines judiciarii*. If in his treatise he gives more substantive law than they do, this is because there is no corpus of English law to which he can refer. His work is, in a sense, romanesque, but he is no romaniser. His vocabulary, a phrase here and there, his cast of mind, rarely a rule of law,[5] will recall to us the schools in which he received his training. But he keeps steadily in view the practice of the king's courts and he does not supplement his English law with passages borrowed from civil or canon law, as in the thirteenth century Bracton will do[6] and as Bracton's counterpart in Scotland, the author of the *Regiam Majestatem*, will do.[7]

To attempt to summarise *Glanville* in a few pages would be to attempt the impossible, but we may, with profit perhaps, say something of the structure and purpose of the treatise.[8] The author or a reviser – it is difficult to be certain – divides his matter into fourteen books.[9] Twelve are devoted to actions for the recovery of property, be it land or chat-

[1] *Governance of Mediaeval England*, pp. 214-15. [2] *Ibid.*, p. 213.

[3] For Henry II's presence at a session of the Exchequer see *Pipe Roll, 29 Henry II*, pp. 138-9; for Henry III's see Madox, *History of the Exchequer*, ii.10-11.

[4] For example, he writes 'Excipi autem possunt iuratores eisdem modis quibus et testes in curia christianitatis iuste repelluntur' (lib. ii, c. 12: Woodbine, p. 66; Hall, p. 72). As we have already indicated (p. 80), this sentence shows that the author expects the judges and officers of the courts to be familiar with Roman-canonical procedure.

[5] Above, pp. 80-2. [6] See Richardson, *Bracton*, pp. 84-6.

[7] *Juridical Review*, lxvii.155-87.

[8] Mr Derek Hall's views differ considerably from ours. It would be inappropriate to discuss the points of difference in detail and the reader would do well to consider them carefully for himself: see Mr Hall's Introduction, pp. xviii-xxx.

[9] The original (*alpha*) text was apparently written without marked divisions, but it was easily divisible into books and chapters. At the same time the text was revised and the style changed (Hall, pp. xviii-xxvii).

tels, to which the plaintiff has a claim. The thirteenth book deals with actions for possession or seisin,[1] the fourteenth with criminal actions. To the legal historian these proportions may seem wrong. The fourteenth book, for example, has been stigmatised by one modern editor as elementary and fragmentary,[2] and, true enough, here, as in other books of the treatise, some details are passed over which might have been given in order to round off the story. Yet it may be that, in writing a practical book for contemporaries, the author felt entitled to assume knowledge on their part which cannot be assumed for us. He was not writing for posterity. But let us examine this fourteenth book a little more closely and try to guess its purpose. Now, it is clear from the earlier books that the treatise is intended to be one of procedure. Apart from a few introductory paragraphs, the first book is devoted to essoins, while the eleventh book is entirely devoted to the appointment and functions of attorneys. Other chapters may include some substantive law, but they are still procedural. As we have already said, the model upon which the treatise is based is an *ordo judiciarius*. We may call these *ordines* elementary – and indeed they are so intended – but we do not call them fragmentary because the substantive law may need to be sought elsewhere. In like manner the fourteenth book is not intended to be a dissertation upon criminal law, but a guide to the procedure in criminal actions, especially where it might be easy for the inexperienced to go astray. The book is short because criminal law, as viewed from Westminster, is, in the main, simple law. There are no essoins, no exceptions, few of the niceties of procedure which fill so much of the first twelve books. The author assumes that we shall know that, in the majority of the cases before us, a man is standing his trial whom the hundred jury have declared to be defamed of a certain felony, and the men from four neighbouring townships have concurred with the hundredors.[3] There is to be no trial in the modern sense of the word. The suspect will go to the ordeal: if he is unfree, to the water; if he is a freeman, to the hot iron.[4] If he fails in the ordeal, he will be hanged or mutilated.

Probably there are but few of these cases to come before the justices. Those guilty of manifest crime will have received short shrift, for criminal justice is still in the main summary and local. But as well as the cases that are presented by hundred juries, there will be some private prosecutions before the justices, appeals of felony or, very exceptionally, appeals of treason. There may also be rumours that come to the ears of the justices – we assume by what we should call delation – and those defamed in this way the justices will deal with *ex officio*.[5] The

[1] The author uses both terms; above, p. 81.
[2] Woodbine, *Glanville*, p. 294: cf. Hall, pp. xxi-xxii.
[3] Cf. Pollock and Maitland, *History of English Law*, ii.644.
[4] *Glanville*, lib. xiv, c. 1 (Woodbine, pp. 174-6; Hall, pp. 171-3).
[5] In later years the delation will be to the hundred jurors (Pollock and Maitland, *op. cit.*, ii.646); but in discussing treason *Glanville* seems to indicate that delation will be to the justices (lib. xiv, c. 1: Woodbine, pp. 174-5; Hall, pp. 172-3).

majority of these cases are commonplace enough; but some few of them are noticed in the treatise because they involve points of interest it is desirable that a justice should know. So our author says more of treason or lese-majesty than of any other felony.[1] If there is an accuser, then the guilt of the accused is determined by a judicial battle or, if battle is for technical reasons impossible, by ordeal. If, however, there is no more than rumour, *fama publica*, the justices will examine witnesses, but the final judgement will be left to God. For if, after examination of all that can be said against the accused, there seems good ground for suspicion, he will go to the ordeal. There is a similar procedure where a man is suspected of concealing treasure trove; but it is noted that there must first be proof that he actually found or received precious metal.[2] The niceties of charges of homicide also require some discussion. An accuser must be of the male kin of the slain man, those nearest of kin having precedence: no woman can be an accuser unless she has been actually present at the death of her husband.[3] Charges of rape, again, are governed by a highly technical procedure and appeals may be compromised by marriage, though not after judgement.[4] The only other felony upon which the author feels it necessary to comment is forgery, and that because, if a royal charter is forged, the offence is a species of lese-majesty and does not fall within the ordinary law.[5]

We trust that, without entering into overmuch detail, we have made it sufficiently clear that procedure in criminal actions is not wholly rational, is not such as an inexperienced judge could be expected to know without instruction. Especially in appeals of felony is detailed knowledge necessary. If the appellor makes a mistake in procedure, if the appellor is not qualified to appeal, the appeal will fail, whatever may be the merits of his case. Where the prosecution is initiated by *fama publica*, there is a different approach. Witnesses may be examined in cases of treason. It is useless to charge a man with concealing treasure unless the existence of treasure is proved. It is no use charging with murder a man who was not caught red-handed and saying that he was not apprehended because he fled. The fact of the flight must be found by a jury.[6] These may not be very bold steps towards rational proof, but they are steps in that direction. We find more evidence of the rational approach when we turn to the thirteenth book.

The thirteenth book is not a particularly long one, but it covers more forms of action than all the preceding books. This is because all the actions can be grouped together: they are, as the author says, solely concerned with seisin and they are all decided by a recognition, that is,

[1] Lib. xiv, cc. 1-2, 7 (Woodbine, pp. 174-7, 179; Hall, pp. 171-4, 176-7).
[2] Lib. xiv, c. 2 (Woodbine, p. 177; Hall, p. 173).
[3] Lib. xiv, c. 3 (Woodbine, p. 177; Hall, p. 174).
[4] Lib. xiv, c. 6 (Woodbine, p. 178; Hall, pp. 175-6).
[5] Lib. xiv, c. 7 (Woodbine, p. 179; Hall, pp. 176-7).
[6] Lib. xiv, c. 3 (Woodbine, pp. 177-8; Hall, pp. 174-5).

by the verdict of a jury, normally of twelve.[1] We first hear of this mode of trial as a definite rule in 1164, when the Constitutions of Clarendon prescribe it for deciding whether land is a lay fee or an ecclesiastical fee.[2] We should notice, for the point is an important one, that in *Glanville* the rule laid down in the Constitutions has been extended to cover a group of cases, all assizes *utrum*. The jurors may be asked to declare whether land was freehold or (as we should say) leasehold, *ut de vadio*, whether an heir is a minor or of full age, whether a man held land in fee simple or in wardship, whether he presented an incumbent in right of his demesne or as guardian of another. With the consent of the parties or by the award of the court any similar dispute may be similarly determined.[3] In the closing years of Henry II's reign it must have seemed that the assize *utrum* was sufficiently flexible to cover a multitude of actions. In like manner the range of the assize of novel disseisin has seemingly been extended beyond what was originally contemplated. Already in 1166 it had been held to cover nuisances: a dike unlawfully constructed, a hedge planted across a pasture or a boundary fence thrown down. Perhaps there was violence in these cases.[4] But in *Glanville* there seems to be an extension of the scope of the assize: to a millpond constructed to a neighbour's harm or to interference with a right of common.[5] Grouped with these actions are that of mort d'ancestor, which originated in the Assize of Northampton,[6] and that of darrein presentment, which has its foundation in the Constitutions of Clarendon, for the first chapter declared that any dispute as to advowsons or presentations to churches was to be decided in the king's court.[7] It is probable that at the time it was assumed that any action arising out of such a dispute would be proprietary, would determine, as between two claimants, who had the better claim to the *jus patronatus*. This question is not decided by the assize of darrein presentment, for, like all the other assizes grouped with it in the thirteenth book, it is regarded, in principle, as preliminary to another, more solemn, action which will decide the better right. We may think that this supposition is becoming transparent when the result of an action of darrein presentment is to secure the presentation of a clerk to a benefice from which it will be impossible to eject him,[8] or when the result of an action of novel disseisin is the levelling of a dike or the

[1] Exceptionally there is a jury of eight when it is necessary to determine the age of a party alleged to be a minor (lib. xiii, cc. 15-17 (Woodbine, pp. 165-7, 283; Hall, pp. 158-60).

[2] Cap. 9: cited above, pp. 29, 104, n. 1.

[3] Glanville, lib. xiii, c. 2: tum ex consensu ipsarum partium, tum etiam de consilio curie considerate, ad aliquam controversiam terminandam.

[4] *Pipe Roll, 14 Henry II*, p. 43: pro quodam fossato iniuste facto; *ibid.*, p. 44: pro sepe quam fecit fieri super pasturam.

[5] Lib. xiii, cc. 34-7 (Woodbine, pp. 172-3; Hall, pp. 168-9).

[6] Lib. xiii, cc. 2-17 (Woodbine, pp. 158-67; Hall, pp. 149-60); Assize of Northampton, c. 4 (*Select Charters*, pp. 179-80).

[7] Lib. xiii, cc. 18-22 (Woodbine, pp. 167-9; Hall, pp. 160-3); *Select Charters*, p. 164.

[8] Lib. xiii, c. 20 (Woodbine, p. 167: and see note, p. 285; Hall, pp. 161-2).

filling-in of a millpond or the restitution of crops or chattels as well as land.[1] And indeed the decisions in all these assizes tend to become final and conclusive. The assize *utrum*, it has been said, became 'the parson's writ of right'.[2]

In little more than a score of years there has been this proliferation of actions all springing from four simple pieces of legislation, two in 1164 – *darrein presentment* and *utrum* – one in 1166 – *novel disseisin* – and one in 1176 – *mort d'ancestor*. Evidently there has been great eagerness on the part of litigants to obtain novel forms of writ and evidently there has been great readiness to devise writs suited to the occasion. Nothing of this is wholly new. Already in 1164 the writ process has a long history behind it.[3] But the legislation of these years has given a new impetus to litigation, coupled as this legislation is with the creation of a judiciary accessible to all men and a readiness to grant a jury in almost any kind of civil action. Rules of procedure have been devised with equal rapidity, and these it is the purpose of the author of *Glanville* to expound. Behind book thirteen there must lie a primitive register of writs, for it is obvious that the justiciar's clerks must, by the 1180s, have had a formula-book at hand: as each variant writ is devised it must be noted down. A good many of the chapters of this book bear indeed a close likeness to sections of thirteenth-century registers of writs.[4] The explanatory matter, the *regulae*, addressed to the junior clerks – the cursitors as they will come to be called – which we find in the registers, have been omitted from *Glanville* as unnecessary for its purpose, but the general likeness remains. The book must, however, make room for instructions of another kind, describing the procedure in court. For although one recognition is very like another, they are differentiated not only by the subject-matter but also by strict rules of procedure. In an assize of novel disseisin no essoins are permitted,[5] in others they are allowed. There are many exceptions that can be pleaded in an assize of mort d'ancestor before the assize can proceed, and the rules regarding essoins are elaborate, for one or both parties may be minors.[6] All such rules of court a justice must know, and while every rule may have a good explanation behind it, the rules are not self-evident.

The rules governing actions *de recto* are more elaborate than those governing the possessory assizes and, in particular, those actions concerning the proprietary right in a freehold. The first twelve books of *Glanville* are therefore more elaborate than the thirteenth, though the respective scales bear no relation to the number of actions of the several kinds that come before the courts. In Glanville's time it is the estab-

[1] Lib. xiii, cc. 34-36, 38, 39 (Woodbine, pp. 172-4; Hall, pp. 168-70).
[2] Pollock and Maitland, *History of English Law*, i.248.
[3] Above, pp. 49-50, 77.
[4] For specimens see *L.Q.R.*, liv.395-9.
[5] Lib. xiii, c. 38 (Woodbine, p. 173; Hall, p. 169).
[6] Lib. xiii, cc. 7, 12-15 (Woodbine, pp. 160-6; Hall, pp. 151-9).

lished rule that no action touching freehold may be heard in any court without a royal writ,[1] and the court in which the action will normally be begun is either a seignorial court or the county court. There the action would, in principle, be decided by battle, and the author of *Glanville* speaks as though battles had been commonly fought not many years before he was writing, battles that had been bloody and mortal.[2] But were these battles many or few, reasonable people had come to regard them as shocking, and the grand assize had been devised as an alternative. This alternative is not, however, compulsory and the law assumes that trial by battle will be the normal course. The choice of the alternative rests upon the tenant, the occupier of the land. That he should have the choice is not so oppressive a rule as might be supposed,[3] for in a great many cases the situation we have to envisage is this, at least in the early years. The man with the better right has been violently ejected by a man who thinks he also has a claim to the land. Such indeed is the historical background, as we have seen. An assize of novel disseisin has been brought and the man with the better right has been reinstated, leaving it open to the disseisor to purchase a writ of right. Should the writ confer upon the disseisor the privilege of forcing his rival to give battle? Since 1179, the law had answered, 'No: the option is given to the tenant'. The tenant may obtain a writ of peace and so force his adversary (the demandant) to abide by the decision of twelve law-worthy knights, the 'recognitors'.[4] Though *Glanville* does not tell us so, behind this stage in the action there is a somewhat elaborate procedure. The tenant goes to the clerk at the Exchequer responsible for the issue of writs of peace. Before this clerk he swears to his identity and to the facts of the case. The writ is then granted to him, and the clerk makes a summary of it on a special roll, known later, and perhaps already under Henry II, as the *rotulus magne assise* – and some of the earliest of these rolls are still preserved. The tenant next takes his writ to the sheriff to whom it is addressed. If the action is in the county court, the case is thereupon dismissed; if in a seignorial court, the sheriff prohibits the court from proceeding. The demandant must now either abandon the action or proceed to obtain a writ for electing recognitors; but before he can do so, he must go to the Exchequer and identify the relevant writ of peace on the roll. Curiously enough, this is not always easy to do. Finally, however, he will get his writ and so

[1] Glanville, lib. xii, cc. 2, 25. (Woodbine, pp. 149, 157; Hall, pp. 137, 148). Note that the reading 'vel eius *insticiarium*' in c. 2 must be wrong: the writ would be issued by the justiciar as stated in c. 25. This rule is stated more succinctly in the *capitula librorum* (prefixed to the *beta* text): Nemo potest alium trahere in placitum de libero servitio vel tenemento sine brevi regis directo ad dominum de quo clamat tenere (Woodbine, p. 37).

[2] *Glanville*, lib. ii, c. 7: 'assisa . . . quo vite hominum et status integritati tam salubriter consulitur . . .' (Woodbine, p. 62; Hall, p. 28).

[3] Cf. Pollock and Maitland, *History of English Law*, ii.63: 'even if all goes swiftly, the tenant has great advantages. He can choose between two modes of trial. . . . The law is too hard upon a demandant, who, it may well be, has recent and well-known facts in his favour. . . .'

[4] *Glanville*, lib. ii, cc. 10-11 (Woodbine, pp. 64-5; Hall, pp. 30-31).

bring the action before the justices.[1] Of these interlocutory proceedings, which may be complicated in ways we need not recite, *Glanville* says nothing, because the justices are not concerned until the recognitors are summoned. But it has seemed desirable to set down here the story in outline in order that an idea might be given of the way in which the law discouraged any adventurer with a shadowy claim who wished to try his luck in a judicial battle. The law, perhaps by devious paths, is becoming rational.

But let us resume. *Glanville* tells us of the further obstacles the law will place in the path of the demandant. When battle had been the rule, the strict qualifications required, at least in principle, for the champions and the essoins allowed to the tenant had been such that the issue might be postponed almost indefinitely, at all events in actions coming before the king's court[2], for we doubt whether the niceties detailed in *Glanville* were scrupulously observed in lower courts. One of the advantages claimed for the grand assize was that there would be occasion for fewer essoins, to the saving to everyone of trouble and expense.[3] But the process of electing the twelve knightly recognitors itself led to intolerable delays. Any of the four knights who were to elect the twelve might essoin and after their essoins the tenant might himself again essoin. 'And so', says *Glanville*, 'the assize might never or hardly ever reach a conclusion.'[4] But supposing all four electors to appear and to proceed to choose the twelve recognitors, the tenant could challenge any and every one of them and it might be a long time before twelve unchallengeable knights could be found. There were various devices for overcoming these difficulties, but the records confirm the impression *Glanville* leaves that, unless the parties were themselves anxious for a decision, the prospects of a successful termination to a grand assize were few and remote.[5] The very evolution of society was against success. As the status of the knight rose, so there were fewer and fewer knights and fewer qualified to serve on recognitions, and as the duties of those few became more onerous, so knights purchased from the king exemption from service, while more and more landowners who were qualified to take up knighthood evaded doing so.[6] At the same time the period of limitation in the assize of novel disseisin receded, in consequence of the negligence of the authorities to adjust it with the advancing years, so that it became possible to apply the assize to circumstances never originally con-

[1] *L.Q.R.*, liv.384-6. The procedure in the thirteenth century is there described, but there can be no doubt that it was substantially unchanged from the twelfth century. When the king became permanently resident in England, however, the chancery followed him in his perambulations over the country (though not abroad), and the parties had then presumably to follow the court to obtain their writs. But in the twelfth century the writs were issued by the justiciar and we have therefore substituted 'Exchequer' for 'chancery'.

[2] *Glanville*, lib. ii, c.3 (Woodbine, pp. 58-9; Hall, pp. 23-5).

[3] Lib. ii, c. 7 (Woodbine, p. 63; Hall, p. 28).

[4] Lib. ii, c. 12 (Woodbine, p. 65; Hall, p. 31).

[5] See Woodbine's notes, *ibid.* pp. 202-3.

[6] *Governance of Mediaeval England*, pp. 130-4

templated and allege not only a recent disseisin but remote facts: its possessory character tended to be lost.[1] Novel disseisin, perhaps in consequence, gained an immense popularity, as the great space allotted by Bracton to the action shows,[2] while recourse to the action *de recto* progressively diminished. A rough index is afforded by the rolls of the grand assize. Under Richard I they are lengthy and full: by the 1260s the entries may be no more than half a dozen in a year[3]; towards the end of the reign of Edward II there may not be one in a year.[4] These entries, it should be emphasised, are of writs of peace, not of writs of right,[5] and they may indicate just as probably that the demandant abandoned his action as that he pursued it – with little prospect, be it added, as the years went by, of its ever coming to trial.[6] What the rolls of the twelfth century do suggest is that in the early years writs of peace were issued in such numbers that a decision by battle came to be a rarity. By a paradox, the grand assize, although it practically passed out of use, did achieve its object of eliminating trial by battle in proprietary actions.

But we must not stay to peer into the future nor can we linger long over those books of *Glanville* we have not yet noticed. Let us note, however, that, by the operation of the Constitutions of Clarendon and the Assize of Windsor, the grand assize is applied to advowsons as well as land. There is no reason to disbelieve *Glanville* when he tells us that before 1179 the better right to the *jus patronatus* would have been decided by battle, and it is an illustration of the spirit of the age that, even after 1179, the decision might lie in the relative prowess of hired champions.[7] But the grand assize also has its oddities when the right to an advowson is in question. The presence of an ecclesiastic is often necessary in court, but if he has no lay fee, the aid of the bishop may be required to compel his appearance. And then, since the conflicting rights of clerks to hold benefices are inextricably intertwined with the question of the ownership of the advowson, there is an inevitable tendency for a dispute as to an advowson to be drawn into court Christian. Already, therefore, writs of prohibition are devised to secure to the king's court the exclusive right to try such actions[8]; the register of writs grows; and procedure becomes more complex. The only other

[1] Pollock and Maitland, *History of English Law*, ii.51-2.

[2] For the distribution of matter in Bracton's treatise, see Richardson, *Bracton*, pp. 56, 58.

[3] The earliest surviving roll, for Richard I, is printed in *Curia Regis Rolls*, i.1-14. For the rolls of Henry III see *L.Q.R.*, liv.387.

[4] Supplementary Close Roll no. 10, printed in *Calendar of Various Chancery Rolls*, pp. 145-56, contains the rolls of the Grand Assize for the reign of Edward II.

[5] Cf. Introduction to *Memoranda Roll, 1 John*, pp. lii-liv.

[6] *L.Q.R.*, liv.386-8. See also the statistics of cases before justices in eyre between 1256 and 1279 in Pollock and Maitland, *History of English Law*, ii.641.

[7] *Glanville*, lib. iv, c. 6 (Woodbine, pp. 77-8; Hall, pp. 46-7). It seems clear that in England, as in Normandy, battle by and even between ecclesiastics might be waged, though not necessarily fought, both before and after 1179 (*Speculum*, viii.388, 391-2). As late as 1329 on a writ of right of advowson battle was waged and the champions appeared before the justices, but the action was compromised (Dugdale, *Origines Juridiciales*, pp. 68-71).

[8] *Glanville*, lib. iv, cc. 9-14 (Woodbine, pp. 78-83; Hall, pp. 48-53).

action which is, in any sense, based upon legislation is dower, for the Assize of Northampton enacted that, on their husband's death, widows should have their dower and such part of the chattels as belonged to them.[1] But although this may have given widows some protection, the elaborate rules embodied in *Glanville* owe nothing to any enactment: they are clearly judge-made.[2] We may apply the same words to practically the whole of the treatise from book 5 to book 12. Behind some of the rules there may be an administrative order, an executive act, but hardly what we should call legislation. Let us take an example where the history behind the law is fairly clear, the law regarding usurers. The king leaves to the Church the duty of correcting living usurers; but he claims the property of dead usurers, and we learn from *Glanville* that an article enquiring into such property has been inserted in the chapters of the eyre. The hundred juries must declare their knowledge of any deceased usurer and a jury from the neighbouring townships will be sworn to testify as to his property and into whose hands it has come.[3] Whence does this prerogative right derive? We suspect that the argument behind it is that usurers have been judaising and that, since in strict law the property of Jews belongs to the king (and he claims his share of it on their death), so the property of Christian usurers who die in their sin belongs to him. But if this is the law, it is recent law: it is apparently no earlier than 1170.[4] The origin of much of the other law in *Glanville* is more obscure, though it may not be of much greater antiquity.

We may take as an illustration the earlier chapters of the eighth book which deal with the action *de fine facto*, that is an action brought by one party to a fine to compel the other party to perform his undertaking.[5] We should perhaps explain that a fine is the record of an agreement by which an action (often fictitious) has been compromised. It has the sanction of the court and, as its Latin name implies, *finalis concordia*, it is final and conclusive. The agreement is engrossed in duplicate upon a piece of parchment and the duplicates are separated by a knife, usually cutting in a wavy line through the word, written in capitals, CIROGRAPHUM, the name given to this form of instrument. The intention is that, when the two parts are fitted together, they shall correspond exactly and that all possibility of fraud, by the substitution of a bogus document, will thus be excluded.[6] We can, without difficulty, trace the history of the fine as it evolved in the English courts, for

[1] Assize of Northampton, c. 4: Et uxor defuncti habeat dotem suam et partem de catallis eius que eam contingit (*Select Charters*, p. 180).

[2] *Glanville*, lib. vi (Woodbine, pp. 87-96; Hall, pp. 58-69).

[3] Lib. vii, c. 16 (*ibid.*, pp. 112-13; Hall, p. 89). See above, p. 85.

[4] *E.H.R.*, xliii.333-6.

[5] *Glanville*, lib. viii, cc. 1-6 (Woodbine, pp. 116-20; Hall, pp. 94-9).

[6] The earliest surviving original fine, Cotton Charters, xi.73, dated 29 June 1176, is reproduced in *Facsimiles of Charters in British Museum*, i, no. 56. In this instance the cut is in a straight line, as in other early chirographs, of which specimens will be found in the same volume.

the parties were careful to preserve their counterparts and a fair number of early fines survive in transcript or original. It was only gradually during Henry II's reign that the formulas given in *Glanville* became settled, and it was not until the judiciary was organised in the late 1160s and the 1170s that it became possible for fines to be levied before justices itinerant in the way *Glanville* assumes. And though fines are known which were levied in the king's court earlier in the reign, the record is not in the later characteristic form but in that of a charter.[1] The definitive formula seems not to have been approached before 1163 and not to have come into common use before the 1170s.[2] It follows that the forms given in *Glanville* both for fines and for writs for commencing an action *de fine facto* were not devised any earlier. But in 1195 the whole background of the law was transformed by the decision that henceforth all fines levied in the king's court should be engrossed in triplicate and that the third copy (or *pes*) should be filed in the Treasury for the purpose of record.[3] The king's court thus assumed a closer control than before; fines became extensively employed, in place of other instruments, for transactions in land; the law relating to them became intricate and highly technical.[4] When *Glanville* was written all this lay in the unseen future. As yet the law is very simple: we are witnessing its first steps.

Let us next glance at another branch of the law which is becoming systematised, that of *status*, as *Glanville* terms it, by which is meant unfree status, villeinage. It is the subject of the fifth book.[5] We must bear in mind that we have before us a treatise on procedure and that it does not pretend to offer any guidance on such difficult questions as the stigmata which mark a man as unfree. In the last chapter of the book there are set out what purport to be the rules for determining whether the offspring of a marriage will be bond or free: for in a village there will be marriages between men and women who, although they may not know it, are, in the contemplation of the law, of different status. This chapter may have borrowed something from Roman law.[6] It seems to be the merest theorising, regardless of the uncertainties of real life. Possibly the author saw no need to go deeply into the problem, no need to give practical guidance to future justices, for in cases of doubt as to a man's status the courts have an easy way out of the difficulty: a jury

[1] For examples see Farrer, *Lancashire Pipe Rolls*, pp. 310-11, *Lincoln Registrum Antiquissimum*, i.65-6, Round, *Ancient Charters*, no. 41. In these cases there may have been a separate instrument of agreement between the parties.

[2] A copy of a fine approaching the settled form and purporting to have been levied in 7 Henry II is included in the record of an action in 1222 (*Curia Regis Rolls*, x.334), but the date appears to be blundered, though it cannot be later than 1169. This fine is printed also in *E.H.R.*, xxv.708, where the date is given as 9 Henry II.

[3] *Feet of Fines, Henry II and Richard I*, p. 21.

[4] Pollock and Maitland, *History of English Law*, ii.96-105; Holdsworth, *History of English Law*, iii.236-45.

[5] Woodbine, pp. 83-7; Hall, pp. 53-58.

[6] So Vinogradoff, *Villainage*, pp. 59-60; but the teaching of *Glanville* appears to be that the Roman rule is *not* to be followed, since the issue of a free woman and an unfree man will be unfree.

may be summoned to decide the question.[1] The courts seem, however, to have been persuaded into some of the oddest of procedural anomalies. A knight, for example, who had been by birth a villein, cannot deraign or be admitted as an oath-helper if the plaintiff thinks fit to challenge him.[2] It is obvious that the knight can bear arms, though the Assize of Arms denies this right to the unfree.[3] But if in the service of the king he ranks with the highest, in the king's courts the taint of unfreedom may still cling to him and make him less than law-worthy. We cannot but suspect that the law in the fifth book is lawyer's law: procedural rules, and not always sensible rules, that do not have behind them much thought, any consideration of the deeper social issues involved.

We must not think too badly of these judges of Henry II, if they seem to us sometimes to fail and falter. They were new to their task and had little to guide them, except perhaps in books of Roman law. They could get no help from the older English lawbooks. And in approaching the problems of status they had the most difficult of tasks. Throughout the Middle Ages the law of status failed to overtake the facts of life. Bracton's law is different from *Glanville's*, but it is just as unreal.[4] The law looks to the past, sometimes to a Roman past, and not to the present. Since the days of the king's grandfather, to which Henry II is so often minded to look back, there has been a social revolution of which seemingly the law has been unaware. In Henry I's day there had still been chattel slavery, still penal slavery,[5] but in ways that are quite obscure to us these forms of servitude had finally disappeared, though even in the thirteenth century men will speak of villeins as having been 'bought'.[6] And among lawyers there is a pretence that the villein has nothing of his own, so that if he agrees with his lord to purchase his freedom, he must do so through an intermediary.[7] We do not suggest that all is make-believe, nor do we deny that unfree status could at times be oppressive or that under its cloak there might be wanton acts of cruelty which the law is slow to redress.[8] But we would give a warning that *Glanville* is not a mirror in which we may see the external world: what we see is the interior of a court of law.

We have said enough of *Glanville* for our present purpose: a fuller commentary might obscure the lesson we wish to draw. The treatise is something quite new in English legal literature and it reflects some-

[1] *Glanville*, lib. v, c. 4 (Woodbine, p. 85; Hall, p. 55).

[2] Lib. v, c. 5 (Woodbine, p. 87; Hall, p. 58).

[3] The Assize of Arms is explicitly limited to freemen: c. 1 applies to 'omnis miles', c. 2 to 'liber laicus', c. 3 to 'omnes burgenses et tota communa liberorum hominum' (*Select Charters*, p. 183). Villeins were not required to provide themselves with arms until 1205: see below, pp. 136-7.

[4] Vinogradoff, *op cit.*, pp. 47-8, and see below, p. 148.

[5] Below, pp. 139-43.

[6] Below, p. 143.

[7] Pollock and Maitland, *History of English Law*, i.427-8; and see Woodbine's notes to *Glanville*, p. 214.

[8] Pollock and Maitland, *op. cit.*, i.415-16; see also the cases cited in the notes to Vinogradoff, *Villainage*, pp. 45-7.

thing that is new in England. Though the legislation of Henry II has its importance, of equal importance is the judicial law-making we have endeavoured to describe. Nothing like this had happened in England before, for the ground had not been prepared. But now there is a corps of judges, the ablest of them, like Geoffrey Ridel and Richard of Ilchester, men who have had some training in Roman law to fit them as ecclesiastical judges. As archdeacons they have passed into the king's service: they become bishops, but they still sit as judges in the king's court.[1] Upon slender foundations they make a great deal of new law in resolving the diverse problems that come before them. They do their work with great rapidity, and they are aided in it by successive justiciars, by Richard de Lucy and Ranulf Glanville, who, although not trained as they have been trained, have great natural abilities. The justiciars are more than the nominal heads of the judiciary, and it is extremely fortunate that they already have at their command a staff of clerks trained in the writing of writs. It cannot be irrelevant that at the beginning of the reign Richard of Ilchester was *scriptor curie*.[2]

Historically *Glanville* is the most important of our mediaeval law-books, more important even than Bracton's treatise: for it records the early years of a new era, while Bracton records its last stages. Bracton lived to see, but he did not record, the beginning of another era, the era of statute law. In itself *Glanville* is not a great monument of jurisprudence nor is it even outstanding among the books of its own class, the *ordines judiciarii*. Tancred's *ordo*, which enjoyed immense popularity throughout Western Europe in the thirteenth century, is more learned, clearer and superior in arrangement.[3] But *Glanville* has a special place of its own amongst us as the first textbook of the English common law, the book in which is recorded the outcome of the decisive years when a worldwide system of jurisprudence was founded.

Before, however, we close this chapter upon the assizes of Henry II, there are some words we would say upon an institution indissolubly linked with them, the English jury. If the day is not yet past, it is passing, when, in speaking of its origin, men paid reverence to Regino of Prüm (whose name would be otherwise unknown to them) or retailed as history the speculations of Heinrich Brunner. We can no longer believe that our jury had Roman or Frankish ancestors, who left descendants in Gaul, whence they passed to Normandy and thence to our own island.[4] We no longer ignore the bleak facts that there is no evidence for the existence of a jury in Normandy before 1133, when, to

[1] This was the cause of much scandal in 1179 when Richard of Ilchester (bishop of Winchester), Geoffrey Ridel (bishop of Ely) and John of Oxford (bishop of Norwich) headed three of the four circuits of itinerant justices: for details see *E.H.R.*, xliii.170-1.

[2] *Pipe Roll, 2 Henry II*, p. 30. Cf. Introduction to *Memoranda Roll, 1 John*, p. lxxxv.

[3] Above, pp. 78-9.

[4] This was the view accepted by, among others, Maitland, *History of English Law*, i.140-3, and by C. H. Haskins, *Norman Institutions*, pp. 196-258. The source of their error was Brunner, whose views were accepted in defiance of the evidence. For recent views on the origin and evolution of the English jury see Van Caenegem, *Royal Writs*, pp. 57-103, and Stenton, *English Justice*, pp. 13-21.

all appearance, it was imported from England, and that there is no evidence for its existence in France until still later.[1] We demand positive evidence, and only in English documents do we find it. We have already mentioned the passage in Ethelred's laws which indicates that in the tenth century the English jury, or at least its ancestor, was introduced into the Danelaw from Wessex. If thereafter the thread of evidence is tenuous, it is reasonably continuous.[2] We must not, however, be so naïve as to expect to find thirteenth-century institutions in the twelfth or the eleventh century. To speak of grand or petty juries under Henry II or even to see their origin there is merely anachronistic. There is nothing to suggest that at that time men saw any difference between one jury and another except in the status of the jurors themselves. The knightly recognitors of the grand assize were obviously superior to the hundredors, and the hundredors to the jurors of the townships, the vicinage. What is most worthy of remark is the variety of questions upon which jurors were expected to give their verdict under Henry II. Of the grand assize we need say no more. Below this level the questions put in legal proceedings have a great range: whether land is a lay fee or an ecclesiastical fee[3]; whether or not a man is of unfree condition[4]; whether a man is of age[5]; whether a man was seised of land when he died or when he went on pilgrimage or entered religion[6]; whether land was held in fee or in wardship[7]; who presented the last incumbent to a church.[8] In criminal proceedings the jury is normally asked to say no more than whether suspicion is justified: this seems the best way of describing the function of the hundred jury, whether under the Assize of Clarendon or the Assize of Northampton.[9] But other questions are put to juries: whether there actually was a treasure, when a man is charged with concealing one[10]; or whether a man charged with murder was actually seen in flight.[11] A jury may be asked to report upon a man's means[12] or to state the extent of his liability to knight service.[13] We do not attempt to list all the possible

[1] The inquest into the estates of the church of Bayeux, conducted by an English earl in 1133, appears to be the first recorded instance of a Norman jury: for the text see *Bulletin de la Société des Antiquaires de Normandie*, xlii.5-80. The frequently cited declaration under the Conqueror concerning the possessions of the abbey of Fontenay (printed in *Gallia Christiana*, xi, Instrumenta, col. 61-65) seems to us to be quite irrelevant to the question: cf. Haskins, *Norman Institutions*, pp. 222-3. As to France see Bongert, *Les Cours laïques du xe au xiiie siècle*, pp. 262-5. Cf. *Governance of Mediaeval England*, p. 205.

[2] Above, pp. 25, 37-8. We exclude the settlement of the dispute regarding the division of fenland between Ramsey and Thornton Abbeys, *c.* 1052, upon which Professor Van Caenegem has laid stress (*Royal Writs*, pp. 69-71).

[3] *Glanville*, lib. xiii, cc. 23-25 (Woodbine, p. 169; Hall, pp. 163-4).

[4] *Ibid.*, lib. v, c. 4 (Woodbine, p. 85; Hall, p. 55).

[5] *Ibid.*, lib. xiii, cc. 15-16 (Woodbine, p. 166; Hall, pp. 159-60).

[6] *Ibid.*, lib. xiii, cc. 2-6 (Woodbine, 158-9; Hall, pp. 149-51).

[7] *Ibid.*, lib. xiii, cc. 13-14 (Woodbine, p. 164; Hall, pp. 156-8).

[8] *Ibid.*, lib. xiii, cc. 18-19 (Woodbine, p. 167; Hall, pp. 160-1).

[9] Cf. Pollock and Maitland, *History of English Law*, ii.642-3; Richardson and Sayles, *Governance of Mediaeval England*, p. 206.

[10] *Glanville*, lib. xiv, c. 2 (Woodbine, p. 177; Hall, p. 173).

[11] *Ibid.*, lib. xiv, c. 3 (Woodbine, p. 178; Hall, p. 175).

[12] *Pipe Roll, 11 Henry II*, p. 64; *14 Henry II*, p. 141.

[13] *Pipe Roll, 12 Henry II*, p. 8; *Governance of Mediaeval England*, pp. 206-7.

questions to which a jury may be asked to give an answer. With the consent of the parties, *Glanville* assures us, almost any justiciable dispute could be referred to a jury.[1] Under Henry II, however, there seems to be no suggestion that anyone accused of a crime wished to put himself upon the country. The question of guilt is the one question never asked of a jury, and seemingly it was never asked until a decision of the Lateran Council of 1215 made it impossible to send men to the ordeal.[2] It was this decision that brought about a great change in the nature of the criminal jury, a change that is almost equivalent to discontinuity and makes any comparison with the past almost meaningless. But the history of civil juries is continuous, and sparse as may be the evidence, it seems possible to trace that history back to the reign of William I and even to the reign of Ethelred.[3] It was in its flexibility and versatility that the English jury proved a suitable instrument for Henry II's justices. The grand assize apart, we doubt whether it ever occurred to any minister or judge that there were different kinds of juries, except in so far as they were differentiated by status. The hundred jurors must be free law-worthy men; but the jurors from the townships would not infrequently have been unfree. Some duties could be given to the one that could not be given to the other, for it was an age when status meant a great deal.[4] But so long as status was respected, a jury might be empanelled for any kind of enquiry, judicial or administrative. What course the history of English law would have taken without the English jury, it is idle to speculate; but that the assizes of Henry II took the form they did because the jury was already available there seems no room for doubt.

[1] *Glanville*, lib. xiii, c. 2 (Woodbine, p. 158; Hall, p. 149): cf. Maitland, *Forms of Action*, p. 35.

[2] Pollock and Maitland, *History of English Law*, ii.599, 647.

[3] Above, pp. 25, 37-8.

[4] The challenge permitted against a knight who had risen from villeinage is a striking example: above p. 116. For others see Pollock and Maitland, *History of English Law*, i.593-4; ii.643.

VI

APOCRYPHA OF THE LAW

We have seen how, in response to the demand for knowledge of King Edward's law, apocryphal tracts began to appear under Henry I.[1] Not surprisingly the enterprise slackened under Stephen, when respect for law declined almost to a mockery during the nineteen cheerless winters that he was king.[2] But with Henry II the rule of law gradually returned and the stream of apocrypha flowed again. The purpose of the authors is often obscure, and few of their inventions had any success. The *Leges Edwardi Confessoris* stands out as a notable exception, both because of its continued popularity until the fourteenth and even the fifteenth century[3] and also because we seem able to discern the intention, a practical intention, of the editor or – if you will – interpolator, who produced the third edition in the early years of Henry II's reign. He was, it would appear, a fervent supporter of the new régime, who provided ancient precedents for innovations, for the doctrine of inalienability, for example, and for the universal obligation placed upon freemen to bear arms.[4] But the intention of other tracts of the same sort is hard to divine. Can the author of Cnut's laws of the forest – a tract we shall shortly discuss – have had any serious purpose? His ingenuity is unquestionable; but did he write in jest or in earnest? The answer eludes us.[5] He is, however, but one among several, perhaps among many; for it is unlikely that we have knowledge of more than chance survivals of these trivia, of a fashionable game that seems to us so purposeless.[6] But not only were fabricated laws attributed to ancient kings, there were fabrications which have been accepted by scholars, even unto our own day, as pieces of genuine legislation of Henry II, however loudly their falsity may seem to proclaim itself upon critical examination.[7] Let us, however, have done with generalities and proceed to particulars, beginning with an expanded version of the *Ten Articles* of William the Conqueror, the original of which appears to us to be, as we have explained, no better than a feeble, if well-meaning, compilation of the middle years of Henry I's reign.[8]

The expanded version of the *Ten Articles*[9] is no better than the original – little more than a conflation of the original with some

[1] Above, pp. 41-9. [2] *Governance of Mediaeval England*, pp. 191-7.

[3] Liebermann, *Über die Leges Edwardi Confessoris*, pp. 122-32.

[4] Above, pp. 57-8, 100-1. [5] Below, p. 128.

[6] Compare the fictitious laws, attributed to Ine and Alfred, in the London collection of the early thirteenth century, which Liebermann entitled *Pseudo-Ine* and *Pseudo-Alfred* (*Über die Leges Anglorum . . . Londoniis collectae*, pp. 12-20).

[7] We describe elsewhere the *Novae Constitutiones* attributed to Henry II: above, p. 93.

[8] Above, p. 46. [9] Text in *Gesetze*, i.489-91.

passages drawn from the *Leges Henrici*,[1] the *Instituta Cnuti*[2] and the third edition of the *Leges Edwardi Confessoris*,[3] with which it is associated in several manuscripts.[4] Among these passages is one prescribing a universal obligation upon all freemen, from earls downwards, to bear arms[5]; but this passage has been in no way adapted to bring it into line with the changes introduced by the Assize of Arms.[6] The inference is then that the compilation was made before 1176.[7] It has no merits of its own and its chief historical interest lies in the evidence it provides for the continued fabrication under Henry II of apocryphal legislation purporting to come from the reigns of earlier kings. It is, however, also of interest to note that, transformed into a charter, the fabrication was accepted in the Exchequer as a genuine piece of legislation by the Conqueror. In other copies it is entitled 'Decreta domini regis Willelmi bastardi et emendationes quas posuit in Anglia'.[8] This title recalls Henry I's coronation charter[9] and indicates, what is, in any case, sufficiently obvious, that the compilation belongs to that considerable group which had their origin in attempts to present the unwritten laws of King Edward. It was not the only fabrication of the kind produced in the 1160s or early 1170s. Independently of the expanded *Ten Articles* there was compiled the tract known as the *Leis Willelme*, though a better title would be a Latin one.

By including the *Leis Willelme* – or, as we should prefer to call it, the *Leges Willelmi* – among the apocrypha of the reign of Henry II we implicitly reject Liebermann's arguments for assigning the tract to a date between 1090 and 1135,[10] and, to begin with, we should perhaps explain why we feel impelled to reject his guidance. If we understand him aright, he believed that there was in existence at that period an original French text of the whole of the tract, which was later translated, not very competently, into Latin.[11] This is a belief we cannot share, and the reason will be plain if we simply place in juxtaposition the Latin and French versions of one clause.[12] For the convenience of the reader we give the French version with the words rendered in their modern form, while preserving their order.

Si quis in periculo mortis ad navem exonerandam, metu mortis, alterius res in mare proiecerit, si suspectum eum habuerit, iura-

[1] Compare chapters 8 and 15 with *Leges Henrici*, cc. 1, 78 (*Gesetze*, i.490-1, 522, 594).
[2] Compare chapter 7 with *Instituta Cnuti* c. 9 (*ibid.*, pp. 490, 315).
[3] Compare chapters 1 and 8 with *Leges Edwardi Confessoris*, cc. 11. 1 A 3, 32 E and 34 and 32 A 9 (*ibid.*, pp. 489-90, 635, 656, 659, 661).
[4] Liebermann, *Über die Leges Edwardi Confessoris*, pp. 119, 127-8.
[5] Chapter 8. In effect this expands chapter 2 which the compiler has retained, with a few additions, from the original *Ten Articles*.
[6] Above, p. 100.
[7] We have already expressed our inability to follow Liebermann in his dating of it some thirty years or so later: above, p. 57.
[8] *Foedera*, i.1-2; *Gesetze*, i.489-91. The title is not given to the exchequer copy.
[9] Chapter 11: 'Lagam regis Eadwardi vobis reddo cum illis emendationibus quibus pater meus eam emendavit . . .'
[10] See Appendix II, below, pp. 170-5.
[11] Liebermann, *Über die Leis Willelme*, pp. 118-30; *Gesetze*, iii.283-4.
[12] *Gesetze*, i.514 (c. 37).

mento se absolvet quod nulla alia causa, nisi metu mortis, hoc fecerit.

Je jetais vos choses de la nef pour peur de mort. Et de ce fait vous ne pouvez me plaider, car loisible est à faire damage à un autre pour peur de mort, quand autrement on ne peut échapper. Et si de ce fait vous me doutez que ce n'est pas pour peur de mort que je ne le fis, je m'en disculperai.[1]

We submit that, while it can be maintained – especially having regard to the context – that the French is derived from the Latin, no one, unless he were influenced by preconceived ideas, could imagine that the Latin was a rendering of the French. This conclusion would be confirmed if comparison were then made with the text in the Digest from which the clause is admittedly derived.[2] It is true that the clause we have selected is quite exceptional in the fact that the French version appears in the first person singular and as the words would be spoken by a defendant in court; but this in no way helps the argument that the Latin derives from the French, for the French is clearly much further from the Digest than is the Latin. This is no place for a philological argument, but, as it seems to us, there are good grounds for believing that no one in England could have written the romanesque section of the *Leges Willelmi* before the second half of the twelfth century, whether in Latin or in French, and this view accords with the conclusion, reached on purely philological grounds, that the French text was written in the period 1150-70.[3] Liebermann was aware of the philological arguments in favour of this date and rejected them[4]; but his own conclusion leads to very great difficulties. We have to suppose, for example, that many years before John of Tilbury made his way to Bologna, before the coming of Vacarius and his fellow Romanists to England, before Roman law was taught at Oxford, there was to be found here a man who had access to the Digest[5] and could find his way through it with sufficient skill to bring together widely separated passages. To convince us that this was possible under William Rufus or under Henry I we should want evidence more solid than philological speculations. But of the coming of Roman law to England we have spoken in a previous chapter.[6]

[1] The original reads: Je jettai voz choses de la nef pur pour de mort; et de ço ne me poez enplaider, kar leist a faire damage a altre pur pour de mort, quant par el ne pot eschaper. E si de ço me mescreez, que pur pour de mort nel feisse, de ço mespurerai. Nothing corresponding to this second sentence appears in the Latin text.

[2] The Latin text is headed 'De iactura metu mortis facta'. The compiler seems to have had particularly in mind the following passage from Dig. 14.2.2.2: Cum in eadem naue varia mercium genera complures mercatores coegissent praeterque multi rectores, servi liberique in ea nauigarent, tempestate graui orta necessario iactura facta erat . . .

[3] Matzke, *Lois de Guillaume le Conquérant*, pp. xxxix-lii.

[4] Liebermann, *Über die Leis Willelme*, pp. 134-5; *Gesetze*, i.492-519; iii.284-5.

[5] We may perhaps venture a reminder that the Digest, after being lost to the West for centuries, was not recovered in Italy and expounded at Bologna until late in the eleventh century. It can scarcely have been at all widely known in England before 1150: see above, p. 73.

[6] Above, pp. 71-87.

There are a good many other passages where, if we attempt to apply the hypothesis of a French text translated into Latin, the hypothesis seems to us to break down hopelessly. But these have no bearing upon the date of either text, and for the moment we pass them over.[1] We turn therefore to another obvious difficulty in the way of accepting an early date for the *Leges Willelmi*. In several passages the author mentions the king's justices,[2] notably where he speaks of the conviction of a sheriff or [hundred] reeve, before the king's justices, for an offence against the men of his bailiwick.[3] The known facts of the evolution of the judicature in England make it impossible to believe that this passage was written before the institution of *justiciarii totius Anglie*, who visited the counties with some regularity, or before these visitations came to be regarded as a matter of course.[4] On these grounds we might have to choose between the second half of the reign of Henry I and the second half of the reign of Henry II for the date of the tract – or rather the first section of it – but not between either of these periods and the reign of William II or the early years of Henry I. This conclusion is inevitable whether we regard the French or the Latin to be the original text.

Let us now describe the *Leges Willelmi* as the text has come down to us. It seems to us evident, though it seems not to have been so evident to others, that it divides itself quite plainly into four sections.[5] The first section consists of twenty-eight chapters and purports to set out the laws and customs, observed under Edward the Confessor, which were granted to the people of England after the Conquest. This is a tract of a not uncommon kind, as we have seen, and it takes its place with the *Ten Articles*, for example, which we have already noticed. It has come down to us quite independently of the other three sections, though only in a French version, and we must conclude that originally it had a separate existence.[6] There follow four short clauses on the status of *coloni* and *nativi*, written by a man with some romanesque learning. Not unnaturally they gave the French translator trouble: he had no notion of what a *colonus* might be as opposed to a *nativus*, though we fancy that *colonus* is just a learned term for socman.[7] The third section, which, for all its difference in character, may possibly be by the author who was responsible for the second, is divided into six chapters and was evidently written by a man with some familiarity with Roman

[1] See Appendix II, below, p. 170-5.
[2] Chapters 2.1, 17.3, 22. There is a similar reference in chapter 31, but this is by a different and later author: see below, n. 7.
[3] Quod si vicecomes vel prepositus convictus fuerit coram justiciariis regis erga homines sue ballie deliquisse (cap. 2.1: *Gesetze*, i.495).
[4] *Governance of Mediaeval England*, pp. 174-7, 197-204, 210-15.
[5] The accepted division is into two or three sections (Liebermann, *Gesetze*, iii.284; Pollock and Maitland, *History of English Law*, i.102).
[6] Apparently it survives in only one, the Holkham, manuscript (Liebermann, *Über die Leis Willelme*, pp. 113-15).
[7] Chapters 29-32 (*Gesetze*, i.512-14). For a corrected text of chapter 31 see Appendix II, below, p. 171.

law. Its contents are hardly more than jottings, dealing with such diverse matters as pregnant women under sentence of death, intestacy, the lawful slaying of women taken in adultery, the penalties for poisoning, jettison of cargo, heirs in common.[1] The fourth section is a rendering of parts of Cnut's code adapted, as even a cursory inspection discloses, from the *Quadripartitus* and the *Instituta Cnuti*, though in the process the language has sometimes been modernised.[2] The compiler or adaptor – however we care to describe him – was a careful writer, who could adorn his text with biblical phrases[3] and on occasion depart quite widely from Cnut's laws.[4] There is no possibility that the French rendering of this section came first, and this conclusion is quite independent of any arguments regarding the other three sections.

So far as the second, third and fourth sections of the *Leges Willelmi* are concerned, all we have said seems to us so unquestionable that we cannot understand how an early date could have been suggested for them or how the French translation could have been assigned to a date no later than 1135. The first section stands apart. Much of it is identifiable with passages from the laws of Alfred and Cnut[5] and, though the source of much is less certain, the parallels to be found in Old English texts show sufficiently well that the author's learning was book-learning, just like the learning of the other compilers of the laws of King Edward. As we have already suggested, the Latin original of this section might possibly have been written under Henry I. No one has claimed, however, that its French version is more archaic than the French versions of the other sections, and indeed the date 1150-70 proposed for the tract as a whole was based upon the language of the first section.[6] The inference is that, after the four sections had been brought together, the three later sections were furnished with a translation, but that the whole translation may belong to the reign of Henry II or Richard I. Only the first section of the Latin text seems to us to have any claim – and that a dubious one – to so early a date as Henry I. The compilation as a whole must, we think, be assigned to the reign of Henry II, though we should not be disposed to tie ourselves down to the limiting date of 1170 suggested for the French text on philological considerations. Other men were expanding and refurbishing old-fashioned tracts in the early years of Henry II, and the work we have here is similar to theirs, though we think the adaptation of Cnut's laws to be rather more carefully done, with some regard to contemporary circumstances. It speaks in favour of the compiler that he took the trouble to collate two Latin versions and make the best he could of the two.

The *Leges Willelmi* never achieved popularity, whether in its shorter

[1] Chapters 33-38 (*Gesetze*, i.514-15).
[2] Chapters 39-52 (*Gesetze*, i. 515-20): see also Appendix II, below, pp. 176-9.
[3] Chapter 40: below, p. 177. [4] Chapter 51: below, p. 173.
[5] The parallels are noted by Liebermann, *Gesetze*, i.493-511.
[6] Matzke, *op. cit.*, pp. xxx-xxxix.

or its longer form, in Latin or in French.[1] Its interest today lies in the fact that it adds to the examples we possess of the continued refurbishing of Old English laws in their twelfth-century Latin form and of their subsequent translation into the vernacular. Its distinguishing mark is a small, and not altogether relevant, admixture of Roman legal learning. That the French version of the *Leis Willelme* was one of the first books of Old English law to be printed was due to its inclusion by the Pseudo-Ingulf in his compilation, for Ingulf was highly valued by our early antiquaries.[2] But, like the Pseudo-Ingulf, the *Leis Willelme* has been over-rated.[3] To suggest that it contains otherwise unknown enactments of the Conqueror seems to us mere fantasy, made credible perhaps by the acceptance of the *Ten Articles* as a similar repository of lost legal texts. Of that apocryphal work we have already said all that it seems necessary to say and we need add nothing more here on the *Leis Willelme*.

Let us now turn to a text that has succeeded in misleading many generations of historians, the so-called Assize of Clarendon. The true text of that assize – subsequent amendments and scribal errors having been eliminated – will be found in a text preserved by Roger of Howden, the text known among historians as the Assize of Northampton of 1176.[4] As we have already explained, once the Assize of Clarendon was given permanence in 1176 and its administration transferred to the recently constituted justices itinerant, it assumed a new and very considerable importance.[5] Not unnaturally the text became the subject of exposition or interpolation, two processes not easily distinguishable in the twelfth century. The pseudo-Assize is the one expository tract that is known to us in an apparently complete, though corrupt, state.[6] Until, however, there has been a far more searching investigation than has yet been undertaken, no one can be certain that other tracts of a similar kind are not lying hidden, to await discovery by a diligent enquirer. One such tract was certainly known to Bracton, who remarks that the assize contained a quite exceptional provision in favour of those who were required to abjure the realm after they had purged themselves by the ordeal of water or of fire – that is, of iron. They were allowed a delay of forty days so that they might seek pecuniary assistance, *subsidia*, from their friends. This privilege, Bracton says, was not granted to any others than those covered by the assize; and he makes it plain that the authority for this statement is the document before him, the *assisa* or *constitutio:* he uses both words.[7] Now

[1] Only one manuscript of the *Leges Willelmi* has survived, and the complete translation was preserved only in the Pseudo-Ingulf (Liebermann, *Über die Leis Willelme*, pp. 115, 118-19.)

[2] For the bibliography see Matzke, *op. cit.*, pp. xvi, xxviii-xxix.

[3] Even by Maitland (*History of English Law*, i.102).

[4] *Gesta*, i.108-111; *Chronica*, ii.89-91: see *Governance of Mediaeval England*, pp. 439-43.

[5] Above, pp. 98-9.

[6] For bibliography and commentary see *Governance of Mediaeval England*, pp. 440*n*, 443-4.

[7] *De Legibus*, fol. 136 (ed. Woodbine, ii.383).

we shall find in Howden's text a provision that those who purge themselves by the ordeal of water may nevertheless be required to abjure the realm if they are defamed of murder or the graver crimes, and that they may take their chattels with them; but there is nothing there of the ordeal of iron or of the exiles' seeking the assistance of their friends.[1] The conclusion is inevitable that Bracton's text was not Howden's text. And though Bracton's text was evidently a modified or interpolated text of the Assize of Clarendon, it was certainly unlike the *textus receptus*, the pseudo-Assize of the Select Charters, which knows nothing of the forty days' grace, nothing of the ordeal of iron.[2]

Howden's text of the Assize of Clarendon, as we have described it, was inserted by him in the first version of his chronicle under the year 1176, for in that year at Northampton the assize of 1166 was revived, amended and given permanence. But while retaining that text in the same place in his revised chronicle, Howden added another text,[3] the pseudo-Assize, as an item in the *Liber de legibus Anglie* which he ascribed to Ranulf Glanville and which he incorporated bodily under the not very appropriate year, 1180.[4] We say that this was hardly an appropriate year, because it was then that Glanville became justiciar and this 'book of the laws of England' is intended to contain the law as it was administered during his nine years of office; and one item, at least, in the book was yet unwritten in 1180 or perhaps in Glanville's lifetime.[5]

It may be well, however, if, at this point, we pause to describe the contents of the book. Beside the treatise known as *Glanville*, which we have already passed under review, there are included the *Ten Articles* of William the Conqueror, the *Leges Edwardi Confessoris*, an Assize of the Forest and the pseudo-Assize of Clarendon,[6] all of which we class as apocrypha. There are other collections of a similar character, mixing indiscriminately genuine and apocryphal texts,[7] betokening a wide interest in these tracts, but an interest devoid of critical acumen. Evidently there was some motive behind them, differing from the antiquarian interest which actuated later collectors; but we are left wondering to what practical end these collections could have been put. We mention them, however, because the very number of these miscellaneous, indiscriminate, collections demonstrates, better perhaps than any other argument could, that the inclusion of the pseudo-

[1] See the text, as we have attempted to reconstruct it, in *Governance of Mediaeval England*, p. 441.

[2] *Select Charters*, pp. 170-3: an unsatisfactory text, but sufficient for our present purpose.

[3] *Chronica*, ii.248-52.

[4] *Ibid.*, pp. 215-52. This legal collection appears to exist in only one of the surviving manuscripts, Royal MS. 14 C 2, perhaps, as Stubbs suggested, Howden's own (*ibid.*, i. pp. lxxiv-lxxvi).

[5] The treatise known as *Glanville*: above, p. 105.

[6] For references see above, n. 4. See also *Governance of Mediaeval England*, pp. 447-8.

[7] *Ibid.*, p. 448. For another miscellaneous collection see that minutely described by Liebermann, *Über die Leges Anglorum saeculo xiii ineunte Londoniis collectae*.

Assize of Clarendon in Howden's *Liber de legibus Anglie* does not confer any *cachet*, does not raise a presumption of authenticity.

If we read the pseudo-Assize carefully, we shall notice that it assumes the existence of justices itinerant. Those accused of crime are to be held in custody until the itinerant justices, before whom they are to make their law, arrive from some other county; and so forth.[1] But since there were no such justices before 1168,[2] it is plain that this text cannot belong to the year 1166. And then we notice that the author has borrowed, not very intelligently, something from the genuine assize as amended in 1176, a clause providing for the law to have retrospective effect and also to continue in effect at the king's pleasure.[3] Now this clause was carefully devised to ensure two ends: that those suspected of crimes committed between 1166 and 1176 should be brought to justice and further that, unlike the assize as originally drafted in 1166, the amended assize should not lapse but should continue in force indefinitely. Nothing of this did the fabricator grasp. Instead he alters the clause to say that the pseudo-Assize of 1166 is to remain in force as long as the king pleases[4] – as if such words would have any significance when the enquiry was confined to crimes committed between 1154 and 1166. We need not attempt here to analyse the text – a sorry and confused jumble, as unlike the genuine legislation of Henry II as could well be imagined, with irrelevancies, perhaps casual accretions, such as a reference to the condemnation of heretics at a council which apparently took place in 1160-61[5] and another to the admission of the lower members of society to houses of religion.[6] There are some details that seem to represent what actually occurred in 1166[7] and others that may reflect the later practice in some counties when the justices came on their eyre.[8] But to distinguish from the rest what may possibly be true of 1166 or of any later time is a difficult and uncertain task. The date of the composition is certainly later than 1176: how much later we are left in doubt, but we do not think it can be subsequent to the reign of Richard I[9] and it seems more likely to belong to the reign of Henry II, when regular eyres were still something of a novelty and the Assize of Clarendon was fresh in men's minds.

No branch of the law seems to have attracted so many fabricators or

[1] Chapters 4, 5, 6, 10, 18, 19. The text in *Select Charters*, pp. 170-3, not infrequently gives a singular where a plural noun is required.

[2] *Governance of Mediaeval England*, pp. 203-4, 212; *E.H.R.*, xliii.168-71.

[3] Chapter 22, with which compare Assize of Northampton, chapter 1: 'Haec autem assisa attenebit a tempore quo assisa facta fuit apud Clarendonam continue usque ad hoc tempus et amodo quamdiu domino regi placuerit . . .' (*Select Charters*; p. 179).

[4] 'Et vult dominus rex quod haec assisa teneatur in regno suo quamdiu ei placuerit.' Cf. *Governance of Mediaeval England*, p. 443.

[5] Chapter 21. For the date of this council see *ibid.*, p. 443*n*.

[6] Chapter 20.

[7] *Governance of Mediaeval England*, p. 443.

[8] *Ibid.*, p. 198.

[9] It is one of the items in the *Liber de Legibus Anglie* which Howden ascribed to Glanville and included in the revised edition of his chronicle. He seems to have acquired it under Richard I. See *Governance of Mediaeval England*, pp. 444-5, 447-8.

elaborators as the law of the forest, and no texts are more difficult to evaluate than those which profess to present an assize of the forest. We can, however, dismiss as a fabrication, without apparent purpose, the pretended *Constitutiones de Foresta* of Cnut. Of this fiction no mediaeval manuscript survives and we are dependent upon sixteenth-century manuscripts and printed editions, for it excited great interest in Tudor times, when its authenticity was not doubted.[1] But without question it belongs to the twelfth century and undoubtedly it was not written before 1184 when the administration of the forests was reorganised and the responsibility for them, which hitherto had been placed upon a single chief justice, was divided between four justices who, with their serjeants, were required to swear to observe the assize,[2] that is Henry II's first Assize of the Forest which, we infer with confidence, was the work of the council of Clarendon in 1165-66.[3] So from 1166, when Alan de Neville went on his first great forest eyre,[4] until 1184, when his successor Thomas fitz Bernard died,[5] this simple assize, coupled with the chapters of the forest eyre,[6] was the only written law of the forest. That our fabricator knew of the reorganisation of 1184 is plain, for in the first chapter of his imaginary 'constitutions', he speaks of the four thegns who henceforward are to have jurisdiction over the forests throughout England and are to be entitled the four *primarii foreste*.[7] He then constructs a framework, composed of excerpts picked out ingeniously from the *Instituta Cnuti*,[8] in which he places fragments of forest lore – if we may use a neutral term – which have but a loose relation to forest law and custom and certainly no textual relation to the true Assize of the Forest. As evidence of the widespread and continued interest in the *Instituta Cnuti*, this composition deserves notice, but beyond this we can hardly say more than that, if it is other than a *jeu d'esprit*, its purpose entirely escapes us.

Let us turn to other purported assizes of the forest. There is nothing to suggest that, while Roger of Howden was working on the first version of his chronicle, he knew of any other assize of the forest than that which he inserted under the year 1184 and which was called, apparently in the copy before him, Henry II's first assize.[9] This may seem to imply that Henry at some time issued another forest assize, but Howden does not insert any other text in his first version and we can be confident that none had come into his hands by 1192, when his first version was finished. But after he had undertaken the work of revision he did acquire a different text and he inserted it under the year 1198, in

[1] *Liebermann, Über Pseudo-Cnuts Constitutiones de Foresta*, pp. 2-10.
[2] *Ibid.*, pp. 28-32.
[3] *Governance of Mediaeval England*, p. 444; above, p. 95.
[4] *Ibid.*, pp. 199-200.
[5] 'Benedict of Peterborough', i.323-4.
[6] For these, to which reference is made in the *Leges Henrici*, see above, p. 44.
[7] *Constitutiones de Foresta*, cap. 1 (*Gesetze*, i.620).
[8] The parallels are noted by Liebermann in *Über Pseudo-Cnuts Constitutiones*, pp. 10-11, 49-55, and *Gesetze*, i.620-6.
[9] 'Benedict of Peterborough', i.323-4.

the belief that it was the code of forest law administered by the justices in eyre in that year.[1] This text includes not only an 'assize', but also certain additional *precepta*. The inference seems to be that, besides being provided with an assize, the justices were given for their guidance certain administrative directions. The point where the assize ends and the *precepta* begin was not indicated by Howden, but it seems probable that the first twelve paragraphs constitute the assize and the remaining five the *precepta*. Some time after 1198 Howden came into the possession of the *Liber de Legibus Anglie* we have already described. This contained yet a third form of the 'assize of the forest'.[2] It lacks the *precepta* and, although it was the third text to reach Howden's hands, it seems to be intermediate between the *prima assisa* and the text he ascribed to 1198. It ends with a clause (incorporated in later versions), stating that the king had given instructions at Woodstock that offenders against forest law were to find sureties, presumably for their good conduct, on the first two occasions, but on the third occasion they should answer with their bodies. Quite clearly this is an addition and no part of the text of the 'assize', but on the strength of the references to Woodstock here and in the obviously spurious title, given not by Howden but in later copies, Stubbs entitled the whole document the Assize of Woodstock and dated it 1184.[3] The date, we may explain, reflects a curious muddle by Howden himself who, when revising his chronicle, expunged from the annal for 1184 the text given there and substituted a reference to the text in the *Liber de Legibus Anglie*.[4]

Whatever authentic legislation or administrative instructions may lie behind Howden's later texts, it is obvious that a fabricator has been at work, and his work has not been improved by copyists with an imperfect command of Latin. The preamble of Stubbs's 'Assize of Woodstock' should itself arouse suspicion. 'Haec est assisa domini Henrici regis filii Matildis in Anglia' it begins, and it goes on to declare that the assize was enacted at Woodstock with the counsel and assent of the archbishops, bishops, barons, earls and nobles of England – in that order.[5] As we have said, it is obviously spurious. The preamble of no

[1] *Chronica*, iv.63-6.

[2] *Ibid.*, ii.243-7.

[3] This title he seems first to have bestowed in the introductory matter prefixed to the text in his *Select Charters* (first edition, 1870), pp. 149-50: His words should be noted. 'The jurisdiction had been resuscitated by Henry II early in his reign, by the appointment of justices who visited the forests at the time that the Justices Itinerant "went the counties" or "circuits". But this, the Assize of Woodstock, is his first formal act concerning them in existence.' In 'Benedict of Peterborough', which, of course, contained a very different 'first assize', Stubbs had not gone beyond calling his spurious text 'Forest Assize of Henry II' ('Benedict', ii. pp. clix-clxiv). The words we have cited from the *Select Charters*, as well as the text, were preserved, with no note of warning, in the revised edition by H. W. C. Davis. An early fourteenth-century version of the 'Assisa foreste facta apud Wodestoke' will be found in Br. Mus. Addl. MS. 5761, fol. 131*b*-132*b*. The Elizabethan copies used by Stubbs are related to this text, but the textual history of this pseudo-assize is complicated and remains to be investigated.

[4] *Chronica*, ii.290.

[5] 'Benedict of Peterborough', ii. p. clxi. The preamble given in Addl. MS. 5761 has not been corrupted, but it is, of course, spurious. It needs hardly to be said that it does not form part of Howden's text, for which see *Chronica*, ii.245-7.

authentic enactment, no authentic instrument, was ever framed in this style. The document then follows, at a distance, Henry's genuine assize, but interpolates a new paragraph,[1] and adds more at the end. It is, however, unnecessary to summarise all the new matter, though we may notice two paragraphs. The ninth is clearly subsequent to the settlement with Cardinal Pierleoni in 1178, when the king's right was acknowledged to proceed against clerks accused of forest offences.[2] The seventh provides that, in every county where there are royal forests, twelve knights are to be appointed to keep the king's vert and venison. These are the 'regarders' of later times; but when they were first appointed, whether under Henry II or Richard I, is not recorded.[3] The twelfth and final clause is, as we have already said, a manifest addition, in direct contradiction to clause one, which is taken from Henry II's original assize. It is possible, though quite unproved, that Richard I or Henry II in his later years did mitigate the savagery of the first assize of the forest on some occasion and that this clause was originally a gloss; but there is overwhelming proof that there was no continued amelioration of the law, which retained all its barbarism until the Charter of the Forest.[4] And that there was an Assize of Woodstock, enacting a law of the forest, in 1184 or any other year and that this fabrication is to be identified with it we can dismiss as chimeras. As for the four clauses that Stubbs saw fit to add to the fabrication, drawn, as he said, 'from copies of the Elizabethan period', we have no shadow of warrant for charging the twelfth-century fabricator with them.[5]

A prolonged discussion of Howden's three texts, endeavouring to date and evaluate the various accretions to the *prima assisa*, would, however, be out of place here. One day this task will be done, when the history of the royal forests in the twelfth century is seriously attempted. Our present purpose is much more limited. It is to remove the so-called Assize of Woodstock from the category in which it has been placed, that of authentic legislation, and to relegate it to the category to which it belongs, that of apocrypha.

[1] Paragraph 4 in the 'Assize of Woodstock'.

[2] Ralf de Diceto, *Opera*, i.410.

[3] In the Charter of the Forest of 1217, c. 5, it is implied that regarders were already in existence in 1154, but this has no evidential value (McKechnie, *Magna Carta*, p. 509; *Select Charters*, p. 345). G. J. Turner assumed that regarders were appointed under Henry II in the manner later customary (*Select Pleas of the Forest*, pp. lxxv-lxxvi).

[4] As we point out in the *Governance of Mediaeval England*, p. 446*n*, there are references to mutilation and the death penalty in the assize attributed by Howden to 1198, articles 1 and 14 (*Chronica*, iv.63, 65), in the 'Unknown Charter' and in the Charter of the Forest (McKechnie, *op. cit.*, pp. 486, 510). We are not prepared to dispute Petit-Dutaillis' contention that in practice the extremity of the law was rarely exacted and that a money composition was preferred (*Studies and Notes Supplementary to Stubbs' Constitutional History*, pp. 193-5), but these references would be meaningless had the law not remained unchanged.

[5] 'Benedict of Peterborough', ii. pp. clxi-clxiv. Stubbs did not think it necessary to warn readers of the *Select Charters* that much of his text was of dubious authenticity, although this was done imperfectly in the revised (ninth) edition, p. 188. Petit-Dutaillis was entirely misled by Stubbs's editorial methods, and his comments on this and other purported forest legislation are consequently pointless (*op. cit.*, pp. 192-5).

In taking our leave of these apocrypha of our law, we are conscious that we are presenting the reader with a half-told tale, historical mysteries with the veil at best but partly drawn aside. Yet it is well that he should know something of this episode, something of this curious divagation of the human spirit when it could find satisfaction in pretences. Let us admit that, with perhaps one or two exceptions, these ephemera are irrelevant to the history of English law, stepping-stones in a miry by-path that leads nowhere. But men have not always thought thus. They have entered into the game without knowing it was a game. They have taken these fables, these *jeux d'esprit*, seriously. The *Ten Articles*, the *Leges Willelmi*, the Assize of Clarendon, the Assize of Woodstock. . . . Think how these falsities have been accepted and interpreted in the work of our most distinguished teachers. For centuries these apocrypha in particular have been doing their bad work and doing it down to our own time – as Maitland said of the *Leges Edwardi*,[1] though this fabrication is of far greater value, despite its fantasies, than any of the four we have named, the four that have been deemed respectable. We can but hope that what we have said of them may lose them that respectability, may in some measure hinder the continuance of their bad work.

[1] *History of English Law*, i.104.

VII

FROM GLANVILLE TO MAGNA CARTA

As we have seen, the system of land laws constructed under Henry II came at the end of a long process of evolution, and it was constructed to last. The system was not, however, rigid. It grew largely by a process of subdivision of forms of action and consequent expansion, while other forms contracted, like the assize *utrum*, and some, like the action *de recto*, virtually disappeared. Of this process we need add nothing to what we have already said.[1] We should, however, make it clear that the law in *Glanville* approached finality so far as law in any rapidly evolving society can be said to be final. There is no reason to suppose that, had Henry II lived – and he was little more than fifty-six when he died – the edifice he and his ministers had created would have been materially extended in his life-time. Consequently it was not to be expected that his successor would be a great legislator, at least in the field of land law; and, as fate would have it, that successor was little better than an absentee landlord whose only interest in his property is its rent.

Richard I issued no coronation charter and, while he could not escape, whenever he was accessible, the constant personal appeals for favour or redress that beset every mediaeval monarch, he took, so far as we can tell, but the slightest interest in administration or in the welfare of his subjects, whether in England or in any of his other dominions. As heir to his father, he inherited not only wealth – which he proceeded to dissipate – but in England and Normandy a system of government and able ministers without their equal elsewhere in Western Europe. He seems, however, to have been but a poor judge of men – except fighting men – though one choice he made was signally good, that of Hubert Walter, who in 1193 became justiciar in succession to the feeble Walter of Coutances and who found that his primary mission was to quell the attempted usurpation of Count John, the direct consequence of Richard's own pococurantism. Inevitably Hubert's second task was to provide remedies for the disorder and unsettlement brought about by years of irresolute government and, then, by civil war. We see repeated, on a smaller scale, the story of Henry II's reign, when twice civil war and disorder were followed by legislation. If we speak of Richard I's legislation, we do so with a qualification, for this legislation does not take the form of royal assizes but of administrative acts which, although they may be called royal edicts, are in reality the acts of the justiciar. It is well to recall that the king paid but

[1] Above, p. 39.

a brief visit to England in 1194. He arrived on 13 March, when his brother's revolt had been all but crushed, and he departed, never to see England again, on 12 May, leaving the settlement of the country in Hubert Walter's capable hands.[1]

Hubert arranged for a general eyre to start in September 1194; but on this occasion the justices had a special task to do and they were given extraordinary powers. Fortunately Roger of Howden has preserved the text of the chapters of the eyre, doubtless because of their exceptional character.[2] They are the first to have been preserved, though we know enough of previous general eyres in the twelfth century to be certain that they repeat the accustomed articles, while greatly extending them.[3] There is to be an enquiry into the outrages against the Jews that had disgraced the early months of 1190 after Richard had departed on his crusade. 'Who were the murderers?' it was to be ascertained, and 'what were the dead Jews' belongings and where were they?', for all the Jews' bonds and debts were to be taken into the king's hand. Any malefactors who had not compounded for their misdeeds were to be arrested. Then there were the arrears of the king's ransom which the justices were to pursue. Since Count John and his followers had suffered forfeiture, many enquiries had to be made so as to ensure that all their possessions should come into the king's hand. Moreover, during the years of unsettlement, the king's demesnes had been neglected: enquiries had to be made into their present state and the steps necessary for restocking them. Jewish affairs had to be regulated upon a permanent basis, and elaborate arrangements were prescribed for recording their loans and repayments in future.[4] Finally, enquiries were to be made into all irregular exactions – *prisae* and *tenseriae* – levied since the coronation by the king's servants, from royal justices down to hundred-serjeants. We pass over other details. It will be seen how administrative and legislative provisions – or what we should regard as such– were run together without distinction. But, in any case, the chapters of the eyre were included by Edwardian lawyers among the statutes, and the earliest surviving text deserves mention. Then in the following year a 'royal edict' was issued, making better provision for the arrest of criminals, who had doubtless prospered and multiplied in the years of disorder.[5] In every county knights were appointed who, to use later terms, might be called keepers or conservators of the peace. Before them every male of fifteen years and upwards was sworn to keep the peace; and this undertaking implied the pursuit of outlaws, murderers and thieves and their delivery to the

[1] For the salient facts of the administration of England under Richard I see our *Governance of Mediaeval England*, pp. 83-4, 170-1, 327-9.

[2] *Chronica*, iii.263-4; *Select Charters*, pp. 252-5.

[3] *Governance of Mediaeval England*, pp. 180, 203; above, pp. 36, 39.

[4] Richardson, *English Jewry under Angevin Kings*, pp. 118-20. Although connected with the eyre, the ordinance regulating the Jewry was a separate document (Howden, *Chronica*, iii.266-7; *Select Charters*, pp. 256-7).

[5] Howden, *Chronica*, iii.299; *Select Charters*, pp. 257-8.

knights who, in turn, delivered them to the custody of the sheriff. The hundred-bailiffs were to be informed of those malefactors whom the hue-and-cry could not run down. To put the edict into effect commissioners were sent round the country, and they did more than see that the edict was implemented locally. They themselves required those sworn to keep the peace to declare before them the names of suspects, and these they proceeded to arrest and lodge in the king's gaols. Once more we see how legislation and administration were intertwined.

According to Roger of Howden, this last measure was successful in clearing the country of many malefactors, though many escaped by flight[1]; but there is little to be learnt from him or from other sources as to the success of the eyre of 1194. The proceedings against ministers who had levied irregular exactions were apparently dropped,[2] for reasons we can guess: too many of those were involved upon whom the administration of justice depended. It had been much the same with the Inquest of Sheriffs.[3] One indication that the country had been pacified and crime and disorder repressed lies, however, in the chapters of the eyre of 1198, which contain no extraordinary provisions.[4] Meanwhile Hubert Walter had turned in another direction and in 1197 had attempted to enforce uniform weights and measures throughout the country,[5] an ideal centuries-old which kings before the Conquest had sought to realise but failed to put into effect.[6] This last was perhaps a more serious effort, and the chapters of the eyre of 1198 contain an article to enquire if the four men appointed in each township to enforce the Assize of Measures had complied with its provisions and if they had attached those who had transgressed against the assize.[7]

Meanwhile Richard was away in France fighting his endless wars against his suzerain and against his feudatories. There is nothing to lead us to suppose that he planned any of the steps taken by Hubert Walter, though it is doubtless to be accounted unto him for righteousness that he appointed as his *alter ego* in England a man of such administrative ability and gave him his full confidence. Any consultations there may have been between king and justiciar on such subjects are likely to have been perfunctory. But there is one ordinance that we may unquestionably credit to Richard, that of 22 August 1194 regulating tournaments, though its main purpose appears to have been the revenue from the licence fees charged to the combatants.[8] We should perhaps notice also the settlement of the limits of ecclesiastical and secular jurisdiction in Normandy; but that was the work of the senes-

[1] Howden, *Chronica*, iii.300.
[2] There is nothing on this matter in the chapters of the eyre of 1198 (*ibid.*, iv.61-2).
[3] Richardson and Sayles, *Select Cases of Procedure without Writ*, pp. xxvi-xxviii.
[4] Howden, *Chronica*, iv.61-2.
[5] *Ibid.*, 33-4.
[6] Above, pp. 23, 27.
[7] Howden, *Chronica*, iv.62
[8] *Foedera*, i.65; R. de Diceto, *Opera*, ii. pp. lxxx-lxxxi; Howden, *Chronica*, iii.268.

chal, William fitz Ralf, and it was left to Richard only to confirm it.[1] England was not affected: a settlement of the same dispute had been made there in 1178.[2]

It is possible that we have not the full tale of all the legislation and administrative orders of these years.[3] The enrolments of Richard's reign that might have told us much are represented today but by the pipe rolls, a few plea rolls and some odd membranes from other rolls.[4] The chronicle of Roger of Howden, valuable as it is, cannot compensate for our losses. It is unlikely, however, that anything of real importance has escaped notice, and one conclusion of great significance seems inevitable. With Hubert Walter's appointment this administrative and legislative activity begins; with his resignation of the justiciarship in July 1198 it comes to an end. Able as his successor, Geoffrey fitz Peter, may have been, his was but a shadow of the greatness that had been Hubert's.

We should not leave the reign of Richard I without mentioning one piece of local legislation that appears to be the very earliest recorded in England. In some year of Henry fitz Ailwin's mayoralty, which seems to have begun in 1193, an 'assize' was issued in London for the prevention of the disastrous fires which swept through the city with alarming frequency. The plan was to limit conflagration by the construction of thick stone party-walls between the wooden houses. The work had to be left to private initiative, but any opposition by neighbours could be overcome by appealing to the court of husting. This early 'London Building Act' is remarkable for its precise detail and shows how the art of drafting legislation had, already before the close of the twelfth century, passed from the king's court to local authorities.[5]

The reign of John was remarkable for two pieces of legislation. Some would say that these were the Great Charter and the grant to the Church of the free election of bishops and heads of religious houses. The latter we should ourselves dismiss as being purely and intentionally delusive, and we should put in its place, as the second enactment of lasting importance, the obligation imposed upon the unfree to bear arms. Of all these three enactments we shall give an account in some detail, but in the first place we should notice that John began his reign

[1] Génestal, *Le Privilegium Fori en France*, ii.95-124. The agreement with William fitz Ralf appears to have been in 1191. Richard's approval could not have been given before 1194, but the date is uncertain (*Governance of Mediaeval England*, p. 312*n*).

[2] R. de Diceto, *Opera*, i.410: cf. *Governance of Mediaeval England*, pp. 309-12.

[3] We pass over legislation, if such it may be called, issued at Chinon and Messina relating to the Crusade (*Gesta Regis Henrici*, ii.110, 130, 139). There seems no evidence that the law of wreck in England was affected by the legislation at Messina which preserved the right of heirs of a wrecked crew. This English *mala consuetudo* was notorious: cf. Gerald the Welshman, *De Principis Instructione* in *Opera*, viii.117-20, and *Traditio*, vii.250, *n.* 28. See above, p. 35, for Henry I's attempt to amend it.

[4] *Memoranda Roll, 1 John*, pp. xvi-xxxv, xlviii-lix; *Select Cases of Procedure without Writ*, p. xi; *Governance of Mediaeval England*, pp. 170-2.

[5] *Liber de Antiquis Legibus*, pp. 207-10. The date (1189) ascribed *ibid.*, p. 206, is not a contemporary statement and cannot be accepted. There are later texts and additions: cf. Weinbaum, *London unter Eduard I und II*, ii.45-8.

by issuing a *constitutio* – which, as we have seen, is a synonym for assize or statute – remedying the worst of the abuses of his brother's reign. This *constitutio* evidently takes the place of a coronation charter and it has this significance, that the abuse is not any of those that figure in the Articles of the Barons of 1215, but the excessive fees that Richard I had demanded for the grant of charters and other instruments under the great seal. The king issues his *constitutio* at the instance of Hubert Walter, archbishop of Canterbury and royal chancellor, and because by his coronation oath he is bound to extirpate entirely evil and wicked customs, he acts to the honour of God and Holy Church and for the peace and tranquillity of clergy and people. The king then announces his intention of returning to the scale of charges in force under Henry II and gives a schedule of them.[1] If, after so grandiloquent a preamble, this seems to us an anticlimax, still the *constitutio* is well worth pondering. In the first place, because in 1199 it could not have seemed to the barons that there were any great evils calling aloud for redress and, secondly, because, whatever straits John was put to during his reign, the scale of charges laid down seems to have been honoured, though Richard had shown how the great seal could be so manipulated as to afford a large and oppressive revenue.[2]

Next we should, we think, remark that, however poorly we may regard John as a ruler, the Interdict, under which the country lay between 1208 and 1214, effectually prevented any legislation in those years, since the assent of the bishops could not have been obtained to any proposals, had the king any to offer, whereas the period between John's return to England from campaigning in France on 13 October 1214 and the outbreak of war with the barons in late August 1215 was largely spent in legislation, though truly of an extraordinary kind. It was, then, only in the early years of his reign that legislation might have been expected of John, had he been a reformer of his father's cast of mind; but it could not have seemed to him or to those around him that any reforms were called for. And apart from an Assize of Money, issued in January 1205, aimed at maintaining the standard of the currency and punishing fraudulent practices,[3] there is nothing of note except the Assize of Arms we shall shortly describe, issued later in that year. These years, it must be remembered, were years of war, and the Assize of Arms, legislation we place second only to the Great Charter in importance, was conceived under the threat of invasion by the French king. This legislation we know, not from a text of John's reign but from a later reference to it under Henry III.[4] For convenience we may call it an 'Assize of Arms', which is indeed likely to have been its actual title. This lost assize is linked with two other instruments that have come down to us and enable us to tell the story in some detail. The first of

[1] *Foedera*, i.75-6; previously printed by Wilkins, *Leges Anglo-Saxonicae*, pp. 354-5.
[2] *Memoranda Roll, 1 John*, pp. xxxv-xxxix.
[3] *Rot. Lit. Pat.*, p. 54*b*.
[4] See below, p. 137, n. 3.

these is entered on the patent roll and is well known from its inclusion in the *Select Charters*.[1] It takes the form of a writ, addressed to the sheriffs in 1205, notifying the passing of two enactments with the assent of the bishops, earls, barons and all the king's lieges of England. The first enactment provides for a restricted call-up of knights, one for every ten knight's fees; and the reason for formal legislation appears to be that there is no limit to the period of service and that the wages of the selected knights are to be found by a levy, so that, in effect, ten knight's fees in every county maintain one knight for an indefinite period. It is, however, the second enactment that is of importance for our purpose. On the occurrence of an invasion, when the first tidings come, all men, whether landowners or not, are to assemble armed, presumably at a place to be appointed by the sheriff. This duty is enforced by drastic penalties: forfeiture in the case of landowners, reduction to serfdom in the case of others. Two points are to be observed. The enactment evidently applies only to freemen; and there is an entire absence of any established organisation. The legislation is panic legislation and could not have been effective. Fortunately there was no invasion and the government had time to make some rational plan to meet an emergency, should it occur. The *constitutio* which embodied this plan does not appear on any surviving chancery roll, but it has been preserved by Gervase of Canterbury.[2] In every county there was to be a chief constable, with a constable in every hundred and constables also in the towns, who were to act in conjunction with the mayor and the constable of the castle, should there be one. All constables, however, were to be at the orders of the chief constable, who was responsible for the organisation of the forces of the shire for the defence of the realm and the preservation of the peace. Service was obligatory upon all men upon attaining the age of twelve. This constitution of 1205 was supplemented the same year by an Assize of Arms, the substance of which is known from documents of 1230, when it was revived.[3] These documents make it quite clear that the unfree as well as the free were now covered by the scheme, extending from those wealthy enough to provide themselves with arms befitting a knight down to those with no more than twenty-shillings' worth of chattels, who were to be armed with bows and arrows or, if they dwelt within a royal forest, with axe or lance.

It seems unlikely that this legislation was rigidly or continuously enforced. Just as Henry II's Assize of Arms seems evidently to have become a dead letter by 1205, so John's enactments of that year do not seem to have been followed by action. The county forces played no part in the civil war ten years later and it is quite evident that, when the scheme was resuscitated in 1230, it was a case of starting afresh,

[1] *Rot. Litt. Pat.* p. 55; *Select Charters*, pp. 276-7.
[2] Gervase of Canterbury, *Historical Works*, ii.96-7.
[3] *Close Rolls, 1227-1231*, pp. 395, 398.

though there is evidence that some at least of those required by the assize to provide themselves with arms, including villeins, had done so.[1] The reason for inaction was doubtless that kings had come to rely upon trained mercenaries.[2] Nevertheless, abortive as John's legislation may have been from a military standpoint, its importance in the history of the law of status is great, for it marks a significant point in the passage of a great part of the population from unfreedom to freedom. Since this is one of the most important changes that can take place in any system of law, it may be appropriate if we devote some pages to an explanation of what the law had been in England and what was the significance of the decision taken in 1205 to impose upon the unfree the obligation to bear arms, in this respect to place free and unfree upon an equality.

The tradition throughout the early Middle Ages had been that only the freeman might bear arms,[3] and a manumission ceremony – an imaginary one, we fear – that is to be found in some of our early law-books bears witness to this.[4] In open court, so it was said, a manumitted man was given sword and spear and all roads and doors were declared open to him. This ceremony, described first by the compiler of the *Leges Henrici*, seems to have been borrowed in all its details from some late version of the *Lex Ribuaria*.[5] And just as the writer gave to a manumitted slave the arms suited to a freeman, so he gave symbolical 'arms of servitude', a billhook or an ox-goad, to a freeman who lost his freedom[6]: and we should perhaps recall that even in 1205 reduction to servitude might be threatened as a penalty for a freeman's refusal to bear arms.[7] Yet we doubt whether the law of the *Leges Henrici* was ever law in England: it seems rather to be the stuff of poetry. Already in the eleventh century the more prosaic charter of manumission was in use.[8] Still, it is true enough that the unfree were denied the privilege or obligation – call it what you will – to bear arms, and this distinction was still made in the Assize of Arms of 1176,[9] and yet again early in

[1] Hence the allowance given in the assessment of villeins to the fifteenth of 1225 for 'armis ad que iurati sunt' (below, pp. 139-40). Other classes have a more general allowance for arms.

[2] *Governance of Mediaeval England*, pp. 72-7.

[3] Guilhiermoz, *L'origine de la noblesse en France*, pp. 379-92. In England in 1198 a defendant pleads that 'ipse liber homo est et quod in jurata domini regis fuit ipse juratus ut liber homo ad habenda arma (*Curia Regis Rolls*, i.67).

[4] *Leges Henrici*, c. 78.1, 2; *Willelmi Articuli Retractati*, c. 15. (*Gesetze*, i.491, 594). We should note that this form of manumission is known only from these two texts and that the second is of no independent value. Extensive enquiry into continental sources has failed to discover any parallel except among the Lombards and the Franks (Fournier, *L'affranchisement dans le droit gallo-franc*, pp. 58-60).

[5] The immediate source we have not discovered. There are some verbal parallels with *Lex Ribuaria*, c. 61.1; but the only reference to the arms of a freedman is in c. 37.2.3, where it is a question of the freedman defending his freedom. That the Lombards symbolically armed a freed slave is known from Paul the Deacon, *Historia Langobardorum*, lib. i, c. 13.

[6] *Leges Henrici*, c. 78.2. Nothing of this is to be found in the *Willelmi Articuli Retractati*, c. 15, though this clearly derives from the *Leges Henrici* at this point.

[7] *Rot. Litt. Pat.*, p. 55: ipsi et heredes sui servi fient in perpetuum.

[8] Below, p. 146.

[9] The three classes covered are *milites*, *liberi laici* and *burgenses*. Text in *Select Charters*, p. 183, from Howden: for date see above, p. 99.

1205. But in that year a revolution took place. We need not credit King John with any enlightened or humanitarian motives. He was neither particularly enlightened nor particularly humane; but in 1205 he was a badly frightened man. He had lost Normandy and, being threatened with invasion, he discovered that his military resources were inadequate to provide for the defence of his kingdom. The artificial distinctions of status could be swept aside in an emergency.

We have declared that the distinctions between free and unfree status were artificial, and we must therefore say more of the legal and social position of the unfree at the end of the twelfth century. Let us put side by side a series of contemporary statements that bear upon the question. Our first citation comes from Richard of Ely, the treasurer under Henry II and Richard I and one of the king's justices. 'By the law of England villeins (*ascripticii*) may not only be removed by their lords from the lands in their present occupation to other places, but they may also be lawfully sold or disposed of in any other way.'[1] This, we take it, any lawyer, any judge who sat on the Bench at Westminster, would have accepted as a correct statement of the legal position. *Glanville* indeed has words to much the same effect, but some words are added regarding a villein's chattels. 'If a man is deraigned by his adversary as a villein (*nativus*), he is adjudged without remedy to his lord, together with his chattels, whatever he may have.'[2] Our next citation is from Howden's account of the assessment of the carucage of 1198, evidently drawn from an official document.[3] The basis of assessment, he tells us, was the sworn statement by a jury of the number of ploughlands in each township. The jury might, and presumably usually did, include both freemen and bondmen (*rustici*). If a jury made a false return, a juror who was a bondman forfeited his best plough-ox to his lord and, over and above this, had to answer to the king from his own property for the deficiency in the tax assessment resulting from his perjury.

It was, as Howden's document indicates, the plain, undeniable fact that a villein – however much he might be at the mercy of his lord – yet had a right to his own property, and it was a truth that sadly vexed the lawyers. When in his *Dialogus de Scaccario* Richard of Ely was asked to explain how it could accord with justice that the lord should lose to the king the chattels of convicted serfs he could find no answer but that the Assize of Clarendon so prescribed. He was, he said, just as puzzled as anyone else to explain the anomaly.[4] And, of course, the anomaly persisted. In 1225 villeins were assessed to the fifteenth and they were

[1] *Dialogus de Scaccario*, lib. i, c. 11 (ed. Johnson, p. 56). For the equivalence of *ascripticius* and *villanus* see lib. i, c. 10 (*ibid.*, p. 53).

[2] Glanville, *De Legibus*, lib. v, c. 4 (ed. Woodbine, p. 86). The *alpha* text is less emphatic (ed. Hall, p. 56).

[3] Howden, *Chronica*, iv.46: *Select Charters*, pp. 249-50. It should be noted that *rusticus* implies unfreedom, for the *liber homo* stands in a different category.

[4] *Dialogus*, lib. ii, c. 10 (pp. 97, 101). Note that Richard of Ely here uses the word *servus*. There is evidently no distinction in his mind between *servus*, *ascripticius* and *villanus*.

given an allowance in respect of the arms they were required to have under the Assize of Arms, their tools and the food and forage needed for consumption on their holdings.[1] Again, in 1232 and 1237 villeins were made directly responsible for their own taxes.[2] And everyone knows the clause in Magna Carta which protected the 'wainage' of the villein from amercement by the king, though quite clearly all his other chattels, which legal theory said were the lord's property, might be diverted to the exchequer.[3] But at the same period villeins were being sold, with their chattels, by their lords, but not, apparently, apart from their chattels.[4]

Before we attempt to explain these anomalies, let us look at a little more evidence and, first, at a letter to the justices of the Bench from Hubert Walter, who had recently resigned the office of justiciar:[5]

> Hubert, by the grace of God archbishop of Canterbury, primate of all England, to his beloved sons in Christ and his dearest friends, the justices of the Bench at Westminster, greeting and unfeigned blessing. This is to let you know that, when we held the office of justiciar, Philip the miller of Barrington made before us a fine with our beloved prior of Llanthony, his lord, whose villein he was, so that he might remove from his land with his brood and chattels. And since, after the fine made before us, the said Philip will not remove from the land as he agreed, we pray that you will see that what was on that occasion enacted before us shall be observed and will distrain the said Philip to surrender the land peacefully to the prior, as is right. And, we pray you, speed the prior's business in this matter and we shall owe you many thanks on his behalf. You know with what affection I regard the prior and his house. Farewell.

Behind this letter there lies an action *de fine facto* brought by the prior of Llanthony, and the result is recorded in the plea roll of the Michaelmas term 1199.[6] It runs as follows:

> Philip of Barrington, who was summoned to appear before the justices to show why he had not observed the fine between himself

[1] *Foedera*, i.177; *Select Charters*, pp. 351-2.

[2] *Close Rolls, 1231-1234*, p. 311; *ibid., 1234-1237*, p. 545; *Select Charters*, pp. 356, 358-9.

[3] Chapter 20. In the issues of 1217 (c. 16) and 1225 (c. 14) it is made quite clear that the villein protected is the villein whose lord is a subject of the king, 'villanus alterius quam noster'. This does not mean that the king's villeins were prejudiced; in practice they were exceptionally privileged (Hoyt, *Royal Demesne*, pp. 192-206).

[4] A number of references are given by Vinogradoff, *Villainage*, p. 151*n*, and Pollock and Maitland, *History of English Law*, i.414*n*.

[5] Hubertus Dei gracia Cantuariensis archiepiscopus, tocius Anglie primas, dilectis in Christo filiis et amicis karissimis iusticiariis de banco Westmonasterii salutem et sinceram benediccionem. Noveritis quod Philippus molendinarius de Berinanton coram nobis, dum iusticiarius eramus, finem fecit cum dilecto nostro priore de Lantonia, domino suo, cuius nativus erat, ut liceret ei a terra sua recedere cum sequela sua et catallis. Et quia idem Philippus post finem illum coram nobis factum non vult a terra illa recedere, sicut convenit, rogamus vos mandantes quatinus coram nobis tunc temporis actum fuit observari faciatis et eundem Philippum distringatis ut terram illam priori pacifice dimittat, sicut iustum est; et ita negocium ipsius prioris in hac parte acceleretis ut vobis pro eo gratias referamus multiplices. Scitis enim quanta affectione ipsum priorem et domum suam diligimus. Valete. (P.R.O., Ancient Correspondence, (S.C.1), vol. i, no. 119.)

[6] *Rotuli Curiae Regis*, ii.44.

> and the prior of Llanthony, made before the lord of Canterbury at Cirencester, regarding five acres with appurtenances in Barrington, came and acknowledged the fine, to the effect that he quitclaimed for ever to the said prior and his successors, on behalf of himself and his heirs, any right that he had in that land, and the said prior quitclaimed for ever Philip's homage and his brood and his chattels.

Now, from one point of view, the fine in this case was a variant form of manumission, interesting to those concerned with the technicalities of legal procedure. But the fine was also a form of conveyance, and the miller's surrender of his five acres implied that he had a title of some sort to them and that, for all that Richard of Ely asserts to the contrary, his lord could not eject him. In law the miller is the tenant and the prior is the demandant and, by coming to court and putting himself in this position, the prior implicitly acknowledged that the miller was a freeman.[1] But that, of course, had already been settled when the parties came to an agreement and before ever they appeared before the justiciar at Cirencester. Yet the prior is in an ambiguous position and the law has put him there: and it may well be that the crafty miller is endeavouring to take advantage of this fact, for if he is a freeman there can be no serious talk of his brood and his chattels. The prior has no right in them and he cannot grant what he does not possess and the miller already owns. This is the kind of tangle the court of chancery had to unravel in the fifteenth century when the courts of common law insisted upon looking at legalities instead of realities. In the twelfth century the justices of the Bench would apparently distrain a man to keep to his bargain, however anomalous it might seem in strict law. At least Hubert Walter thought the judges might take this step, and none knew the law of England better than he. What pressure was, in fact, put upon the miller we do not know: perhaps the threat of distraint was enough. We can but surmise what lies behind the record.

And now it may be helpful if we turn back to certain passages in the *Leges Willelmi* which owe nothing to the older legal tracts, but are an independent statement of the law relating to villeinage, written, it would seem, in the first half of Henry II's reign.[2] We give a translation.

> Socmen and other tillers of the soil are not to be harassed to pay more than is due and customary, nor is it lawful for lords to remove socmen from their lands so long as they render the services due.
>
> Villeins may not depart from their lands nor resort to ruses for defrauding their lord of the services due to him. If, however, anyone of them should depart, none may receive him or his chattels nor retain him; but he should be made to return to his own lord with all

[1] A villein, it was held not long after, could not be a party to a fine. 'Non potest cirographum fieri quia non est certum utrum sint villani necne' (*Curia Regis Rolls*, iv.19). Earlier it had been alleged by an intervener that a party to a fine 'villanus est . . . et non potest cirographum facere in curia domini regis' (*ibid.*, ii.133, 238).

[2] *Leges Willelmi*, cc. 29-32 (*Gesetze*, i.512-14). For date and correction of text see above p. 123, and Appendix II, p. 171.

his possessions. If other landlords do not compel strange villeins to return to cultivate their lands, the justices will do so. No one, on account of any remission freely made to him by his lord, may withdraw a service due to him.

The first paragraph, as we understand it, applies to those personally free, even though some of them, the socmen, may be tied to the soil, *ascripticii glebae*.[1] The implication is that the lords may wish to deprive free cultivators of their land, presumably because it would be more profitable if it were allotted to villeins. On the other hand, their fear is that villeins may remove themselves or may be recalcitrant and, if they do not take their departure, may refuse to perform their services. The writer thinks that the justices should help, and by the time that *Glanville* was written the writ *de nativo habendo* was a writ of course,[2] and indeed writs to similar effect seem to have been freely granted under Henry I.[3] On the other hand the king's courts seem never to have been disposed to enforce the performance of predial services: remedies were to be had in the lord's own court or he might eject a villein for good reason.[4] But the prospect of ejection was no deterrent and its enforcement no remedy if the villein could betake himself elsewhere and leave behind a vacant, unprofitable holding, and this is a contingency the writer has in mind. It is well to remember that fugitive villeins might be able to find other lords who had land that could be turned to profitable use and also that there was a labour market in towns. Economically the villein was not everywhere entirely dependent upon his lord.

And now perhaps we may attempt to explain the anomaly that, while the king recognises the villein's ownership of his chattels, the law – or should we say the lawyer? – recognises the right of the villein's lord to the villein's chattels. Let us ask what happens when a lord sells a villein or in some other way transfers the ownership to a third party. Now it seems evident that, as in the case of the miller of Barrington, the villein is inseparable from his brood and his possessions. A lord, said Bracton, may not usurp, without a judgement of the court, a villein's brood or chattels; but if he recovers the body of the villein, then he will recover what follows the body, namely the brood, lands and chattels.[5] There is no chattel slavery in England in the later twelfth century. But

[1] We translate *coloni* as 'socmen': for this equivalence see Vinogradoff, *English Society*, p. 435. *Colonus* is found in *Quadripartitus* as a translation of geneat in Ine, cc. 19, 22, and is given as an alternative to *villanus* (*Gesetze*, i.97, 99). But geneat, a comparatively rare word, seems in general to mean a ceorl who was a member of a noble's (or priest's) household (Chadwick, *Anglo-Saxon Institutions*, pp. 137-9). *Colonus* was beyond the understanding of the French translator of the *Leges Willelmi*.

[2] *Glanville*, lib. xii, c. 11 (Woodbine, p. 153; Hall, pp. 141-2). The terms of the writ to the sheriff are important: facias habere M.R. nativum et fugitivum suum cum omnibus catallis suis et cum tota sequela sua. The next clause shows that the assumption is that the fugitive had settled elsewhere, for the writ does not apply where the villein is to be found in the king's demesne.

[3] Cf. Bigelow, *Placita Anglo-Normannica*, pp. 94-5, 220; Van Caenegem, *Royal Writs in England*, pp. 336-44, 467-71.

[4] Pollock and Maitland, *History of English Law*, i.377-8. And see a case in *Bracton's Note Book*, no. 1237 (iii.251) where the court declares that 'dominus rex non vult se de eis intromittere'.

[5] *De Legibus*, fol. 198-198*b* (Woodbine, iii.103-4).

men had been sold openly in England in 1086; in the market at Lewes they were ranked with horses and oxen.[1] Under Henry I slaves were exported from Bristol.[2] These facts are, we fear, undeniable; and they mean, if they mean anything, that men and women might be separated from their children and sold like cattle, just as they might be in the United States little more than a century ago. But there was a growing sentiment in England in the eleventh and twelfth centuries that chattel slavery was wrong and that at least the export of slaves to heathen lands was wrong. What men understood to be the laws of Edward the Confessor forbade the practice[3]; and it is evident that the sale of slaves ceased in the course of the twelfth century while the sale of serfs continued. We may say, in other words, that the status of the slave was assimilated to the status of the unfree. But the sale of a serf seems to mean in practice the sale of his services. The institution of chevage, the payment due from a villein who has leave to reside away from the manor, serves to confirm this view. When King John threatens landless freemen that he will reduce them to servitude, he gives point to his threat by telling them that they will have to pay chevage at the standard rate of fourpence a year.[4] That is the mark of serfdom. There is no suggestion of any other disability. The serf, it is true, was liable to tallage by his lord; but in this respect he did not differ from the townsman, the burgess, of whose freedom there was no question.[5] And tallage might be arbitrary and oppressive. But this right of the lord's in itself implies the ownership by the serf of his means of livelihood. Let us recall the words of the flatterer to the knight: 'Men ought always to pluck and pillage the churl; for he is like the willow, which sprouteth the better that it is often cropped'.[6] But we are told of this as of an evil deed. And though lords might behave thus and might do so lawfully, no decent man would condone such conduct which, if not punished in this world, would be punished hereafter. Moral issues apart, the unfree were never so much at the mercy of their lords as legal theory implied. The value of the serf lay in the profit to be made out of him, and that could come only from his labour on the land. This seems to be the implication of Richard of Ely's words. It was only exceptionally that villeins were removed from their holdings and, if they were, it was in exchange for other holdings. And as for selling a villein, since he could not be sold as a chattel, since he could not be separated from his brood,

[1] D.B. i.26 a 1: Qui in burgo vendit equum dat preposito nummum et qui emit alium. De bove obolum. De homine iiii. denarios quocumque loco emat infra rapum.

[2] Malmesbury, *Vita Wulfstani*, p. 43; Hermann, *De Miraculis sancte Marie Laudunensis*, lib. ii, c. 21.

[3] The source is II Cnut c. 3, which derives from V Ethelred c. 2 or VI Ethelred c. 9; the derivative texts from Cnut include *Quadripartitus*, *Instituta Cnuti*, *Consiliatio Cnuti*, *Ten Articles* c. 9, *Leges Willelmi*, c. 41 (*Gesetze*, i.238-9, 250, 310-11, 488, 515).

[4] *Rot. Litt. Pat.*, p. 55: ipsi et heredes sui servi fient in perpetuum reddendo singulis annis iiii. denarios de capitibus suis. See Maitland's comment, *History of English Law*, i.424.

[5] *Ibid.*, pp. 638, 663. For many facts and some speculations regarding urban tallage see Hoyt, *Royal Demesne*, pp. 107-23.

[6] *Ancrene Riwle*, English Text, p. 37. Note that the French text (p. 72) reads 'vilein' for 'churl', and the Latin text (p. 23) 'rusticus'.

since the king, if not the lawyer, recognised his right to his own possessions, what could be sold but his services, even if he were removed to another manor?[1]

When we come to the reign of Edward I the villein seems to be advancing towards economic equality with the freeman. We find that, at least in some parts of England, those legally unfree are dealing with land – buying, selling and leasing – in exactly the same way as freemen. Let us cite from a recent commentary on the land charters relating to the estates of Peterborough Abbey: 'the charters combine in the same transaction the free and the unfree, villeins and villein land with freemen and free land'.[2] And it has been argued that the unfree were doing much the same in the twelfth century.[3] The argument would be stronger if it were better supported by documents; but it is not one we would, with any confidence, undertake to controvert. There may be more than a grain of truth in it. If villeins had not yet arrived at economic equality with freemen, Time was on the march and villeins were marching with it. And then there is the consideration that villeinage was not always and everywhere obviously recognisable. Whether a man was a villein and whether land was held in villeinage were questions open to dispute,[4] so that if we say that in the twelfth century there were transactions in land by villeins, we may be describing transactions by men, who thought themselves free, in land that the parties did not recognise as held in villeinage.

As time went on, though the courts were impelled to uphold a lord's well-supported claim to his villein,[5] the inclination of the judges was to give a casting vote for freedom. Bracton's teaching on the fugitive villein suggests rather the formidable obstacles in the way of the lord's recovering his property than the danger the fugitive ran of losing his liberty.[6] A lord must be very wary of asserting his claim to a villein who has left the manor and has established a claim to freedom, even though the fugitive ventures to return to his 'nest'. Any rash interference with the liberty of the venturer may result in the payment of heavy damages.[7] Nor does the king, in his public capacity, consider himself

[1] Maitland took the view that sales of villeins were sales of their persons: a villein might be 'sold as a chattel' (*History of English Law*, i.414). The terms of a grant may mislead.

[2] Postan, Introduction to *Carte Nativorum*, p. xxx. This is stated as an 'impression': but later it seems to be asserted as a fact. We must in general assume the lord's licence, though doubtless there were informal transactions in land: cf. Pollock and Maitland, *History of English Law*, i.382.

[3] Postan, *op. cit.*, pp. xlix-lviii.

[4] See *Curia Regis Rolls*, iv.19, cited above, p. 141, n. 1.

[5] *Curia Regis Rolls*, passim: *see* indexes *s.v.* Villeinage. Professor R. H. Hilton has reviewed the evidence from the printed plea rolls and monastic surveys and concludes that the status of the villein had deteriorated generally over the country by the middle of the thirteenth century (*Past and Present*, pt. xxxi, 3-19). Such a generalisation seems to conflict with evidence such as we adduce.

[6] Bracton, *De Legibus*, fol. 6*b*, 7 (Woodbine, ii.36-7).

[7] *Year Books of 1 & 2 Edward II*, pp. 11-13. This is the well-known case of Simon of Paris, who served as sheriff of London. He returned to his villgae of Necton, where he was claimed as a villein and required to serve in the office of reeve. On his refusal, he was arrested and held in custody from the hour of terce to vespers. He brought an action for assault and imprisonment and recovered damages of £100.

bound by the trammels of the landlord's claims over the persons or possessions of the unfree. The doctrines of *Glanville* and of Richard of Ely are not for him. The chattels of the felonious villein escheated to the king, not to the lord; the villein paid his own taxes; the villein stood in arms by the side of the freeman and the arms were those he provided from his own resources. What those arms were depended upon his wealth and not upon his status, or, to put the facts in another way, his military status depended upon his wealth and not upon his status at law. We may think that, from the king's standpoint, it was well that the villein provided his own arms, for where the lord provided the members of his household with arms, he was so likely to pawn or sell them, when pressed for money, that the law expressly forbade him to do any such thing.[1] If then the villein was protected in the possession of his holding, as in practice he was, although not by the king's courts; if by the king he was otherwise treated as a freeman; by the end of the thirteenth century there could have been little in many, if not in the majority of cases, to distinguish him from a freeman of the lower orders, except in the heavier burden of the services demanded of him, and these were progressively commuted for money payments.[2] If the cases on the plea rolls of the king's courts suggest that lords were anxious to recover the bodies of fugitive villeins,[3] we may doubt very much whether their real motives were not very different. A London sheriff, a respected merchant, would have made but an indifferent agricultural labourer: his purse was more likely to excite his lord's covetousness than his services.[4] Money was the universal solvent. And though villeinage and villein services lingered on here and there until the seventeenth century – for the progress of events was widely uneven from county to county, from manor to manor – yet by the fifteenth century they had become anomalous.[5]

The forces that were making, if not for freedom, for an easing of the disabilities of unfreedom were at work, if but feebly, in the centuries before the Conquest. The fugitive villein was a problem as old as the reign of Henry I,[6] just as the fugitive slave must have been in the tenth and eleventh centuries.[7] To the unfree, flight was the remedy for oppression, whether in mediaeval Europe or in nineteenth-century America. The slave watched his opportunities. To the freeman the Danish invasions were a disaster that might lead to his own enslave-

[1] Et nullus ex quo arma hec habuerit ea vendat . . . nec dominus suus ea aliquo modo ab homine suo alienet, nec per forisfactum, nec per donum, nec per vadium, nec aliquo alio modo: Assize of Arms (1176), c. 4 (*Select Charters*, p. 183).

[2] It is now believed that the commutation of labour services for a rent began very early and was 'wholesale' in the twelfth century (Postan, *op. cit.*, pp. xliv-xlv.).

[3] It would appear from the defended cases on the *Curia Regis Rolls* that the alleged villeins were, at least as a rule, people of substance.

[4] Above, p. 144, n. 7.

[5] Page, *End of Villainage*, pp. 72-99. For the late survivals under Elizabeth see Savine in *Trans. R. Hist. Soc.*, New Ser., xvii.235-89; further examples are given by H. E. Malden, *ibid.*, xix.305-7.

[6] Hence the frequency of writs for recovering fugitive villeins: above, p. 142.

[7] This is evident from the law of Athelstan; above, p. 18.

ment. To the slave they offered the prospect of freedom and not only freedom but honour. Archbishop Wulfstan laments that slaves who had fled to serve in arms with the Danes had to be treated by the English as thegns.[1] The world was turned upside down. When the Danes ruled in England that prospect was over; but there was still open to the bold the prospect of flight, of finding in a far country a less oppressive lord. For whatever reason the slave's lot seems to have become less harsh. Manumission, at least of penal slaves, had long been considered a pious deed,[2] and manumission seems not to have been infrequent before the Conquest and for some time afterwards. It is noteworthy, however, that surviving acts of manumission of the eleventh century are, with rare exceptions, in English and that formal deeds in Latin do not seem to appear until late in the twelfth century.[3] There is a well-known passage in Domesday Book, telling how William Levric had set free twelve *servi*,[4] and this has been hailed as an act of Norman benevolence.[5] But on other manors of William's the *servi* were still unfree in 1086.[6] Elsewhere the evidence of Domesday Book suggests that, when the number of ploughs was reduced, the *servi* were sold off like any other redundant farm-stock.[7] No one explanation will elucidate the varying numbers, the increases and decreases, of different social classes on so many pages of Domesday Book. One explanation, however, we can safely exclude in the absence of direct evidence – Norman benevolence. We have to remember that in the Old English polity slaves might purchase their freedom,[8] and the inference is that these conditions continued, and that here we may have another possible explanation of the isolated act of enfranchisement by William Levric. And whatever manumissions had been purchased or – to take the benevolent view – freely given, there were still chattel slavery and penal servitude under Henry I,[9] while the evidence of Domesday Book, uncertain as it may often be, does point conclusively to the loss of status by many men, if only for a time, as the result of the Conquest.[10]

We must beware of reading too much into the nomenclature of

[1] *Sermo Lupi ad Anglos*, lines 104-8.

[2] For the law of Athelstan see above, p. 18.

[3] Thorpe, *Diplomatarium*, pp. 621-44; Earle, *Land Charters*, pp. 253-64; Madox, *Formulare*, p. 416. For Latin charters see *ibid.*, pp. 416-20.

[4] D.B. i. 167 *b* 1: xii. servos quos Willelmus liberos fecit.

[5] Poole, *Obligations of Society*, p. 14; Loyn, *Anglo-Saxon England*, p. 350.

[6] D.B. *loc. cit.* Leckhampton: Ibi iiii. servi. Shipton: iiii servi, sine caruca.

[7] The evidence from Essex indicates that, where *servi* were kept, it was at the rate of two to a ploughteam and that the *servi* acted as ploughmen – as indeed may be deduced from Ælfric, *Colloquy*, lines 23-35. The evidence is summarised by Round, *V.C.H.*, *Essex*, i.361-3. Where the ploughs have decreased in number the *servi* have decreased by twice the number. Where, as at Walden, the ploughs have increased, there is a corresponding increase in *servi*. The rate of two *servi* to a plough was not uniform throughout England. In some counties it was higher (Vinogradoff, *English Society*, p. 464).

[8] Above, pp. 145-6.

[9] For chattel slavery, see above, p. 143. For a threat of penal slavery to clerical concubines in 1127, see Florence of Worcester, *Chronicon*, ii.87-8.

[10] This is particularly well illustrated by the decline in the numbers of socmen: for details see Darby, *Domesday Geography*, *Eastern England*, p. 375; *South-East England*, p. 613.

Domesday Book. Tables have been prepared, maps have been drawn, showing the distribution of *servi* in England and, whatever value we give to Domesday classifications, there can hardly be room for doubt that the grossest forms of servitude steadily increased as one went west from Kent to Cornwall.[1] And yet we may doubt whether *servus* implied the same status in the two counties, whether a man whom a Kentish steward considered a serf, a slave, would be considered such in the West Country.[2] The incidence of slavery, if we were to put our trust in Domesday nomenclature, would seem to be more than twice as high in Kent as in Sussex,[3] yet at the beginning of the fourteenth century it was being said in the king's court that in Kent there was no villeinage. There it could not exist, for every child was born free.[4] It may be that there is exaggeration in statements such as this[5]; but that they do not broadly represent the truth is not to be supposed, nor, on the other hand, is it easy to believe that there was a unique acceleration of the process of liberation in this corner of England, that the monks of Canterbury or of Rochester, let us say, had been less tenacious of their rights than monks elsewhere were wont to be. The more we probe Domesday classifications, the greater are our doubts whether they afford a basis for statistical comparisons, except occasionally of local changes; but otherwise only for comparisons of the most general and vaguest kind.[6] We do not doubt, however, that the *servi* of Kent as elsewhere represent for the most part the enslaved of past centuries and, using that as a key word, let us give an example of the kind of historical comparison, imprecise though it may be, which we think can usefully be made. In the Domesday Book of 1086 we find on the estates of St Paul's, London, *villani*, *bordarii*, *cotarii* and *servi*, while in the Domesday of St Pauls's of 1222 we find *tenentes* of various kinds, *cotarii* and *nativi*,[7] besides the occasional local descriptive names of *akermanni* and *hidarii*.

[1] See the map, based upon Ellis's figures, in Seebohm, *English Village Community*, facing p. 85. Sir F. Pollock's explanation, that there is a relation between the incidence of slavery and the survival of conquered British inhabitants, may have an element of truth (*Land Laws*, pp. 216-19). But there are reasons for supposing that the surviving British population in Kent was not inconsiderable: see below, Appendix I, pp. 159-61.

[2] We speak of a 'steward' because we find it impossible to believe that either the commissioners or the hundred juries were responsible for the returns in Domesday Book, whatever part they played in checking the information. There was no conceivable means in the eleventh century of ensuring uniformity in the answers (or returns) delivered to the commissioners. And what detailed information did a hundred-jury have? The inevitable inference is that the returns were in the first place made by or on behalf of the landowners concerned. Cf. *Governance of Mediaeval England*, p. 207*n*.

[3] Darby, *Domesday Geography: South East England*, p. 617.

[4] *Year Books, 30 & 31 Edward I*, p. 168; *33 Edward I*, p. 15. It is in the latter place that a Kentish ancestor established a man's freedom 'quia esset impossibile servum procreare liberum'.

[5] Somner, *Gavelkind*, pp. 73-5; Vinogradoff, *Villainage*, pp. 205-8; above, p. 51.

[6] As an example of the difficulties of classification, let us take *bovarius*, a ploughman. We can be certain that he was unfree and in Essex he is given the generic name of *servus*. But there are entries elsewhere where *servi* and *bovarii* are found upon the same manor. E.g. D.B. i. 172 a 2 (Garstone, etc.): Ibi ii. *servi* et vi. *bovarii*. At Huntington, Salop, iiii. *servi* has been corrected to iiii. *bovarii* (D.B. i. 256 b2). In these instances there must be a distinction. Is it occupational or social? For what seems evident confusion in classifying men as *servi*, *coliberti* and *villani* see Maitland's note in *Domesday Book and Beyond*, p. 34.

[7] *Domesday of St. Paul's*, pp. xxi-xxvi.

The nomenclature of 1086 will certainly no longer fit the conditions of 1222. Where earlier there had been a marked distinction between *villani* and *servi*, under Henry III men made no difference between *villanus*, *servus* and *nativus*. *Servus* had, in fact, lost its meaning, though lawyers still tried to employ the word as it was employed by Justinian.[1] We cannot doubt that, whatever setbacks there may at times have been, in a century and a half from the Conquest there had been a general advance in status, even though the distinctions between the classes had been maintained. A like social movement must, we think, have taken place in the century and a half preceding the Conquest. The masses of slaves postulated by the laws of Athelstan and Edmund are no longer to be found in 1086.[2] The Danish wars may have accelerated, rather than retarded, the movement towards freedom: we can but conjecture. But whatever the forces at work, the disabilities of the majority of the unfree seem unquestionably to have decreased. Even in the remote West the fully enslaved are but a comparatively small minority.[3]

In this continuous movement over three centuries legislation had played no part until the reign of John. What the position of the slave was under so humane a king as Alfred we have already remarked. He was treated with a barbarity that placed him below the level of common humanity.[4] But in 1205 it is insisted that the unfree without distinction – *servus*, *nativus*, *villanus*, call him what we will – shall, so long as he has the money to pay for them, bear arms on an equality with a freeman. If he is wealthy enough he has a duty to provide himself with the arms, and consequently the horse, of a knight.[5] This is perhaps only the legal recognition of economic and social facts; but of its significance there can be no doubt.

We may be thought to have lingered over-long in our discussion of John's legislation of 1205, but, before we pass to his later legislation, which became possible after the relaxation of the Interdict, we should perhaps notice two enactments, one of the least significance in itself and one of great importance, not, however, for England, but for Ireland. The first is a 'constitution' or 'assize' – it is given both titles – regulating the price of bread at Winchester.[6] This assize was made by

[1] Bracton provides an outstanding example in his adaptation of *Institutes*, lib. iii, tit. 28: see Richardson, *Bracton*, pp. 110-11. He is not, of course, consistent: see above, p. 142.

[2] Above, pp. 20-1.

[3] Ellis, *Introduction to Domesday Book*, pp. 432-84. About a fifth of the recorded population in Devon and Cornwall, nearly a quarter in Gloucestershire, less than a sixth in Somerset.

[4] Above, p. 16.

[5] For the knight who had been a villein see *Glanville*, lib. v, c. 5 (above, p. 116). Bracton's teaching appears to be theoretical: a knight cannot be claimed as a villein unless he has been degraded by judgement of the court (*De Legibus*, fol. 190*b*: Woodbine, iii.85). The implication is, of course, that a villein might become a knight. We must beware of the different connotations of *miles* in different contexts and at different periods. A knight of the mid-twelfth century and one of the mid-thirteenth century might be persons of very different status. Cf. *Governance of Mediaeval England*, pp. 100-1, 128-31. But we think that in 1150 the mere fact of bearing arms would imply freedom.

[6] *Rot. Litt. Pat.*, p. 41.

common counsel of the king's barons at Easter after the death of Queen Eleanor. But despite the solemnity with which it is clothed, this is a trivial regulation, doubtless devised to keep down the price of bread while the court was in the neighbourhood of Winchester,[1] a regulation with many forerunners.[2] Chance – for there can be no more than the vagary of a clerk to account for its enrolment – has preserved it on the patent roll; but it conveys a warning that, just as chance played its part in preserving a document of so little value, chance may have led, as it did in later reigns,[3] to the neglect of enactments of greater value and that we must admit the possibility that John legislated more frequently than surviving records disclose. This is indeed more than a possibility, as is shown by the other enactment we would mention here. In 1210 John took with him to Ireland 'men of discretion and learned in the law and, at the instance of the Irish, he commanded and established that English laws should be observed in Ireland'. The instrument which embodied this decision is found in no surviving enrolment and we know of it only by the reference to it we have cited from the patent roll of sixteen years later.[4]

We have said that the Interdict and the consequent absence of most of the bishops would in any case have prevented the consideration of legislation in England, even if John had had a mind for it. We have seen that legislation had in the past been largely the aftermath of times of crisis and, oddly perhaps, the Interdict of itself provoked no internal crisis. John's quarrel with the papacy evoked, in fact, a good deal of sympathy on the part of the barons towards the king and, though he managed to quarrel with some of the more prominent of them in the course of the years the Interdict endured, yet he could look back upon those years as a period of domestic tranquillity.[5] The situation was changed, in the first place by the conclusion of peace with Innocent III and secondly by the disaster of Bouvines, for although the king was not personally involved, the defeat of the emperor rendered vain all John's plans for the reconquest of Normandy and drove him back to England, a vanquished and dishonoured man. The bases of such support and sympathy as the barons had given him disappeared; and though he had made his peace with the papacy, he was far from an accord with Stephen Langton, over whose election to the see of Canterbury the quarrel with the Church had arisen. The root of the quarrel had been the king's claim to the right in law to determine the

[1] Where it was for a good many days in April and May 1204: see Hardy's *Itinerary* prefixed to *Rot. Litt. Pat.*

[2] Above, pp. 102-3.

[3] An excellent example is the earliest known legislation regarding the Jewry in 1233 (*L.Q.R.* liv.392-4; Richardson, *English Jewry*, pp. 293-4). It was largely a matter of chance in the thirteenth century whether legislation was enrolled or not: see Richardson and Sayles, *The Early Statutes*, pp. 6-21.

[4] *Patent Rolls, 1225-1232*, p. 96. Cf. Richardson and Sayles, *Irish Parliament in the Middle Ages*, pp. 12-15, 21-3.

[5] *Rot. Litt. Pat.*, p. 182: Cum comites et barones Anglie nobis devoti essent antequam nos et nostram terram dominio vestro subicere curassemus.

appointment of bishops. Langton had been elected in defiance of that claim, and the Interdict had resulted from John's insistence upon his right.[1] It may be well to recall certain words of the Constitutions of Clarendon which testify that John was making no novel claim: 'the election of archbishops, bishops, abbots and priors must be made in the king's chapel, with the king's assent and by the advice of those notabilities of the kingdom whom he shall appoint for this purpose'.[2] On more than one occasion before Langton's election Innocent had refused to recognise John's claim; but in 1213, while there was no formal abandonment by the pope of his opposition, yet one of the understandings upon which peace was concluded had been that the king should have his own way in filling episcopal vacancies. And to Langton's chagrin a cardinal, Nicholas of Tusculum, had been sent from Rome to fill vacant sees as the king desired.[3]

After John had returned, a beaten man, to England on 13 October 1214, Langton, believing apparently that the hour was now favourable, asked him to concede that the election of prelates should be freely made, that is the election of bishops and the heads of abbeys and priories of royal foundation. Consequently, at a prolonged meeting with the barons in November, the archbishop's request was, with their counsel, ostensibly granted.[4] In form, the king renounces any custom or right which prevented the free election of prelates, major and minor, but there are saving clauses which negative the apparent concession. The king retains the custody of vacant churches and monasteries; his licence must be obtained before an election takes place; and his approval is required to the person elected. It is true that there are verbal limitations upon the king's absolute discretion. He is not to refuse or delay his licence to elect, nor is he to refuse his approval to the person elected save for reasonable cause. But these are no more than words and, as succeeding centuries were to show, in the matter of appointing bishops, at least, the king's will prevailed. For we must distinguish between the appointment of bishops, which had a political significance, and the appointment of heads of religious houses. Kings in the past, and notably Henry II, had made and unmade abbots of royal monasteries as had seemed good to them.[5] But though the king might make bishops, he could not, as Henry himself declared, unmake them[6]; and no king could be indifferent to the selection of prominent members of his council, who, as past experience had shown, might

[1] *Governance of Mediaeval England*, pp. 338-47.

[2] Constitutions of Clarendon, cap. 12: Et cum ventum fuerit ad consulendum ecclesiae debet dominus rex mandare potiores personas ecclesiae et in capella ipsius domini regis debet fieri electio assensu domini regis et consilio personarum regni quas ad hoc faciendum vocaverit (*Select Charters*, p. 166). The deficiencies of this deplorable drafting we have endeavoured to explain above, p. 65. The sense is sufficiently clear.

[3] *Governance of Mediaeval England*, pp. 356-7.

[4] *Ibid.*, pp. 455-7.

[5] *Ibid.* p. 421.

[6] *Chronicon Mon. de Bello*, p. 91: Verissimum est episcopum non posse deponi. Henry continued 'sed ita, manibus pulsus pretensis, poterit expelli'.

prove to be thorns in his side. So while it is possible that the concession of free elections did mean less interference with the choice of heads of religious houses,[1] kings continued to have the first, as well as the final, word in the choice of most bishops, except only as the king's desires might have to be accommodated with the views of the pope as the system of papal provisions evolved. Royal influence was weakest under Henry III, but free election of bishops by their chapters there rarely was, save in quite exceptional circumstances.[2]

The charter is dated 31 November 1214, but it has a curious subsequent history. John, it would seem, desired to obtain papal confirmation of the charter, embodying a concordat that was all in his favour. Agreement to this end was secured at a great council in January 1215 and, in order to make it appear that there had been no delay in submitting the concordat to the pope, the date of the charter was altered to 15 January. After mature consideration Innocent confirmed the charter, much to John's satisfaction, and it was again confirmed by Magna Carta in June.[3] But all reference to it was omitted in subsequent issues of the Great Charter, on the first and second occasions, be it noted, with the approval of Cardinal Guala, the pope's representative.[4] Langton, of course, was still in exile on these occasions; but this is by the way. In view of its history we find it extremely difficult to understand how importance has come to be attached to a charter which conferred an illusory privilege upon the Church, a privilege, moreover, that was not confirmed in subsequent reigns. We cannot say that after John's reign it ceased to be law, for it had made no alteration in the law. It was never more than a simulacrum.

And so we come at last to John's Great Charter. It is, in truth, of far greater political interest than of legal interest, and unfortunately it has been so misrepresented by the fabricators of historical myth that its meaning, and especially its legal meaning, has been obscured. Of the political import of the Charter we need say nothing: we have said as much as is necessary elsewhere.[5] Of its legal import we need but say at this point two things. During what little remained of John's reign the Charter was of no effect because, after some insincere negotiations with the barons, he repudiated it. Consequently in law it was as though the Charter had never been.[6] It lived on, it is true, but in the first place as a political aspiration and then as a draft which, after successive revisions in Henry III's reign, attained definitive form in 1225,[7] the form in which it reached the Statute Book.

[1] *Governance of Mediaeval England*, p. 358.

[2] The whole question of the appointment of bishops under Henry III has been examined by Miss Gibbs and Miss Lang in *Bishops and Reform, 1215-1272*. Their conclusions on free elections are stated succinctly at pp. 92-3, 139-42.

[3] *Governance of Mediaeval England*, pp. 357-8.

[4] The variants are conveniently shown in McKechnie, *Magna Carta*, pp. 190, 497-9.

[5] *Governance of Mediaeval England*, pp. 383-8.

[6] *Ibid.*, pp. 389-90.

[7] Text in McKechnie, *Magna Carta*, pp. 497-508; Bémont, *Chartes des Libertés Anglaises*, pp. 45-60.

It is doubtless a platitude to remark that in order to understand the Charter in any of its successive versions, it is imperative to read the text. But quite clearly many of those who have commented upon the Charter have not read it with understanding. How else can we account for such grotesque misstatements as that the purpose of the barons in demanding the Charter was 'to undermine the whole fabric of the new judicial system'?[1] Both the Articles of the Barons, upon which the Charter is based, and the Charter itself are clamant in their insistence upon more and more royal justice. The barons' complaint was that the administration of justice had been the sport of the king's caprices: there had been arbitrary restrictions and interruptions in the functioning of the courts. The Bench at Westminster had, however, recently been reconstituted, and the barons demanded that it should be maintained there or at some other fixed place. They also demanded frequent and regular visitations by justices of assize. There is not the slightest ambiguity about these demands or about the terms of the Charter.[2] Any misinterpretation is due entirely to the interpreters, to that intellectual blindness which arises from preconceptions and the senseless repetition of attractive myths.[3]

A detailed discussion of the clauses of the Charter would not be very profitable unless we were to tell how in a revised form the Charter did become law: and that is a story we hope to tell in a later volume. As granted by King John, the Charter embraced transitory political provisions and trivialities as well as weighty general principles of law. Considered as a statute, it may well be thought to be ill-constructed and ill-drafted, not such an instrument as a skilled lawyer would prepare. But this is to view the Charter, the original Charter, in a wrong light. It is, as contemporaries called it, a *concordia*, a *forma pacis*, in modern language a treaty: as such it is intended to be inclusive of grievances, great and small, and it results in a disorderly jumble of unco-ordinated demands.[4] Yet one note runs through it: the re-establishment of the rule of law. At an early stage in their negotiations with the king, the barons had made this demand, but they had put it in the form of a demand that Henry I's coronation charter should be observed.[5] They could hardly have meant that the laws of Edward the Confessor should be enforced. The law the barons wanted was the law

[1] These words were used by Sir Maurice Powicke to summarise the views of one school of historians: they do not represent, as he supposed, the views of G. B. Adams. See our note in *Governance of Mediaeval England*, p. 388.

[2] With chapters 17-19 and 40 of the Charter of 1215 compare the Articles of the Barons, cc. 8, 13, 30, and see our commentary in *Governance of Mediaeval England*, pp. 383-7.

[3] There has been a curious combination of the denigration of the baronial leaders and a hagiographical cult of Langton, both in defiance of the evidence, as we have pointed out in *Governance of Mediaeval England*, pp. 338, 349-54, 368-71.

[4] *Ibid.*, p. 361.

[5] *Histoire des Ducs de Normandie*, pp. 145-6. The anonymous author of this work, the 'Minstrel of Béthune', was in John's service and is a strictly contemporary witness. Wendover's apocryphal story of Langton's 'discovery' of Henry I's charter, absurd as it may be, is in its way confirmation of the Minstrel's statement that the barons' demands were based upon Henry's charter. The canon of Barnwell more directly confirms his statement (Walter of Coventry, *Memoriale*, ii. 215).

that had been built up with their concurrence, step by step, in the twelfth century, the law embodied in *Glanville*. But Henry I's charter was the most widely known of any political document at the time: it circulated in both Latin and French.[1] If in its terms it expressed the needs of a bygone day, the principle underlying it was as pertinent in 1214 as in 1100: it guaranteed the barons against arbitrary rule and it restored to them accustomed and established law. They wished John to say, as Henry had said: 'I will do away with all the evil customs with which the kingdom of England has been unlawfully oppressed . . . I establish firm peace throughout the kingdom and I order that it shall henceforth be kept'.[2] And though in the Articles of the Barons and in the Great Charter there is no word of Henry I or of the laws of the Confessor, nevertheless it might well be claimed that the Charter expressed the spirit of Henry's charter in contemporary terms.

But the Great Charter has another significance. It is a landmark in the history of legislative procedure. Hitherto all legislation had been from above. It is true that the Constitutions of Clarendon had been debated with what we may perhaps call the episcopal opposition before they reached their statutory form[3]; but, as the assizes of 1166 and 1176 were to be, so the Constitutions had been legislation from above, whatever counsel the king may have taken beforehand with ministers and magnates, whatever assent he had wrung from the bishops subsequently. The Great Charter creates a new pattern. The king may have refused to accept it as law in 1215; but the Articles of the Barons are yet the basis of the Great Charter of 1216 and the revisions of 1217 and 1225. That pattern must have been in the minds of the barons of a later generation when they presented to the king the petitions that resulted in the Provisions of Oxford; and though the great Edwardian statutes were legislation from above, legislation based upon petition from below became the characteristic form of parliamentary law-making in the fourteenth century.

Yet, though we may see in the Charter of 1215 the harbinger of a new era, let us remember that the new era was brought to birth by the death of King John, who had followed to the grave his friend and defender Pope Innocent III. Had their will prevailed, the old era would have persisted and the Great Charter would have come down to us, if it had come at all, as a historical curiosity. It is, therefore, not without justification that we end our present story here, even though

[1] When Liebermann established the text of the charter he was able to draw upon no less than twenty-eight manuscripts representing early copies (*Trans. R. Hist. Soc.*, N.S., viii.21-48). The charter had originally been circulated to every county (*ibid.*, p. 22). The French text was printed by Liebermann, *ibid.*, pp. 46-8: the date he assigns to it (p. 37) is, in our view, much too late.

[2] Et omnes malas consuetudines quibus regnum Anglie iniuste opprimebatur inde aufero. . . . Pacem firmam in toto regno meo pono et teneri amodo precipio (Coronation Charter, cc. 1 and 12). Henry must have made much the same declaration verbally at his coronation (*Traditio*, xvi.163-5).

[3] Above, p. 65.

we end at a point where we seem to be beginning a new chapter that should tell how the Great Charter did finally become law and the foundation of our Statute Book. Clio's web is indeed endless and seamless, but the pattern changes, and the *tempus guerrae* which endured from Easter 1215 to Michaelmas 1217 marks a great break in the pattern. When we resume our narrative we shall be telling a new story.

APPENDIXES

BIBLIOGRAPHY

INDEXES

APPENDIX I

KENT UNDER ÆTHELBERHT

In the sixth and seventh centuries Kent was on much the same level of civilisation as Merovingian Gaul. It seems probable that the 'Jutish' invaders of Kent had included a no slight proportion of Franks[1] and that Hengist and his successors had maintained close relations with the Franks across the Channel. The easy communications ensured by the narrow seas meant that Kent was nearer in time to northern Gaul than to any but the nearest English kingdoms and much nearer in culture, and it should occasion no surprise to find English moneyers at work in Quentovic in the sixth century.[2] It is clear that Eormenric, king of the Kentish people (†565)[3] had been in close diplomatic contact with Charibert, king of the Franks (†567), and it is well to remember that, when Augustine landed in Thanet, a Frankish bishop had been in residence at the Kentish court for more than thirty years,[4] where, it is evident, he was highly honoured and where he struck gold coins in his own name.[5] The speech of the Kentings and of the Franks was so nearly allied that they had little difficulty in understanding one another,[6] less difficulty probably than a Londoner today experiences in grasping Lowland Scots. To an Italian both Franks and Kentings were doubtless barbarians; but the fears of Augustine and his companions at the prospect of a journey to Britain[7] are evidence, not of the isolation or rudeness of Kent, but rather of the isolation and ignorance of the Romans. Nor must we assume without question that Christianity implied any cultural superiority over paganism. Though Gaul was nominally Christian, its rulers did not feel the aversion from the worship of idols that Bede, for example, did. If Christ was a superior god, He was just a god among other gods.[8] Nor did conversion to Christianity mean a revolution in manners or morals among the people at large. What Christianity meant to the Franks is abundantly

[1] Hawkes, 'The Jutes in Kent' in *Dark-Age Britain*, pp. 91-111.

[2] Sutherland, *Anglo-Saxon Gold Coinage*, p. 27, *n.* 4.

[3] Bede's date, 560, for the accession of Æthelberht (*Historia Ecclesiastica*, lib. ii, c. 5: Plummer, i.89), which seems to be generally accepted, must be rejected on chronological grounds: see below, p. 165. There seems no reason to question the date in the Anglo-Saxon Chronicle (Thorpe, i.30-1; Plummer, i.19).

[4] Assuming that he came over with Bertha in 565 or an earlier year (below, p. 165). Miss Deanesly suggests that he was dead or a very aged man in 597 (*Augustine of Canterbury*, p. 30). But this is on the assumption that a strict canonical rule for the consecration of bishops was observed by the Merovingian Franks – which seems unlikely.

[5] For the 'Leudardus' coin or 'medalet' see below, p. 159, n. 6.

[6] See Plummer's note on Bede, *Historia Ecclesiastica*, lib. i, c. 25, in vol. ii, p. 41. His argument is strengthened by the archaeological evidence (Hawkes, *loc. cit.*).

[7] Bede, *Hist. Eccl.*, lib. i, c. 24 (Plummer, i.42-3).

[8] We cite the example of Raedwald: below, p. 166.

depicted by Gregory of Tours. Unfortunately there was no contemporary writer in Kent to depict the manners of his countrymen, and the impression we get of a better ordered and more peaceful country, at least during the long reign of Æthelberht, may be mistaken. The glimpse we have later of Kent in the last quarter of the seventh century, torn by a bloody feud between King Hlothere and his nephew Eadric,[1] suggests that only under an exceptionally strong and able ruler were peace and order likely to be maintained. Bede's story of Queen Æthelburh's fear, fifty years earlier, lest her husband Edwin's son and grandson should be murdered by Oswald of Northumbria, with the connivance of her own brother King Eadbald,[2] is only too like an echo from Gregory of Tours. As we have said, Kent and Merovingian Gaul were on much the same level of civilisation.

This common level of the two countries is best illustrated by the numismatic evidence which has hardly yet reached the textbooks.[3] This shows that Kent and Gaul had an interchangeable gold currency in the sixth and seventh centuries and, as we have already mentioned, that English moneyers worked in Gaul, while it seems not unlikely that Frankish moneyers worked in Kent. The authority under which the moneyers worked is imperfectly understood. The acceptance of their coins on both sides of the Channel depended upon the maintenance of a recognised standard, and the moneyers were primarily goldsmiths. Some issues appear, however, to have been made under the authority of King Eadbald.[4] Minting coins of recognisable types and with intelligible inscriptions implies not only a relatively high degree of culture but a certain standard of literacy. Without central control over dies, there will, however, inevitably be degenerate coin-types and meaningless inscriptions, the unskilful imitations of standard (or generally acceptable) coins by illiterate workers: and provided these copies are of the requisite weight and fineness – and even if they fall short – they will pass. But it nevertheless remains true that the better coins imply both literacy and skilled craftmanship.

The idea, which seems to be current, that in some unexplained way the mission under Augustine introduced the Kentings to the knowledge of the Roman alphabet, and so led to the transition of Anglo-Saxon from a spoken to a written language, involves a series of improbable assumptions. Some would apparently assert that the Roman clergy were wholly responsible.[5] The weighty and, as it seems to us, conclusive arguments against such a view we have already stated. Such an

[1] Bede, *Hist. Eccl.*, lib. v, c. 26 (Plummer, i.268).

[2] *Ibid.*, lib. ii, c. 20 (Plummer, i.125-6).

[3] An exception is Loyn, *Anglo-Saxon England and the Norman Conquest*, pp. 73-4.

[4] For this paragraph see Sutherland, *op. cit.* For the antecedents see his paper 'Coinage in Britain in the Fifth and Sixth Centuries' in *Dark-Age Britain*, pp. 3-10.

[5] E.g. Whitelock, *English Historical Documents*, p. 327: 'but it was not until after the adoption of Christianity that any of this mass of legal custom was written down'. This is a restatement of Plummer's words: above, p. 1. Whence the Roman clergy acquired their knowledge of the pagan runic alphabet is not explained.

achievement, moreover, could hardly have failed to have been recorded, for it would have rivalled the work of Ulfilas in devising the Gothic alphabet. Yet Bede knows nothing of it nor have any religious vernacular writings survived from so early a period. Bede does tell us of Bishop Felix (†647) who, at the instance of Sigeberht, king of the East Angles, founded schools after the manner of the Kentings; but he makes no suggestion that these Kentish schools owed anything to Augustine.[1] His silence seems very significant. Can there be the least likelihood that he would have denied the credit to Augustine if credit were due? On the other hand there is hardly room for doubt that the Kentings, whatever their origin, were, like other related Germanic tribes, acquainted with the runic alphabet when in the fifth century they made themselves masters of East Kent.[2] The numismatic evidence indicates that by the sixth century they had become acquainted with the Roman alphabet.[3] And while no English written document remains from the sixth and seventh century, the characteristics of the English script, though owing something perhaps to contact with the surviving British Christians, are likely to have been largely determined by contact with the Franks. That the runic characters wyn and thorn were introduced from Frankland seems, however, out of the question.[4] When King Chilperic wished to enlarge the Latin alphabet with symbols for sounds not adequately represented there, he ordered the use of four characters which Gregory of Tours calls Greek but which may, in fact, be runes, though not of a type otherwise known.[5] This reform seems, however, to have been abortive. It would appear therefore that the introduction of runes into the insular script was a device of the Kentings themselves. They were, it would appear, using runes as well as the Latin alphabet on their coins in the sixth century.[6] We have already set out the arguments which permit the inference that, long before Augustine, English was being written in Kent. This was

[1] *Hist. Eccl.*, lib. iii, c. 18 (Plummer, i.162).

[2] There is an extensive literature on the origin and evolution of the runic alphabets: a convenient summary is Elliott, *Runes: an Introduction* (1959), with bibliography.

[3] Runic inscriptions are also found on coins minted in England (Sutherland, *op. cit.*, *passim*; Elliott, *op. cit.*, pp. 77-8).

[4] The Kentish laws are written in the *Textus Roffensis* in the later insular script, which employs runic characters. Though more than 500 years distant from the original text of the laws of Æthelberht, the indication is that his scribes used the same runes. Otherwise, if only Roman characters had been employed, it seems quite unlikely that any copyist would have troubled to convert 'w' and 'th' into the corresponding runes. The more recent printed texts (but not Hearne, Wilkins or Thorpe) convert 'wyn' into 'w' and are therefore misleading, for, curiously enough, they preserve 'thorn'. The facsimile edition by Sawyer makes verification easy. For the first page of Æthelberht's laws in the *Textus Roffensis* see our frontispiece.

[5] *Historia Francorum*, lib. v, c. 44. For these characters, see Arntz, *Handbuch der Runenkunde*, pp. 116, 249*n*.

[6] This assumes that the *tremisses* of Merovingian type, but with runic inscriptions, are correctly assigned to Kent: see preceding note 3. Some runes are found on Merovingian gravestones (Arntz, *op. cit.*, p. 116). There is also a form of L on some Merovingian coins, and in particular on the Leudardus 'medalet', which may represent a runic character for l, though it resembles the character for n. Cf. Evans in *Numismatic Chronicle*, ser. vi, vol. ii, 25-6, and Sutherland, *op. cit.*, pl. 1.

presumably on papyrus,[1] and probably in a Merovingian hand. The Kentings could not have been unacquainted with the schools of Gaul. It was during his exile there that the East Anglian Sigeberht came to appreciate learning, and they were schools on the Frankish model that he wished to introduce into his own kingdom.[2] Bishop Felix found them nearer at home – in Kent. Any writing, such as was practised in Kent in the sixth century, has, however, long ago perished and any trace of Merovingian influence has, in any case, been swept away by the triumph of the insular English script. One cannot therefore clinch the argument with a demonstration, but we are not the first to come to much the same conclusion as that to which we have been led. Long ago John Earle saw the difficulty of ascribing the literacy of the Kentings to Augustine's mission. 'Perhaps', he said, 'it is most reasonable to suppose that the adoption of the Roman alphabet was very gradual and that the Saxons may have begun to use it, at least in Kent, before the reign of Æthelberht.'[3]

It might be thought that Augustine and the other early bishops of the English church would wish to obtain written evidence of the grants made to them by Æthelberht and, indeed, in later centuries it was pretended that copies of Æthelberht's charters could be produced. But these are, without exception, fabrications, based upon Bede's narrative and later practice,[4] and it is now generally agreed that English royal charters do not go back beyond the time of Theodore of Tarsus, who became archbishop of Canterbury in 668.[5] He, or members of his entourage, adapted the current Roman written forms to hitherto unwritten English practice, obtained the approval of rulers and benefactors to their use, and so gave England landbooks and book-land. With what ceremonial forms, if any, Æthelberht's grants to Augustine and his companions were clothed is quite unknown, nor can we be at all certain that he had any thought that he was alienating land either by the erection of churches or by the endowment of the clergy, if indeed this happened. Such an idea as making a grant to a saint – embodied in the least implausible of the spurious charters fathered upon him[6] – was, we may be sure, beyond his comprehension, even though precedents may be found in Italy[7] and though such formulas may conceivably have been known to members of the Roman mission.

[1] Papyrus would also be used by the Roman mission as it was by the Roman curia, and the papal letters to Æthelberht and Bertha were doubtless on papyrus. But the Merovingian kings also used papyrus, though little has been preserved, the earliest specimen apparently being from 625. For a brief account see Giry, *Manuel de diplomatique*, p. 494. It is quite likely that the Kentish laws were written in uncials on parchment, since they were intended for permanent reference.

[2] Bede, *Hist. Eccl.*, lib. iii, c. 18, *ut supra*.

[3] Earle, *Anglo-Saxon Literature*, p. 78.

[4] Levison, *England and the Continent in the Eighth Century*, pp. 174-225.

[5] *Ibid.*, p. 232; Stenton, *Latin Charters of the Anglo-Saxon Period*, p. 31.

[6] In favour of St Andrew's, Rochester. It was accepted as genuine by Kemble and by Earle, who gives the best text of it (*Land Charters*, pp. 3-4). It is no. 3 in Birch, *Cartularium Saxonicum*.

[7] Levison, *op. cit.*, pp. 223-5.

There is no evidence that in the formulation of English charters, any more than in the formulation of English laws, Augustine and his companions had the slightest influence. Any such suggestion rests upon the assumption that Æthelberht was baptised in 597 and that his conversion led, in turn, to the adoption of Roman practices, Latin charters, Italian script, grammar schools, foreign craftsmen. . . . Actually, the situation of the missionary bishops was uncertain and insecure, their influence small. Bede's story of their resolution after Æthelberht's death teaches a plain lesson. 'They would return to their own country, where they could freely serve the Lord, rather than reside without profit among barbarians who rejected the faith.'[1]

The archaeological evidence, which has been interpreted as demonstrating the dependence of the mission on the resources of the Mediterranean world, appears on the contrary to testify to the level of culture in Kent and to indicate that here, if nowhere else in England, something of Roman-British craftsmanship survived. Such remains of Kentish churches as can be ascribed to the late sixth or early seventh century are romanesque and have their nearest parallel in the Roman-British church excavated at Silchester.[2] To account for this similarity it has been suggested that masons were imported from Gaul or Italy.[3] That Frankish masons were better than Kentish we may perhaps doubt. But that masons should be brought from southern Gaul or from Italy seems the wildest of improbabilities. How workmen from these distant countries could be recruited and who would recruit them or what inducement could be offered them to make such a long, toilsome and hazardous journey are essential questions neither asked nor answered. Apparently there were no skilled masons at the time in Northumbria and, in their absence, Edwin, a generation later, erected a timber church[4] – an obvious alternative, equally available in Kent but rejected in favour of masonry. The necessary inference is that there were skilled masons in Kent in the sixth century, as evidently there must have been when, after the church of St Peter and St Paul had been completed by his successor, Laurence, a tomb was erected over Augustine's final resting-place.[5] This conclusion lends plausibility to the suggestion that not only were there in Kent a good many descendants of the British population, but that the practice of the Christian religion had survived among them. They may have been too poor to keep their churches in good repair; but if Bede's testimony is worth anything, it means that some of the churches were in such a state that

[1] *Hist. Eccl.*, lib. ii, c. 5 (Plummer, i.91-2).

[2] This seems first to have been pointed out by Sir Charles Peers (*Antiquity*, iii.65-74).

[3] Clapham, *English Romanesque Architecture before the Conquest*, p. 25. His second chapter, 'Church building under the Heptarchy', pp. 16-38, is a fuller survey than Peers'. It groups with the Kentish churches those at Bradwell, Essex, ascribed to Cedd 'after 653', and at Brixworth, Northants, 'about 670'. The problem whence the masons came in these cases is not canvassed.

[4] *Hist. Eccl.*, lib. ii, c. 14 (Plummer, i.114).

[5] *Ibid.*, lib. i, c. 33; lib. ii, c. 3 (Plummer, i.75, 86).

they could be restored to meet Roman standards of worship.[1] This inference is borne out by what Bede tells us of the church of St Martin in which Queen Bertha worshipped and which was made available to the Roman mission.[2] The dedication shows that the church was a fifth-century edifice.[3] The fact that the dedication was remembered points to continuous worship. It seems extravagant in any case to suppose that repairs would have been feasible to humble structures that had been abandoned for a century and a half to the ravages of the English climate, even if the remains had still been distinguishable. The survival of a depressed Christian community of British origin among the Kentings would lend some colour of truth to Augustine's otherwise incredible statement that at Christmas 597 he had baptised more than 10,000 converts.[4] It will be remembered that under Æthelberht there were not – as happened later elsewhere – wholesale forcible conversions to ensure that large numbers of nominal catechumens were available for the rite.[5]

We are brought at this point to the question of Æthelberht's conversion. We have conscientiously examined and can but reject the generally accepted story because it is in conflict with the available evidence. If this involves also the rejection of Bede's story, we are but following in the footsteps of the most distinguished of Bede's editors, Charles Plummer, who found reason for doubt or disagreement in a good many passages of the *Ecclesiastical History*. Great as is our debt to Bede, we must remember that he was writing more than a century after the event and that he could do nothing else than put what seemed to him a plausible interpretation upon such documents as came to his hand and such hearsay evidence as could be supplied by his correspondents. On some matters we are better informed than he was, for we possess not merely a few letters of Gregory the Great, but a quite extensive correspondence. This shows conclusively that by June 601 no news of Æthelberht's baptism had reached Rome. The accepted date, 2 June 597, rests upon no better authority than that of Thomas of Elmham, a monk of St Augustine's, Canterbury, who was writing in the fifteenth century.[6] Bede appears to give, doubtless *per incuriam*, the impossible date of 595 for Æthelberht's reception of the faith,[7] and his assertion that Æthelberht was converted can be no more than an

[1] Bede's words are (*Hist. Eccl.*, lib. i, c. 26): 'donec rege ad fidem converso maiorem praedicandi per omnia et ecclesias fabricandi vel restaurandi licentiam acciperent' (Plummer, i.47; and see his note on the construction of churches, ii.101-2).

[2] *Hist. Eccl.*, lib. i, c. 26 (p. 47).

[3] See Plummer's note, *ibid.*, ii.43. On this and two other Canterbury churches of Roman-British origin, see M. Deanesly, *Augustine of Canterbury*, pp. 36-7.

[4] Pope Gregory can be only repeating Augustine's statement when he gives this figure in July 598 to Eulogius, bishop of Alexandria (*Gregorii I Registrum*, ii.31; Haddan and Stubbs, *Councils*, iii.12).

[5] *Hist. Eccl.*, lib. i, c. 26 (Plummer, i.47). For wholesale forcible conversion see Plummer's notes, ii.44, 105.

[6] Elmham, *Hist. Mon. S. Augustini Cantuariensis*, p. 137.

[7] *Hist. Eccl.*, lib. ii, c. 5 (Plummer, i.90): 'Defunctus . . . post xx et unum annos acceptae fidei'.

inference[1] – an inference made without access to the pope's letter to Queen Bertha of June 601, which puts the king's baptism by that date, or at any time, very much in doubt,[2] for though Gregory's correspondence continues until 604, Æthelberht and Bertha drop out of it entirely, explain this silence how we may. Bertha indeed may have died not very long after June 601, before Gregory himself died in 604. It seems certain that, left a widower, Æthelberht married a young pagan woman, who, we have good reason to believe, was the daughter of an English royal house.[3] She followed pagan customs and on Æthelberht's death in 616 married his son Eadbald, himself, significantly enough, a pagan.[4] Upon his conversion, which had apparently taken place by 624, Eadbald repudiated her and married a Frankish, that is to say a Christian, princess.[5]

Æthelberht's second marriage and Eadbald's paganism tell very strongly against Bede's assumption that Æthelberht was baptised or was ever indeed a true convert. There are indeed some pieces of evidence apparently telling in favour of Bede's hypothesis: a letter of Boniface IV to Æthelberht; the inscription on Augustine's tomb; Æthelberht's sepulture in a consecrated building; and the faith of Æthelberht's daughter. Let us examine them. All we know of the papal letter is what Bede tells us, that in 610 Mellitus brought back with him from Rome a letter to Æthelberht and the people of England[6]: a letter purporting to be this is manifestly a fabrication[7] and is evidence that nothing was known of the original at Canterbury. Since Bede gives no hint of its contents, we may be sure that he did not find it useful or informative. Just as in 601 Pope Gregory wrote to Æthelberht,[8] who seems certainly not then to have been baptised, so we cannot assume that, when Pope Boniface wrote to him, at the instance of Mellitus, in 610, the king had been baptised in the interval. The inscription on Augustine's tomb, cut long after his death when apparently the year had been forgotten, stated, according to Bede, that Augustine 'Aedilbertcum regem ac gentem illius ab idolorum cultu ad

[1] *Ibid.*, lib. i, c. 26 (Plummer, i.47).

[2] For the pope's letter to Bertha see *Registrum*, ii.304-5 (Haddan and Stubbs, *Councils*, iii.17-18). The evidence has been examined minutely by S. Brechter, who reaches the conclusion that this letter shows that 'im Juni 601 war König Ethelbert noch nicht getauft' (*Die Quellen zur Angelsachsenmission Gregors des Grossen*, pp. 240-6: the words quoted are at p. 247, *n.* 132). Miss Deanesly must have misunderstood Archabbot Brechter when she attributes to him the belief that 'Æthelberht's baptism had taken place, probably at Easter 601' (*Pre-Conquest Church in England*, p. 49). Mr R. A. Markus has attempted to controvert Brechter (*Journal of Ecclesiastical History*, xiv.16-30). Mr Markus believes – and we agree – that the pope's letter to Bertha was probably unknown to Bede (p. 21); but he seems hardly to appreciate how damaging Bede's ignorance is to his credibility.

[3] So far as we have information, English kings appear invariably to have married women of royal blood: they must have been numerous (cf. Chadwick, *The Heroic Age*, p. 380*n*).

[4] *Hist. Eccl.*, lib. ii, c. 5 (Plummer, i.90: and see his note at ii.88).

[5] Emma, daughter of the king of the Franks (Florence of Worcester, *Chronicon*, i.259, whence William of Malmesbury, *Gesta Regum*, i.15).

[6] *Hist. Eccl.*, lib. ii, c. 4 (Plummer, i.88).

[7] Elmham, *op. cit.*, p. 86.

[8] *Registrum*, ii.308-10; Haddan and Stubbs, *Councils*, iii.30-1.

Christi fidem perduxit'.[1] Since the claim that Augustine had converted the Kentish people is, on Bede's own showing, false or, at least, grossly exaggerated, the claim that Æthelberht was converted may be no more reliable. It is true that an earlier writer than Bede, a Whitby monk, had asserted that Æthelberht had been 'ad fidem Christi correctus',[2] but he was merely repeating the tradition already recorded on Augustine's tomb. We have Bede's word for it that Æthelberht's tomb was in the south *porticus* of the church of St Peter and St Paul, where he lay beside Bertha.[3] But Bertha's body had, almost certainly, lain outside the church until the *porticus* was finished and consecrated. Thomas of Elmham indeed states so positively, and though his stories are largely fictional, there seems no need to call this statement into question.[4] He also states that Bishop Liudhard's body was similarly translated,[5] but this, unfortunately, can hardly be more than a pious guess, for Bede knows nothing of the tradition. So far as Æthelberht is concerned, it seems unlikely that his pagan wife and his pagan son and successor would wish for a Christian burial at a time when the very future of Christianity in Kent was trembling in the balance. On the other hand, the Canterbury monks would, when more prosperous times came, wish the south *porticus* of their church to be a royal burying place.[6] The balance of probabilities points to a later translation of Æthelberht's body. His tomb is no sure evidence of his faith.

The story of Æthelberht's daughter affords an excellent illustration of the difficulties which confronted Bede, and still confront us, in seeking to arrive at some certainty in interpreting the evidence. The daughter, Æthelburh, was a Christian[7] and is said to have been a virgin when in 625 she was married to the pagan king of the Northumbrians, Edwin. Who was her mother? Because of her faith she has been taken to be the daughter of Bertha. But when was Bertha and when was Æthelburh born? For some knowledge of Bertha's life we have a better authority than Bede, namely Gregory of Tours, who was acquainted with her mother, Ingoberg, in her old age. Gregory believed Ingoberg to be about seventy when she died in 589, so we may put the date of her birth at approximately the year 520.[8] Her only child, Bertha, was married to Æthelberht before he had succeeded his father as king of the Kentish people.[9] There seem to be no grounds for disputing the date, 565, given for his accession in the Anglo-Saxon

[1] *Hist. Eccl.*, lib. ii, c. 3 (Plummer, i.86).

[2] The Life of Gregory the Great, appended to Plummer's edition of *Hist. Eccl.*, ii.290.

[3] *Hist. Eccl.*, lib. ii, c. 5 (Plummer, i.90).

[4] Elmham, *op. cit.*, p. 132.

[5] *Loc. cit.*

[6] Bede's words imply that this was the intention from the beginning; but he must be reading history backwards (*Hist. Eccl.*, lib. i, c. 33: Plummer, i.70).

[7] We have contemporary evidence in the letter to her from Boniface v (*Hist. Eccl.*, lib. ii, c. 11: Plummer, i.104).

[8] Gregory of Tours, *Historia Francorum*, lib. iv, c. 19; lib. ix, c. 26 (pp. 125, 377).

[9] Gregory's words in the latter passage are conclusive: 'relinquens filiam unicam quam in Chancia regis cuiusdam filius matrimonio copulavit'. This was pointed out by Sir

Chronicle.[1] Clearly a marriage in the period 560-565 fits in well enough with the other data we have, except perhaps the date given in the Chronicle for Æthelberht's birth, 552,[2] though a political marriage, for such it evidently was, when Æthelberht was twelve or so and Bertha perhaps nearly twenty is not at all unlikely. That Bertha was born between 540 and 550 seems, in any case, an inevitable inference.

At this point we begin to run into our difficulties. In applying to Æthelburh the description *virgo*, Bede seems to write as though she was, at the time of her marriage, still a girl and this impression is confirmed when we learn that she bore Edwin four children between 625 and 633.[3] In the absence of any evidence to the contrary we should suppose that she was born in the early years of the seventh century. But by then Bertha must have been about sixty. We are never directly told that Æthelburh was Bertha's daughter; but that she was allied to the Frankish royal house is hardly open to question, since after Edwin's death she sent the children of her family for safety to King Dagobert, her *amicus*, by which must be meant her kinsman.[4] That she was the child of Æthelberht's second marriage seems impossible, since we are expressly told that Eadbald's second wife was Frankish and therefore Christian, the necessary inference being that his first wife (and stepmother) was English, while her (to Christians) incestuous marriage to Eadbald shows that she was pagan.[5] It is hardly necessary to adduce the further consideration that, if Æthelburh had been the daughter of a pagan mother and a dubiously Christian father and the sister of a pagan brother, it is quite unlikely that she should have been brought up as a Christian.

We do not pretend to have the material for resolving the doubts and difficulties left by the available sources. What seems quite certain is that Bede was reduced to guessing from very inadequate premises and that he is no infallible guide. Moreover, for all his honesty of purpose, he had a weakness for hagiography. There is an apt illustration in his

[1] Both Bede and the Anglo-Saxon Chronicle, which depends, of course, largely on Bede, are hopelessly at variance with themselves. Bede gives the year of Æthelberht's death as 616 and says that he reigned 56 years (*Hist. Eccl.*, lib. ii, c. 5: Plummer, i.89). The Anglo Saxon Chronicle E, *s.a.* 616, copies this statement (Thorpe, i.41; Plummer, i.22-3), though F gives the length of the reign as 53 years. Hence the year 560 commonly accepted as the beginning of the reign. But *s.a.* 565 the Chronicles E and F both give this year as the commencement of Æthelred's reign and say that he reigned 53 years (Thorpe, i.31; Plummer, i.19). This would make the year of his death 618. The probability is that he reigned 51 years, but no satisfactory explanation has been given of the discrepancies.

[2] Chron. F only (Thorpe, i.29; Plummer, i.17). This date is independent of Bede and is the more to be trusted.

[3] *Hist. Eccl.*, lib. ii, cc. 9, 14 (Plummer, i.97-9, 114.)

[4] *Ibid.*, lib. ii, c. 20 (Plummer, i.125-6: and see his note at ii.117).

[5] Above, p. 163.

Arthur Evans in *Numismatic Chronicle*, ser. vi, vol. ii, p. 24. The consequences do not seem to have been appreciated by English historians, who suggest a misleadingly late date for the marriage: cf. Stenton, *Anglo-Saxon England*, p. 105, 'Before 588 Æthelberht . . . had married Bertha'.

story of Paulinus. To justify the pagan-Christian marriage of Edwin and Æthelburh, Bede duplicates the story of the conditions imposed when Bertha married Æthelberht and gives Æthelburh a bishop, Paulinus, as companion, just as Bertha had Bishop Liudhard for companion. This is the kind of duplication that is always suspect.[1] The miraculous elements introduced later into the story do not increase one's confidence in its veracity.

In our endeavour to reconstruct, as best we can, the cultural environment in which were promulgated the first known vernacular English laws we may appear to be unduly sceptical; but, in the absence of corroboration, it seems quite impossible to accept Bede's interpretation of the course of Kentish history in the sixth and seventh century. Where we have better evidence – and we have evidence unknown to Bede – we must accept it, even though it means the rejection of a story familiar and dear to many of us. That Æthelberht was tolerant, and perhaps sympathetic, towards Christianity we do not doubt, nor that he would wish to gratify Bertha. It is evident that at Rome there was great hope that Christian wives would influence pagan husbands.[2] But pagan wives doubtless wielded their influence also. Æthelberht's conversion is, on such evidence as we have, very much in doubt. His attitude may indeed have been ambiguous. We must remember that there were those who, like Rædwald, king of the East Angles, thought it not impossible both to serve Christ and to remain faithful to the gods of their fathers. Perhaps Æthelberht, like Rædwald, was in his later years seduced by his pagan wife and became less friendly towards Christianity.[3] This might better explain the revulsion from the new religion which, according to Bede, marked the accession of Eadbald, who, for his sin, was afflicted by Heaven with fits of insanity.[4] Perhaps we may permit ourselves the comment that, insane or not, it would have been graceful to credit him, pagan though he was, with the same tolerance that his father had shown in permitting the continuance of a cult he himself rejected.

The concluding section of the laws attributed to Hlothere and Eadric raises the problem of the position of the Kentish kings in London,[5] and we venture to re-open the question. It may be best to state our tentative conclusions at the outset. The Middle Saxons, perhaps the obscurest of all the early groups of invaders, seem never to have obtained possession of the city,[6] which came under the authority

[1] Compare 'ut ritum fidei ac religionis suae cum episcopo' (*Hist. Eccl.*, lib. i, c. 25) with 'ut fidem cultumque suae religionis. . . . Itaque . . . ordinatur episcopus' (*ibid.*, lib. ii, c. 9: Plummer i.45, 98).

[2] As witness Pope Gregory's letter to Bertha (above, p. 163, *n.* 2) and the letter from Boniface v to Æthelburh (*Eccl. Hist.*, lib. ii, c. 11: Plummer i.104-6). The latter has a charming touch: the pope reinforced his admonitions with presents of a silver mirror and a gold-mounted ivory comb.

[3] For Rædwald see *Hist. Eccl.*, lib. ii, c. 15 (Plummer, i.116).

[4] *Ibid.*, lib. ii, c. v (Plummer, i.90-1).

[5] Above, pp. 10, 12.

[6] The evidence of Saxon burials adduced by Sir Mortimer Wheeler is as conclusive as archaeological evidence can be (*London and the Saxons*, pp. 54-5).

of the Kentish kings at the end of the fifth or the beginning of the sixth century. Nor did London form part of the territory of the East Saxons, another obscure people. That the bishop of the East Saxons had a church in London was due to the historical accident that, in consequence of a marriage alliance, Sæberht, the king of the East Saxons, was exercising there authority delegated to him by Æthelberht. The East Saxon kings do not seem to have had sovereignty over London at any time, and it would have been a most unsuitable place from which to administer their kingdom. That their residence in London was exceptional is suggested by Bede's words in which he speaks of *urbs Lundoniae in qua tunc ipse [Sebbi] manebat*. Sebbi, who was king of the East Saxons under Wulfhere of Mercia, was then infirm and was ending his days in pious retirement.[1] Nor does it seem to have been necessary – it was hardly convenient – for a bishop of the East Saxons to have his stool in St Paul's. Cedd, though he is placed second in the list of bishops of London, is never so called by Bede, but bishop to the East Saxons.[2] It is not certain that he even visited London: his interests lay elsewhere. Plummer aptly applies to him and his successors Wharton's words: *nullam cathedram sive certam sedem sibi positam habuerunt*.[3]

The problem of the position of the Kentish kings in London is posed not only by the laws of Hlothere and Eadric but also by Bede's account of the building by Æthelberht of a church there for Mellitus, conclusive evidence that the Kentish king exercised jurisdiction in the city. Let us go back a century and a half. The Anglo-Saxon Chronicle, under the year 457, records a victory by Hengist over the Britons at Crayford: the Britons retreated upon London. The chronicle says that they thereupon forsook Kent.[4] If so, they must have returned, for in 473 Hengist had another great victory over them, when they fled 'like fire.'[5] The inference must be that in the latter year the Britons were still in possession of London and presumably had a considerable hold on West Kent. Nothing more is said of any action by Hengist or any of his successors against the Britons or against London, and the city does not come again into written history until 604, when Æthelberht is said to have constructed the church of St Paul's. At that date, as presumably he had done for many years, Æthelberht exercised supreme authority over London, though, as we have noted, the direct ruler was Sæberht his nephew.[6] There is nothing, however, to suggest that, before the marriage of Æthelberht's sister, Ricula, to Sledda, Sæberht's father, any king of the East Saxons had ruled London,[7] nor does there seem

[1] *Hist. Eccl.*, lib. iv, c. 11 (Plummer, i.226).
[2] *Ibid.*, lib. iii, c. 22 (Plummer, i.172): 'episcopus in gentem orientalium Saxonum'.
[3] Plummer, *Hist. Eccl.*, ii.178.
[4] Thorpe, i.22-3; Plummer, i.12.
[5] Thorpe, *loc. cit.*; Plummer, i.15.
[6] *Hist. Eccl.*, lib. ii, c. 3 (Plummer, i.85).
[7] For the marriage see *Hist. Eccl.*, *loc. cit.* For the name of Ricula's husband see William of Malmesbury, *Gesta Regum*, i.98, where Sledda is called the first king of the East Saxons. See also the genealogical table in Florence of Worcester, *Chronicon*, i.250, upon which Malmesbury's account appears to be based.

any real evidence that any East Saxon king did so after Sæberht's death in 616 or 617.[1] When we hear of East Saxon kings again in connexion with London, it is as dependants of the Mercian king, and it was the king of the Mercians, Wulfhere, who sold the bishopric of London to Wine, apparently in 666.[2] But somewhere in the period 673-686, the Kentish king was maintaining a reeve in London, and there the men of Kent were freely resorting to trade.[3] This may have been the result of the marriage of a daughter of Earconberht of Kent with Wulfhere.[4] After the death of Wulfhere in 675 Kent was devastated by his successor Ethelred,[5] and the kings of the Mercians were certainly in control of London early in the eighth century.[6] But there seems to have been an interval when the enemy of Kent was not the Mercian king, an interval during which Kent had suffered severely at the hands of the West Saxon kings.[7] The inference seems inevitable that in the second half of the seventh century there was a fluctuating contest between Kent and Mercia, and perhaps Wessex, for the possession of London, a contest that could end only in the victory of the stronger power. There is nothing to suggest that the East Saxon kings counted for anything in the struggle.[8]

But apart from documentary evidence, the unity of Kent and London during much of the sixth and seventh centuries is testified by the gold coinage, common to both and to Gaul, which continued to be minted under Æthelberht's successor, Eadbald.[9] This fact, too, lends

[1] The date is conjectural. It depends upon the acceptance of the date assigned for Æthelberht's death by Bede and the Anglo-Saxon Chronicle. See Plummer's note, *Hist. Eccl.*, ii.85.

[2] *Hist. Eccl.*, lib. iii, c. 7 (Plummer, i.141). We reject as unhistorical the story of the three sons of Saba, whom Bede identified with Sæberht. The direct speech used by the interlocutors shows that the story is fiction. Only two sons of Sæberht are known to history (Florence of Worcester, *op. cit.*, i.250, 262, whence Malmesbury, *loc. cit.*: for Florence's source see Chadwick, *Studies on Anglo-Saxon Institutions*, p. 276). The historical details introduced by Bede do not make the story more convincing: abstracting the introductory words and the two sentences 'Qui expulsus . . . disponentes', we are left with a folktale of three wicked, unnamed sons who, although unbaptised, demand the host from an unnamed prelate. They come to the appropriate bad end in battle with the Gewisse, a tribal name which Bede himself says elsewhere was obsolete (*Hist. Eccl.*, lib. ii, c. 5; lib. iii, c. 7; lib. iv, c. 15; Plummer, i.91-2, 139, 236). Bede's story influenced Chadwick in his tentative reconstruction of the East Saxon genealogy. He did not know of the evidence showing that the Kentish Eadbald was the ruler of London (see below, n. 9). This in itself upsets his hypotheses. But we can only express our disagreement with his suggestions regarding both Essex and Middlesex (*op. cit.*, pp. 275-9).

[3] Above, p. 10.

[4] Florence of Worcester, *op. cit.*, i.252, 265; Malmesbury, *op. cit.*, p. 78.

[5] *Hist. Eccl.*, lib. iv, c. 12; v, c. 24 (Plummer, i.228, 354). The date 674, usually adopted, appears to rest on no authority: see Plummer's note, *ibid.* ii.187. And 675 is also the date in the Anglo-Saxon Chronicle (Thorpe, i.58-9; Plummer, i.34-5).

[6] Earle, *Land Charters*, pp. 27-8 (from *Textus Roffensis*); see also Robertson, *Anglo-Saxon Charters*, p. 2, a similar grant a little later.

[7] *Anglo-Saxon Chronicle.*, *s.a.* 686-7, 694 (Thorpe, i.62-3, 66-7; Plummer, i.38-41); Florence of Worcester, *Chronicon*, i.40, 44.

[8] That they exercised some jurisdiction in parts of Middlesex is possible (cf. Stenton, *Anglo-Saxon England*, p. 203), but this is irrelevant. London and Middlesex do not seem to have been administered together except under Athelstan and perhaps for some time before and after (above, p. 18).

[9] Above, p. 158. The inscription on the coins attributed to Eadbald should apparently read Audubald, though the 'b' and 'a' are transposed (Sutherland, *Anglo-Saxon Gold*

support to Bede's description of London under Æthelberht as 'a market place for many peoples coming by land and sea',[1] and indicates that the description would hold good at the beginning as well as at the end of his long reign.[2] If so, the interval between 473, when the Britons were evidently in London, and 565, when Æthelberht acceded, is too short to permit us to suppose, as has been argued, that London had been deserted by the Britons and that an urban trading community had been slowly and painfully evolved by barbarous and untutored English settlers.[3] Some form of commendation by the Britons to the Kentish kings is much more likely, involving the preservation in London of a cultured life on the same level as that of the Kentings, who, on the evidence, appear to have been a people of mixed British and Jutish stock – whatever we are to understand by Jutish.[4] The Romans and the Franks knew them as *Angli*.[5]

[1] *Hist. Eccl.*, lib. ii, c. 3 (Plummer, i.85).

[2] Cf. the sequence of stages in the use and production of gold coinage in England proposed by Mr Sutherland, *op. cit.*, pp. 66-7.

[3] This was, in substance, Haverfield's view, which was controverted by Wheeler, *London and the Saxons*, pp. 28-91. Some of Wheeler's arguments have not stood scrutiny (see the review by J. N. L. Myres in *Journal of Roman Studies*, xxvi (1936), pp. 87-92). But his general thesis has stood the test of subsequent investigations and is now hardly disputed.

[4] T. C. Lethbridge, arguing from different premises, reaches a conclusion similar to our own (*Dark-Age Britain*, pp. 121-2).

[5] To the papal curia all the kings and peoples of England were *Angli*. This is the invariable usage of Gregory the Great: see the references in the *Registrum*, collected in the Index, ii.476. See also Bede, *Hist. Eccl.*, lib. ii, c. 4, c. 10 (Plummer, i.88, 100). The moneyer, presumably Kentish, working at Quentovic was *Anglus* (Sutherland, *op. cit.*, p. 27, *n.* 4). Gregory of Tours, however, speaks of 'Chancia': for reference see above, p. 164, n. 9.

Coinage, p. 95). Compare the various spellings of the name in the manuscripts of Bede: these spellings include Audubaldus (Plummer, i.104; ii.452). There can therefore be little doubt about the identification and consequently it seems clear that Eadbald ruled in London, for the coins were struck there. Mr Kent has argued that no coins were struck in England before the last decades of the seventh century. But since he ignores both Eadbald's coinage and the evidence of Æthelberht's laws that money was circulating in Kent in the sixth century, his argument is unconvincing (*Anglo-Saxon Coins*, pp. 1-22).

APPENDIX II

LEGES WILLELMI AND *LEIS WILLELME*

IN chapter six we have expressed our view forcibly that the *Leis Willelme* is a French rendering of the *Leges Willelmi*.[1] To fly in the face of the unanimous opinion of modern scholars may seem to need more justification and a closer examination of the texts than was possible in that chapter without making it unreadable to many, perhaps the majority, of our readers. For those who are not content with the one example we have given and our assurance that it is fairly representative we offer more detailed proof and a critical examination of the examples adduced in support of the argument that the French version is the original.

First let us give further instances where it is impossible to regard the Latin as a translation of the French. Thus, in chapter 3 the *Leges Willelmi* reads[2]:

> quod consilio aut ope sua non fugerit et quod eum habere non potest ad justiciam.

The corresponding words in the *Leis Willelme* are:

> ne par lui ne s'en est fuid ne aver nel pot.

Whence came the *consilio aut ope* or the *ad justiciam* of the Latin?

The difference is even greater in chapter 5. We give two corresponding passages[3]:

> Si prepositus hundredi equos aut boves aut oves aut porcos vel cuiuscunque generis averia vagantia restare fecerit, is qui veniens sua clamaverit dabit preposito pro ove denarium, pro porco ii. denarios, pro bove vel equo iiii. denarios, ita tamen ut ultra viii. denarios non tribuat, quotquot averia sibi restitui petierit.

> Cil ki aveir rescut u chevals u bos u vaches u berbiz u pors, que est forfeng apelé en engleis, cil kis claimed durrad al provost pur la rescussiun viii. deniers, ja tant n'i ait, mes qu'il i oust cent almaille ne durrad que viii. deniers, e pur un porc i. denier e pur i. berbiz i. denier e issi tresque a viii., pur chascune i. denier, ne ja tant n'averad ne durrad que viii. deniers.

If this is not a clumsy, defective, repetitive version of the Latin, we are at a loss how else to describe it. Is the alternative suggestion to be that a highly gifted translator took this very imperfect piece of vernacular prose and transformed it into Latin which is at least intelligible?

[1] Above, p. 121-3. [2] Liebermann, *Gesetze*, i.494-5. [3] *Ibid.*, pp. 496-7.

Take again chapter 25, where the Latin reads:[1]

> Omnis qui sibi vult justiciam exhiberi vel se pro legali et justiciabili haberi, sit in francplegio.

For this the French offers (chapter 20.3)[2]:

> e puis seint tuz les vilains en franc plege.

These are, we think, the most telling examples witnessing to the priority of the Latin text in the first section of the tract[3]; but in other chapters we find omissions in the French of words that seem undoubtedly to have stood in the original: *were suum* (c. 7), *legitimam* (c. 12).

Let us now turn to chapter 31 in the second section where the Latin text, as it has been transmitted, gives no intelligible meaning. With the aid of the French translation it is not difficult, however, to re-establish the true reading: we correct one word and repair an omission:

> Si domini terrarum non procurent *alienos* culturos ad terras suas colendas *revenire*, justiciarii hoc faciant.

We italicise the words we have supplied: *alienos*, in place of *idoneos*, is justified by *altri* of the French and *revenire* by *venir*.[4] We may note that in this passage we have again an omission in the French: *colendas* is not translated.[5] Now, as in chapter 31, so in chapter 45 a misreading can be corrected by reference to the French: *videant* should plainly be *vocant* or *advocant*. The complete passage is given below.[6] We draw especial attention to it in view of the notion put forward by Liebermann, and accepted by scholars such as Maitland and Bémont, that since the French text reads correctly *voist* or *voest* (the subjunctive of *vochier*: our verb, to vouch), the occurrence of *videant* in the Latin betrays the ignorance or stupidity of the supposititious translator from the French.[7] We fear that our comment will seem elementary; but there is no help for it.

[1] *Ibid.*, p. 511.
[2] *Ibid.*, p. 506.
[3] For Matzke's explanations of the differences in chapters 3 and 5, on the assumption that the Latin is the translation, see *Lois de Guillaume le Conquérant*, p. xxx. He offers no explanation in regard to chapter 25.
[4] It is possible that the Latin verb was *venire*, as in a writ of 1116: 'precipio firmiter quod faciatis venire ad dominium ecclesie mee', where *venire* means to come back or to be restored (*Monasticon*, ii.496; *Regesta*, no. 1131.)
[5] *Gesetze*, i.513. For Matzke's explanation see *op. cit.*, p. xxxi. Liebermann attempted to explain the defective Latin in *Archiv*, cvi.125. Later (*Gesetze*, iii.291) he brought into comparison Dig. 50.6.6.11: Coloni . . . liberantur ut idoniores praediis fiscalibus habeantur. (We supply a fuller citation than his.) This might justify the reading *idoneos*, though the sense of chapter 31 would still be defective; but, in any case, the sense of the passage in the Digest is the direct contrary of that in the *Leges Willelmi*. And if the latter is the work of a learned lawyer, what becomes of Liebermann's thesis that it is a translation from the jejune French? He felt the difficulty and sought to evade it (*Archiv*, cvi.121-3; *Gesetze*, iii.283-4).
[6] Below, p. 178.
[7] *Archiv*, cvi.119; *Gesetze*, i.518; Pollock and Maitland, *History of English Law*, i.103*n*; Bémont's preface to Matzke's *Lois*. Matzke, of course, himself believed the French to be the original. So also Miss A. J. Robertson, *Laws of the Kings of England*, pp. 226-7.

The Latin text that survives in Harley MS 746 is a copy made a century and a half after the original was written and it has many imperfections, due to the carelessness of successive generations of copyists. Doubtless the scribe of the Harleian manuscript should not have written *alta* for *alia* or *duos* for *suos*[1] or *idoneos* for *alienos*. He should not have lapsed into haplography and allowed his eye to wander from 'viii den.' in his exemplar to 'iii den.' lower down, with the consequence that he omitted fifteen words or so from chapter 10.[2] Of course not. But neither should the French translator or his copyists have botched their work rather more. They should not have omitted whole chapters or transposed sentences.[3] Normally we accept such accidents as inevitable in derivative texts and we form an opinion of the work of an author after doing our best to relieve his text of the faults for which he was not responsible. By that test we ourselves judge the author – or authors – of the Latin original to have been reasonably competent by twelfth-century standards and the translator of the text into French to be far less competent. And so we do not suppose our latinist – be he singular or plural – to have been ignorant of the meaning of common French words, while we have come to the conclusion that the translator knew less Latin than he should have done. But that is just what we should expect in the twelfth century. What we should not expect to find at that period is an original tract on law written in French.

It may be suggested that we have not met all of Liebermann's arguments. Has he not demonstrated that, at least in the first section of the tract, the presence of French forms in the Latin betrays a French origin of the text?[4] We have already set out some fairly lengthy passages which, to our mind, demonstrate that the Latin is certainly not a translation from the French: these passages Liebermann ignored. But let us run through his examples. One we may give at length: Alii iiii. equi erunt palefridi et chascuri . . . alter erit palefridus, alter chacur' (c. 20): for Liebermann the key words were *chascuri*, *chacur*. But the scribes responsible for the pipe rolls also wrote *chascurs*, *chascuris*, and a good many other French words, intermixed with their Latin.[5] So our author wrote *ores*, for which there was no convenient Latin equivalent. And one of his copyists wrote *murdre* instead of *murdrum* and likewise *en gaige* for *in gagio* or some other of the many variants of *vadium*: but such lapses, and much worse, are common on the part of scribes. Doubtless the author wrote *hora* and *manet*, where we should not expect a stylist to use these words – two other examples of Liebermann's which hardly

[1] Below, pp. 177-9.

[2] *Gesetze*, i.500-1. The first translator had the complete text of this chapter before him and thus reveals the lacuna.

[3] As in chapters 9, 17, 19, 35.1, 40 (*Gesetze*, i.498, 504, 514, 516). We cannot refrain from citing Matzke's comment upon the disordered state of the French text of chapters 51 and 52: 'on voit que l'ordre du texte français est mauvais et que le traducteur l'a rétabli' (*op. cit.*, p. xxxiv).

[4] *Archiv*, cvi.119. Cf. Matzke, *op. cit.*, pp. xxx-xxxi, xxxvi-xxxix.

[5] *Governance of Mediaeval England*, p. 278*n*.

help his argument. It is noteworthy that outside the first section Liebermann could support his thesis with only two examples: one, the common mediaeval Latin word *sursisa*, and the other, a scribal error of *videant* for *advocant*, with which we have already dealt. The sum of his examples[1] might have added a little unnecessary weight to the inevitable conclusion that the first section was composed independently of the other sections. But that is all. Liebermann, however, seems to have convinced himself that the French text was not only the original but homogeneous, and he was blind to all evidence to the contrary.

Let us now turn to the fourth section which Liebermann believed to have been translated, or rather adapted, into French straight from the Old English of Cnut's Laws.[2] As we have already said, this section is an adaptation of selected paragraphs from two Latin renderings of Cnut's Laws, the *Instituta Cnuti* and a section of the *Quadripartitus*: we fully demonstrate this fact with a representative selection of passages subjoined to this appendix. The compiler, be it noted, is no mere copyist. He does not cling to the language of his exemplars; but nevertheless he adopts sufficient of their vocabulary to show that they were, in truth, his sources. Sometimes he prefers the *Instituta*, sometimes the *Quadripartitus*. What is abundantly clear is that he does not draw directly upon Cnut's Laws or any French rendering. But perhaps we should elaborate this last point by adducing a conclusive piece of evidence. In the Latin and the French the amount of any penalty is precisely the same, but there are variations between these two texts and the Old English Cnut. Thus, where the Old English text reads 120 *s.* the French and Latin read 40 *s.*; where the Old English text reads 60 *s.*, the French and Latin read 40 *s.* Further it should be observed that the compiler of the *Leges Willelmi* was thoroughly confused by the different ways of reckoning a shilling.[3] There were twelve pence in the pre-Conquest English shilling, but five pence in the West Saxon and four pence in the Mercian shilling. The compiler of the *Instituta Cnuti* consistently reckons Cnut's shillings as four pence and converts them into current shillings of twelve pence, so that, with the Old English Cnut before him, he converts 120 *s.* into 40 *s.*, 60 *s.* into 20 *s.*, 30 *s.* into 10 *s.* The compiler of the *Quadripartitus*, on the other hand, always preserves the Old English reckonings. With the *Instituta* and the *Quadripartitus* before him, the author of the *Leges Willelmi* chooses now the former, now the latter. In chapter 39 he chooses the 40 *s.* of the *Instituta*. In chapter 42 his choice falls on the *Quadripartitus*, but he falls into error: reckoning twelve pence to the shilling and twenty shillings to the pound, he writes £6 for 120 *s.*, but he transcribes 30 *s.* without change; where, however, he should write lx. *s.*, he writes xl. *s.*, and this error is faithfully copied in the French. This confirms, if confirmation were

[1] We have not included one of Liebermann's examples, the differences between the numerals in chapter 28, but merely refer to Matzke's explanation (*op. cit.*, p. xxxix) which is the precise reverse of Liebermann's.

[2] *Archiv*, cvi.129.

[3] *Ibid.*, pp. 130-2.

necessary, that the French text is not derived from the Old English. It is also of interest to note that, where the Old English Cnut, the *Instituta* and the *Quadripartitus* all speak of a man's going to the triple ordeal if he is accused simultaneously by three men, the author of the *Leges Willelmi* follows his Latin authorities at such a distance that – evidently with deliberation – he says something very different: one who is accused by four men must purge himself twelve-handed – *purget se manu xii* – that is, he must find eleven compurgators.[1] The French, of course, follows the Latin of the *Leges*.

We need not labour the argument further, but some concluding remarks may be useful. The *stemma* constructed by Liebermann to show the affiliation of the texts is a figment of the imagination. Most of the items in the *stemma* are, on his own showing, hypothetical: they are, in truth, purely imaginary.[2] The Latin text was, as we have said, composed of four disparate sections. Why and how they came to be put together, there is no telling. Guessing would not be helpful. They do not form an organic whole. The French translation found in the Pseudo-Ingulf obviously lies between an earlier translation of the first section and an imperfect Latin text, the ancestor of the Harleian manuscript.[3] It looks as if a second translator added a translation of the second, third and fourth sections and then revised the translation of the first section to make it accord more or less with the defective text of the Latin he had before him. He even committed the absurdity of striking out a line or two from the French translation of chapter 10 because there had been a careless omission by the copyist of the Latin text.[4] He made relatively few other changes; but one is of some interest: he changed the earlier *socheman* into *vilain* as a translation of *villanus* (c. 16).[5]

The French translation under the title of the *Leis Willelme* has been accorded a quite unjustifiable importance by the philologists. The first section of the *Leges Willelmi* might possibly, but very dubiously, be assigned to the reign of Henry I. It is quite unlikely, however, that the first translation can be ascribed to that reign. Matzke attributed it to the period 1150-70 on philological grounds. He drew no distinction between the first translation and the later continuation, though all his evidence was drawn from the first section.[6] Liebermann's date 'at least a generation after 1066'[7] or more widely 1090-1135[8] – again without distinction between the first translation and the continuation – seems

[1] With II Cnut, c. 30, compare *Leges Willelmi*, c. 51 (*Gesetze*, i.390-1, 519).

[2] *Archiv*, cvi.123; *Gesetze*, iii.284.

[3] Liebermann gives the three texts (*Gesetze*, i.492-520). Matzke's French text is reconstructed from the Holkham MS. and the variant printed texts of the Pseudo-Ingulf: see his explanation, *op. cit.*, pp. lii-liv. He gives the Latin text of Harl. MS. 746.

[4] *Gesetze*, i.500-1.

[5] *Ibid.*, p. 502.

[6] *Op. cit.*, pp. xxxix-lii.

[7] *Gestze*, iii.284.

[8] *Gesetze*, i.492-519. In *Archiv*, cvi.154, Liebermann suggested 1100-1120 as the probable date.

to us misguided. Whatever distance of time separated the two translators, it is evident that the resources of the philologist are inadequate to determine or even to remark it. Our own belief is that both the first translator and the continuator were working at much the same period and under the same impulse as the translator of the *Ten Articles* and the *Leges Edwardi Confessoris*, who was working in 1190-93.[1] Similar texts translated at the same period were the coronation charters of Henry I, Stephen and Henry II.[2] We doubt whether this period could be dated any closer than the last quarter of the twelfth century and then with some margin at either end.

It is right that we should add these final words. Thanks to Liebermann's magnificent apparatus, it is a comparatively simple matter to check his own hypotheses. That a hypothesis should occasionally be found wanting is a minor blemish on his work, though the consequences may be important. To follow Liebermann unquestioningly, without giving due weight to the apparatus he has supplied for criticism and verification, is to pay him the poorest of compliments.

[1] Described, and extracts printed, by Liebermann in *Zeitschrift für Romanische Philologie*, xix.77-84. The translator refers to Richard I 'ki s'en alat à Jérusalem e ne esteit mis uncore venu'. Richard left England on 12 December 1189 and returned on 13 March 1194. The translation of the *Ten Articles* is reprinted in *Gesetze*, i.488-9.

[2] In Harl. MS. 458. The text of Henry I's charter was printed by Liebermann in *T.R.H.S.*, N.S., viii.46-8. We cannot, however, accept the date, 'the middle of the thirteenth century', which he assigns to the manuscript (p. 37).

ADDENDUM

PARALLEL TEXTS OF *LEGES WILLELMI* AND *LEGES CNUTI*

There are subjoined selections in parallel columns from the fourth section of the *Leges Willelmi*, the *Instituta Cnuti* and the *Quadripartitus*. Our justification for using the title *Leges Cnuti* to cover these Latin versions of the Laws of Cnut is that it is found in a heading to the so-called *Consiliatio Cnuti*,[1] the text of which we do not give because it was not employed by the author of the *Leges Willelmi*. We prefer this Latin title to the more familiar *Leis Willelme* because it emphasises that the original text was in Latin. We can justify it by reference to Harley MS 746, whence we have taken our extracts, which prefaces the text thus: 'Iste sunt leges et consuetudines quas Willelmus rex post adquisitionem Anglie omni populo Anglorum concessit tenendas. . . .'[2] If there is no early authority for the Latin title, there is none for the French either. The extracts from the *Leges Cnuti* are borrowed from Liebermann's edition,[3] but we have made some changes in orthography for the sake of uniformity and we have put in square brackets some variant readings and glosses which may have been before the author of the *Leges Willelmi*. The numbering of the paragraphs in all cases follows Liebermann's. We have put in italics words in the *Leges Cnuti* which correspond with words in the *Leges Willelmi*.

LEGES WILLELMI	INSTITUTA CNUTI	QUADRIPARTITUS
[39.1] Qui vero falsum iudicium fecerit vel iniusticiam foverit odio vel amore vel peccunia sit in regis forisfacto de xl solidis, nisi purgare se possit quod melius iudicare nescivit, et insuper libertatem, si habuit, amittat illam, nisi a rege eam redemerit.	[15.1] Si *quis iniustas* leges adinverit aut *iudicaverit*, aut causa *odii* aut adquisitionis *pecunie*, *sit* reus *regi xl solidis* in lege Anglorum, *nisi* iuramento affirmaverit se rectius *iudicare nescisse*, et postea careat *libertate* sua *nisi* eam *a rege redimat* ad velle regis	Si *quis* ammodo [deinceps] unlagam [id est non legem] erigat vel *iniustum iudicium* iudicet pro lesione vel aliqua *pecunie* susceptione, sit erga *regem* cxx *solidis* reus in Anglorum laga [lege], nisi cum iuramento audeat inveritare quod hoc rectius *nescivit*, et dignitatem suam legalitatis semper *amiserit*, *nisi* [si non] *eam redimat* erga *regem* sicut ei permittet
[39.2] In Danelahe erit in forisfactura de sa[4] laslite.	[15.1a] *In lege Danorum* erit reus *forisfacture* quam Dani vocant *lahslit*.	*In Denalaga lahslictes* reus sit nisi se allegiet [si non iuret] *quod melius nescivit*.

[1] *Gesetze*, i.618.
[2] The *Leges Willelmi* is on folios 55*b*-58*b*.
[3] *Gesetze*, i.309-71.
[4] *Sic* MS.

LEGES WILLELMI	INSTITUTA CNUTI	QUADRIPARTITUS
NE QUIS PRO PARVO DELICTO MORTI ADIUDICETUR [40] Prohibemus ne pro parvo forisfacto adiudicetur aliquis homo morti, sed ad plebis castigacionem alia[1] pena secundum qualitatem et quantitatem delicti plectatur. Non enim debet pro re parva deleri factura quam ad ymaginem suam Deus condidit[2] et sanguinis sui precio redemit.[3]	[2.1] Interdicimus etiam *ne pro parva re* Christiani *morti* traduntur, scilicet pro latrocinio aut pro talibus rebus, sed alio modo corrigantur propter alias ne culpe inulte remanent.	*Prohibemus ne* Christianus *aliquis pro* penitus *parva re* saltem ad *mortem* seducatur [id est contempnetur aut preiudicetur] sed exquiratur pro necessitate populi iusticie pacificans nec [ne] *pro* levi *re* dispereat opus manuum *Dei* et *suum* ipsius *pretium* quod profundi *redemit.*
NE CHRISTIANI EXTRA TERRAM VEL PAGANIS VENDANTUR [41] Inhibemus etiam ne quis Christianum in alienam patriam vendat et maxime infidelibus. [41.1] Cavendum enim valde est ne anime in dampnacionem vendantur pro quibus Christus vitam impendit.	[3] Et *prohibemus ne Christiani* genti[li]bus *extra* hanc *terram* venundentur [*vendantur*] nec in *paganismo ne anima* Christiana, *quam* ipse *Christus* suo sanguine redemit, pereat.	Precipimus ne *Christiani* passim in exilium venundentur [*vendantur*] vel in gentilitatem ne forte pereant *anime quas* propria *vita* sua mercatus est dominus noster Iesus *Christus.*
DE HIIS QUI IUSTUM IUDICIUM REPELLUNT [42] Qui legem equam et iustum iudicium subire renuit forisfacturam reddat ei cuius erit iuris illam accipere. [42.1] Si adversus regem vi libras, si adversus comitem xl solidos, si in hundreto vel in cuiuscumque curia qui eam ex libertate habere debet debet xxx solidos anglicos.	[15.2] *Qui* rectum *iudicium et iustam legem* abnegat sit *forisfactus ei cui* iustum est: *si regi,* det illi xl *solidos,* si *comiti* xx *solidos, si hundredo* x *solidos,* si contra omnes hos omnibus reddat.	Et *qui* recte legi *iusto iudicio* refragabit, reus habeatur erga *eum cui* pertinebit, erga *regem* sic cxx solidis, sic erga *comitem* lx *solidis,* sic erga *hundretum xxx solidis,* sic erga singulum eorum, si sic accidat in Anglorum lege.
[42.2] In Danelahe qui rectum iudicium subire contempserit erit in forisfactura de suo laslite.	[15.1a] Per *legem Danorum lahslit* reddat.	*In Denalaga lahslite.*

[1] MS. alta.
[2] Gen. i.27: Et creavit Deus hominem ad imaginem suam.
[3] Apoc. v.9: et redemisti nos Deo in sanguine tuo.

LEGES WILLELMI	INSTITUTA CNUTI	QUADRIPARTITUS
NE QUIS ALIQUID SINE TESTIBUS EMAT [45] Nemo emat vel vivum vel mortuum ad valentiam iiii denariorum sine iiii testibus aut de burgo aut de villa campestri.	[24] Volumus etiam ut nullus *emat* aliquid ultra *quatuor denarios valens* nec rem *vivam* nec *mortuam* nec iacentem *sine quattuor* idoneis *testibus*, nec infra *burgum* nec extra.	Et *nemo* aliquid *emat* supra *iiii denarios valens*, mobile vel inmobile, nisi habeat credibile testimonium *iiii* hominum, sit in civitate, sit extra.
[45.1] Quod si aliquis rem postmodum calumpniatus fuerit et nec testes habuerit nec warantum, et rem reddat et forisfacturam cui de iure competit.	[24.1] Et si non tot nec tales testes habuerit, et aliquid tale in manu vel potestate eius inventum fuerit, et ipse *warantem* voluerit vocare, non ei valeat neque liceat, sed *reddatur* calumnianti quod suum est aut valens et insuper iterum tantum valens *et forisfacturam*[1] *qui* eam iuste habere debet.	Et si tunc super eum intercietur et tale testimonium non habeat, non liceat ei advocare, sed *reddat* repententi captale suum et secundam solutionem, *et forisfacturam cui* pertinebit.
[45.2] Si vero testes habet [ad]vocant[2] rem tercio, et quarta vice aut rem diracionet aut amittet.	[24.2] Quod*si* tales *testes habuerit* quales supra diximus, warentem vocet, et ille vocatus vocet alium, si potest, et tertius[3] adhuc *tertium vocet*, si potest, et tertius suum faciet, si valet: quodsi non valet reddatur ei qui [quod] iuste habere debet.	*Si* testimonium *habeat*, sicut prediximus, tunc liceat inde *ter advocari*, et *quarta vice* proprietur aut reddatur ei cuius erit.

[1] *Supply* ei.
[2] MS. videant
[3] *Read* alius.

LEGES WILLELMI	INSTITUTA CNUTI	QUADRIPARTITUS
UT DOMINUS IN FRANCPLEGIO HABEAT SUOS[1]		
[52] Omnes qui servientes habent eorum sint francplegii, quod si rectati fuerint ad rectum in hundredo eos habebunt.	[31] *Omnis dominus habeat* familiam suam in proprio *plegio* [suo] ut *si* aliquis eorum calumpniatus fuerit, respondeat *hundredo* in quo calumniatus est, sicut iustum sit.	Et *habeat omnis dominus* familiam suam in *plegio* suo, et si accusetur in aliquo, respondeat *in hundredo* ubi compellabitur, sicut recta lex sit.
[52.1] Quod si infra rectacionem aliquis fugerit, dominus solvat were.	[31.1] *Si* post calumpniam evaserit, *dominus solvet* eius *were* regi et plegii quod calumniatus est . . .	*Quodsi* accusatur et *fugiat*, reddat *dominus* eius *weram* [id est pretium nativitatis] hominis illius.
[52.2] Et si calumpnietur quod per eum fugerit, aut purget se manu sexta aut erga regem emendet. Et is qui fugerit uthlagetur.	[31.1a] *Et si* ipse dominus *calumniatus* fuerit quod *eum* sponte *fugere* permiserit, si ille est liberalis, id est thegen, acceptis quinque similibus *purget se*. Si non poterit purgare se, persolvat *regi* were suum. Et homo est exul ab omnibus.	*Et si* dominus accusetur quod eius consilio [suo] *fugerit*, adlegiet se cum v tainis [id est nobilibus] et ipse [idem] sit sextus. Si purgatio frangat ei, solvet *regi* weram suam. *Et qui fugit* extra legem habeatur.

[1] MS. duos.

BIBLIOGRAPHY

Standard works of reference are not included. Articles and separate volumes are cited under the name of the author or the title, and titles of Journals or Series are included only in special cases.

ABBREVIATIONS

A.H.R.	*American Historical Review.*
B.I.H.R.	*Bulletin of Institute of Historical Research.*
B.J.R.L.	*Bulletin of John Rylands Library.*
E.E.T.S.	*Early English Text Society.*
E.H.R.	*English Historical Review.*
L.Q.R.	*Law Quarterly Review.*
M.G.H.	*Monumenta Germaniae Historica.*
T.R.H.S.	*Transactions of Royal Historical Society.*
V.C.H.	*Victoria County History.*

ADAMS, G. B. *Council and Courts in Anglo-Norman England* (New Haven, 1926).
ÆLFRIC. *Colloquy*. Ed. G. N. Garmonsway (London, 1939).
ALEXANDER, J. J. 'The Dates of County Days' in *B.I.H.R.*, iii (1926), 89-95.
ALLARIA, A. 'English Scholars at Bologna' in *Dublin Review*, cxii (1893).
Ancient Charters. Ed. J. H. Round (Pipe Roll Soc., London, 1888).
Ancrene Riwle. English text, ed. Mabel Day; French text, ed. J. A. Herbert; Latin text, ed. Charlotte D'Evelyn (London, E.E.T.S., 1952, 1944, 1944).
Anglia Sacra. Ed. Henry Wharton (London, 1691).
Anglo-Saxon Charters. Ed. A. J. Robertson (Cambridge, 1939).
Anglo-Saxon Chronicle. Ed. B. Thorpe (Rolls Ser., London, 1861).
See *Two of the Saxon Chronicles*.
Anglo-Saxon Laws. *See* Attenborough; Liebermann; Robertson.
Anglo-Saxon Writs. Ed. F. E. Harmer (Manchester, 1952).
Annales Monastici, vol. iii (Dunstable). Ed. H. R. Luard (Rolls Ser., London, 1866).
Anniversary Essays in Mediaeval History. By students of Charles Homer Haskins (Boston, New York, 1929).
See David.
ARMITAGE ROBINSON, J. *Somerset Historical Essays* (London, 1921).
ARNTZ, H. *Handbuch der Runenkunde* (Halle, 1944).
ATTENBOROUGH, F. L. *See* Liebermann.

BECKET. *See* Materials; Radford; Thomas Saga.
BEDE, *Opera Historica*. Ed. C. Plummer (Oxford, 1896).
[Cited as *Historia Ecclesiastica*].
BENEDICT OF PETERBOROUGH. *See* Roger of Howden.
BIGELOW, M. M. *Placita Anglo-Normannica* (London, 1879).
BISHOP, T. A. M. *Scriptores Regis* (Oxford, 1961).

BISHOP, T. A. M. and CHAPLAIS, P. *Facsimiles of English Royal Writs to A.D. 1100* (Oxford, 1957).

BOEHMER, H. 'Das Eigenkirchentum in England' in *Texte und Forschungen für Englischen Kulturgeschichte: Festgabe für Felix Liebermann* (Halle, 1921).

BONGERT, YVONNE. *Recherches sur les cours laïques du xe au xiiie siècle* (Paris, 1949).

BOUMAN, C. A. *Sacring and Crowning* (Groningen, 1957).

BRACTON, HENRY OF. *De Legibus et Consuetudinibus Angliae.* Ed. G. E. Woodbine (New Haven, 1915-42).

— *Bracton's Note Book.* Ed. F. W. Maitland (London, 1887).

BRECHTER, S. *Die Quellen zur Angelsachsenmission Gregors des Grossen* (Münster in Westf., 1941).

BROOKE, G. C. *English Coins* (London, 3rd. ed., 1950).

BUCHNER, RUDOLF. 'Die Lex Salica eine Falschung der Zeit Karls des Kahlen?' in *Deutsches Archiv für Erforschung des Mittelalters*, ix (1951), 59-78.

BUCKLAND, W. W. *Roman Law of Slavery* (Cambridge, 1908).

— *Text-book of Roman Law* (Cambridge, 1932).

Calendar of Various Chancery Rolls (London, 1912).

CAM, H. M. *Studies in the Hundred Rolls* (Oxford, 1921).

Canterbury. *See* Gervase.

Carte Nativorum: a Peterborough Abbey Cartulary of the Fourteenth Century. Ed. C. N. L. Brooke and M. M. Postan (Oxford: Northampton Record Soc., 1960).

Cartularium Monasterii de Rameseia. Ed. W. H. Hart and P. A. Lyons (Rolls Ser., London, 1884-94).

Cartularium Saxonicum. Ed. W. de G. Birch (London, 1885-93).

CHADWICK, H. M. *The Heroic Age* (Cambridge, 1926).

— *Studies on Anglo-Saxon Institutions* (Cambridge, 1905).

Chartes des Libertés anglaises. Ed. Charles Bémont (Paris, 1892).

CHENEY, C. R. *From Becket to Langton* (Manchester, 1956).

Chronicles of the Reigns of Stephen, Henry II and Richard I. Ed. R. Howlett (Rolls Ser., London, 1885-90).

Chronicon Abbatiae de Evesham. Ed. W. D. Macray (Rolls Ser., London, 1863).

Chronicon Abbatiae Rameseiensis. Ed. W. D. Macray. (Rolls Ser., London, 1886).

Chronicon Monasterii de Abingdon. Ed. J. Stevenson (Rolls Ser., London, 1858).

Chronicon Monasterii de Bello. Ed. J. S. Brewer (Anglia Christiana Soc., London, 1846).

Chroniques des Comtes d'Anjou et des Seigneurs d'Amboise. Ed. Louis Halphen and René Poupardin (Paris, 1913).

CHURCHILL, I. J. *Canterbury Administration* (London, 1933).

CLAPHAM, A. W. *English Romanesque Architecture before the Conquest* (Oxford, 1930).

Close Rolls, 1227-1272. (London, 1902-1938).

Consiliatio Cnuti. Ed. F. Liebermann (Halle, 1893).

Corpus Juris Canonici. Ed. Erich Friedberg (Leipzig, 1876-82).

Councils and Ecclesiastical Documents relating to Great Britain and Ireland. Ed. A. W. Haddan and W. Stubbs (Oxford, 1869-78).

Councils and Synods, 1205-1313. Ed. F. M. Powicke and C. R. Cheney (Oxford, 1964).

Coventry. *See* Walter.

Crown Pleas of the Wiltshire Eyre, 1249. Ed. C. A. F. Meekings (Wiltshire Archaeological and Natural History Soc., Devizes, vol. xvi (1961)).

Cunningham, W. *The Growth of English Industry and Commerce during the Early and Middle Ages* (Cambridge, 5th Ed., 1910; reprinted 1922).

Curia Regis Rolls (London, 1923-).

Daniel of Morley. 'Philosophia' in *Archiv für die Geschichte der Naturwissenschaften*, viii (1917), 6-40; ix, 50-1.

Darby, H. C. *The Domesday Geography of Eastern England* (Cambridge, 1952).

— and Campbell, E. M. J. *The Domesday Geography of South-East England* (Cambridge, 1962).

Dark-Age Britain: Studies presented to E. T. Leeds. Ed. D. B. Harden (London, 1956).
See Hawkes; Lethbridge.

David, C. W. 'The Claim of King Henry I to be called learned' in *Anniversary Essays . . . Haskins*, pp. 45-56.

Deanesly, Margaret. *Augustine of Canterbury* (London, 1964).

— *The Pre-Conquest Church in England* (London, 1961).

Derville, M. T. *The Level and the Liberty of Romney Marsh* (Ashford, 1936).

de Zulueta, F. 'William of Drogheda' in *Mélanges de droit romain dédiés à Georges Cornil* (Paris, 1926), pp. 641-57.
See Vacarius, Vinogradoff.

Dialogus de Scaccario [By Richard of Ely]. Ed. and trans. C. Johnson (Edinburgh, 1950).

Diceto. *See* Ralf.

Diplomatarium Anglicum. Ed. B. Thorpe (London, 1865).

Domesday Book (London, 1783-1816).
See Darby; Ellis.

Domesday of St. Paul's of the Year MCCXXII. Ed. W. H. Hale (Camden Soc., London, 1858).

Duggan, Charles, *Twelfth-Century Decretal Collections and their importance in English History* (London, 1963).

— 'Richard of Ilchester' in *T.R.H.S.*, 5th. Ser., xvi (1966), 1-21.

Douglas, D. C. *William the Conqueror* (London, 1964).

Dugdale, William. *Origines Juridiciales* (London, 1666; 3rd ed., 1680).
See Monasticon.

Durham. *See* Simeon.

Eadmer, *Historia Novorum*. Ed. M. Rule (Rolls Ser., London, 1884).

Earle, J. *Anglo-Saxon Literature* (London, 1884).

— *Handbook to the Land-Charters and other Saxonic Documents* (Oxford, 1888).

Eckhardt. *See* Liebermann.

Ekwall, E. *Street-names of the City of London* (Oxford, 1954).

Elliott, R. W. V. *Runes: an introduction* (Manchester, 1959).

Ellis, H. *General Introduction to Domesday Book* (Record Comm., London, 1833).

Elmham. *See* Thomas.

English Historical Documents. Ed. D. C. Douglas (London, 1953-). Vol. I. (*c*. 500-1042): ed. D. Whitelock (1955).

Epistolae Cantuarienses, 1187-1199. Ed. W. Stubbs (Chronicles and Memorials, Richard I, vol. ii: Rolls Ser., London, 1865).

EVANS, Sir ARTHUR, 'Notes on Early Anglo-Saxon Gold Coins' in *Numismatic Chronicle*, 6th ser., ii (1942), 19-41.

Eyre of Kent, 6 and 7 Edward II, vol. i. Ed. F. W. Maitland, L. W. Vernon Harcourt and W. C. Bolland (Selden Soc., London, 1908). See *Year Books*.

Facsimiles of Royal Charters. *See* Warner.

Feet of Fines: Henry II and Richard I (Pipe Roll Soc., London, 1894, 1898).

Fleta. Ed. H. G. Richardson and G. O. Sayles (Selden Soc., London, 1953-).

FLORENCE OF WORCESTER, *Chronicon*, Ed. B. Thorpe (Eng. Hist. Soc., London, 1848-49).

Foedera, Conventiones, Litterae et Cuiuscunque Generis Acta Publica. Ed. T. Rymer (Record Comm., London, 1816-69).

Foliot. *See* Gilbert.

FOREVILLE, RAYMONDE, *L'Église et la Royauté en Angleterre sous Henri II Plantagenet* (Paris, 1943).

FOURNIER, MARCEL. *Essai sur les formes et les effets de l'affranchisement dans le droit gallo-franc* (Paris, 1885).

GABEL, LEONA C. *Benefit of Clergy in England in the Later Middle Ages* (Northampton, Mass., 1929).

GALBRAITH, V. H. *The Making of Domesday Book* (Oxford, 1961).

— 'Royal Charters to Winchester' in *E.H.R.*, xxxv (1920), 382-400.

GALE. *See* Historiae.

Gallia Christiana, tom. xi (Paris, 1721).

GÉNESTAL, R. *Le Privilegium Fori en France* (Paris, 1924).

GERALD THE WELSHMAN, *De Principis Instructione Liber* in *Opera*, ed. J. S. Brewer, vol. viii, 3-329 (Rolls Ser., London, 1861-91).

GERVASE OF CANTERBURY. *Historical Works*. Ed. W. Stubbs (Rolls Ser., London, 1879-80).

Gesta Regis Henrici Secundi et Ricardi I. *See* Roger of Howden.

GIBBS, M., and LANG, J. *Bishops and Reform, 1215-1272* (Oxford, 1934).

GILBERT FOLIOT, *Epistolae*. Ed. J. A. Giles (Patres Eccl. Angl., Oxford, 1845).

GIRY, ARTHUR, *Manuel de Diplomatique* (Paris, 1894).

GLANVILLE, *De Legibus et Consuetudinibus Regni Angliae*. Ed. G. E. Woodbine (New Haven, 1932); ed. G. D. G. Hall (Oxford, 1965).

Gregorii I Papae Registrum Epistolarum. Ed. P. Ewald and L. M. Hartmann (M.G.H., Berlin, 1891-99).

GREGORY OF TOURS. *Historia Francorum*.
[Our page references are to *Histoire des Francs*, ed. H. Omont and G. Collon; 2nd ed. by R. Poupardin (Paris, 1913). There is an English translation of this text by O. M. Dalton, with introduction and notes (Oxford, 1927).

GREGORY OF TOURS. *Historia Francorum—continued*
Later editions:
Ed. B. Krusch in *M.G.H.* (1937-51).
Ed. R. Buchner, with German translation (Berlin, 1956).
Ed. R. Latouche, with French translation (Paris, 1963)].
GUILHIERMOZ, PAUL. *Essai sur l'origine de la noblesse en France au moyen âge* (Paris, 1902).

HARDY, T. D. *Itinerary of King John* (prefixed to *Rotuli Litterarum Patentium*, q.v.).
HARMER. See *Anglo-Saxon Writs*.
HASKINS, C. H. *Norman Institutions* (Cambridge, Mass., 1918).
See *Anniversary Essays*.
HAWKES, C. F. C. 'The Jutes in Kent' in *Dark-Age Britain* (q.v.), 91-111.
HENGHAM, RALPH OF, *Summae*. Ed. W. H. Dunham (Cambridge, 1932).
HENRY OF HUNTINGDON. *Historia Anglorum*. Ed. T. Arnold (Rolls Ser., London, 1879).
HERMANN OF TOURNAI. *De Miraculis Sanctae Mariae Laudunensis* in Migne, *Patrologia Latina*, clvi (1853), 962-1018.
HILTON, R. H. 'Freedom and Villeinage in England' in *Past and Present*, no. 31 (July 1965), pp. 3-19.
Histoire des ducs de Normandie et des rois d'Angleterre. Ed. F. Michel (Soc. de l'Hist. de France, Paris, 1840).
Historiae Britannicae, Saxonicae, Anglo-Danicae Scriptores XV. Ed. T. Gale (Oxford, 1691).
Historia Ecclesiastica. See Bede.
Historians of the Church of York. Ed. James Raine (Rolls Ser., London, 1879-94).
HOLDSWORTH, W. S. *History of English Law* (London, 1922-52).
HOLLISTER, C. W. *The Military Organisation of Norman England* (Oxford, 1965).
HOWDEN. *See* Roger.
HOYT, R. S. *The Royal Demesne in English Constitutional History, 1066-1272* (New York, 1950).
Huntingdon. *See* Henry.

Imagines Historiarum. See Ralf de Diceto.
Inquisitio Comitatus Cantabrigiensis. Ed. N. E. S. A. Hamilton (Roy. Soc. of Literature, London, 1876).

JACOB, E. F. *Studies in the Period of Baronial Reform and Rebellion, 1258-1267* (Oxford, 1925).
JOHN OF SALISBURY. *Letters*. Ed. W. J. Millor, H. E. Butler and C. N. L. Brooke (Edinburgh, 1955).
— *Epistolae*. Ed. J. A. Giles (Oxford, 1848).
JOHN OF WORCESTER. *Chronicle*. Ed. J. R. H. Weaver (Oxford, 1908).

KANTOROWICZ, E. H. ' "Inalienability": a Note on Canonical Practice and the English Coronation Oath in the Thirteenth Century' in *Speculum*, xxix (1954), 488-502.

KANTOROWICZ, H. *Studies in the Glossators of the Roman Law* (Cambridge, 1938).
KENT, J. P. C. 'From Roman Britain to Saxon England' in *Anglo-Saxon Coins: Studies presented to F. M. Stenton*. Ed. R. H. M. Dolley (London, 1961).
KNOWLES, D. *The Episcopal Colleagues of Archbishop Thomas Becket* (Cambridge, 1951).
KUTTNER, S., and RATHBONE, E. 'Anglo-Norman Canonists of the Twelfth Century' in *Traditio*, vii (1949-51), pp. 279-358.

Lancashire Pipe Rolls. Ed. W. Farrer (Liverpool, 1902).
Land Charters. *See* Earle.
Leges Anglo-Saxonicae ecclesiasticae et civiles. Ed. David Wilkins (London, 1721).
Leges Willelmi. *See* Liebermann; Lois.
LE PATOUREL, J. 'The Plantagenet Dominions' in *History*, l (1965), 289-308.
LETHBRIDGE, T. C. 'The Anglo-Saxon Settlement in Eastern England' in *Dark-Age Britain* (q.v.), 112-22.
LEVISON, W. *England and the Continent in the Eighth Century* (Oxford, 1946).
Lex Ribuaria. Ed. Franz Beyerle and Rudolf Buchner (*M.G.H.*, 1954).
[This supersedes the numerous earlier editions: for bibliography, see Karl A. Eckhardt, *Lex Ribuaria* (Göttingen, 1959).]
Lex Salica. *See* Buchner; Stein.
Liber de Antiquis Legibus. Ed. T. Stapleton (Camden Soc., London, 1846).
LIEBERMANN, F. 'A contemporary manuscript of the "Leges Anglorum Londoniis collectae"' in *E.H.R.* xxviii (1913), 732-45.
— 'Eine Anglonormannische übersetzung des 12. Jahrhunderts von Articuli Willelmi, Leges Edwardi und Genealogia Normannorum' in *Zeitschrift für Romanische Philologie* (Halle), xix (1895), 77-84.
— *Die Gesetze der Angelsachsen* (Halle, 1903-16).
[The following are based upon Liebermann's texts:
The Laws of the Earliest English Kings. Ed. F. L. Attenborough (Cambridge, 1922).
The Laws of the Kings of England from Edmund to Henry I. Ed. A. J. Robertson (Cambridge, 1925).
Gesetze der Angelsachsen, 601-925. Ed. K. A. Eckhardt (Göttingen, 1958).]
— 'On the Instituta Cnuti Aliorumque Regum Anglorum' in *T.R.H.S.*, New Ser., vii (1893), 77-107.
— *The National Assembly in the Anglo-Saxon Period* (Halle, 1913).
— *Quadripartitus, ein Englisches Rechtsbuch von 1114* (Halle, 1892).
— 'The Text of Henry I's Coronation Charter' in *T.R.H.S., New Series*, viii (1894), 21-48.
— *Über das Englische Rechtsbuch Leges Henrici* (Halle, 1901).
— *Über die Leges Anglorum saeculo xiii ineunte Londoniis collectae* (Halle, 1894).
— *Über die Leges Edwardi Confessoris* (Halle, 1896).
— 'Über die Leis Willelme' in *Archiv für das Studium der Neueren Sprachen und Litteraturen* (Brunswick), cvi (1901), 113-183.
— *Über Pseudo-Cnuts Constitutiones de Foresta* (Halle, 1894).
See Boehmer; *Consiliatio Cnuti*.

Lincoln. *See Registrum Antiquissimum.*
Lois de Guillaume le Conquérant. Ed. J. E. Matzke (Paris, 1899).
LOYN, H. R. *Anglo-Saxon England and the Norman Conquest* (London, 1962).
LYTTLETON, GEORGE (Lord), *The History of the Life of King Henry the Second* (Revised ed., London, 1777).

MCKECHNIE, W. S. *Magna Carta* (Glasgow, 1905; 2nd ed., 1914).
MADOX, T. *History and Antiquities of the Exchequer of England* (London, 2nd ed., 1769).
— *Formulare Anglicanum* (London, 1702).
Magnus Rotulus Scaccarii, 31 Henry I. Ed. J. Hunter (Record Comm., London, 1833).
[Cited as Pipe Roll].
MAITLAND, F. W. *Select Passages from the Works of Bracton and Azo* (Selden Soc., London, 1895).
— *Domesday Book and Beyond* (Cambridge, 1907).
— *Forms of Action at Common Law* (Cambridge, 1909).
— *Roman Canon Law in the Church of England* (London, 1898).
See Bracton, Pollock.
MAKOWER, F. *The Constitutional History and Constitution of the Church of England* (London, 1895).
MALDEN, H. E. 'Bondmen in Surrey under the Tudors' in *T.R.H.S.*, New Ser., xix (1905), 305-307.
MARKUS, R. A. 'The Chronology of the Gregorian Mission to England' in *Journal of Ecclesiastical History*, xiv (1963), 16-30.
Materials for the History of Thomas Becket. Ed. J. C. Robertson and J. B. Sheppard (Rolls Ser., London, 1875-85).
MATZKE. *See* Lois.
Memoranda Roll, 1 John. Introduction by H. G. Richardson (Pipe Roll Soc., London, 1943).
Monasticon Anglicanum [*curante* Dugdale]. Ed. J. Caley, H. Ellis and B. Badinell (London, 1846).
Munimenta Gildhallae Londoniensis, vol. ii, part i (Liber Custumarum). Ed. H. T. Riley (Rolls Ser., London, 1860).
MURRAY, K. M. E. *The Constitutional History of the Cinque Ports* (Manchester, 1935).
MYRES, J. N. L. *See* Wheeler.

NAVEL, H. 'L'Enquête de 1133 sur les Fiefs de l'Évêch deé Bayeux' in *Bulletin de la Société des Antiquaires de Normandie*, xlii (1935), 5-80.
Niger. *See* Ralf.
NORGATE, KATE. *England under the Angevin Kings* (London, 1887).

Old English Miscellany. Ed. R. Morris (*E.E.T.S.*, London, 1872).

PAGE, T. W. *The End of Villeinage in England* (American Hist. Assoc., New York, 1900).
PAGE, W. *London: its Origin and Early Development* (London, 1923).
Patent Rolls of Reign of Henry III [1216-1232]. (London, 1901-3).
PAUL THE DEACON. *Historia Langobardorum.* Ed. G. Waitz (*M.G.H.*, 1878).

PEARSON, KARL. *The Chances of Death* (London, 1897).
PEERS, C. R. 'The earliest Christian Churches in England' in *Antiquity*, iii (1929), 65-74.
PETER OF BLOIS. *Epistolae*. Ed. J. A. Giles (vols. 1 and 2 of *Opera:* Oxford, 1846-7).
PETIT-DUTAILLIS, CHARLES. *Studies and Notes Supplementary to Stubbs's Constitutional History* (Manchester, 1908-29; reprinted 1930).
Pipe Rolls, 5 Henry II-16 John (Pipe Roll Soc., London, 1884-1959). [For earlier roll see *Magnus Rotulus*.]
Pleas before the King or his Justices. Ed. D. M. Stenton (Selden Soc., London, 1949, 1953).
PLUCKNETT, T. F. T. *Early English Legal Literature* (Cambridge, 1958).
POLLOCK, FREDERICK. *The Land Laws* (London, 1883; 3rd ed., 1896).
POLLOCK, F., and MAITLAND, F. W. *History of English Law before the Time of Edward I* (Second ed. Cambridge, 1898; reprinted 1911, 1923, 1952).
POOLE, A. L. *From Domesday Book to Magna Carta* (Oxford, 1955).
— *Obligations of Society in the Twelfth and Thirteenth Centuries* (Oxford, 1946).
POOLE, R. L. 'The Publication of Great Charters by the English Kings' in *Studies in Chronology and History* (Oxford, 1934), 308-318.
POST, GAINES. *Studies in Medieval Legal Thought* (Princeton, 1964).
POUZET, PH. *L'Anglais Jean dit Bellesmains, Évêque de Poitiers, puis Archévêque de Lyon* (Lyons, 1927).
POWICKE, F. M. 'The Oath of Bromholm' in *E.H.R.*, lvi (1941), 529-48.

RADFORD, L. B. *Thomas of London* (Cambridge, 1894).
RALF DE DICETO. *Opera Historica*. Ed. W. Stubbs (Rolls Ser., London, 1876). [Vol. i contains 'Imagines Historiarum'.]
RALF NIGER, *Chronicles*. Ed. R. Anstruther (Caxton Soc., London, 1851).
RAMSAY, J. H. *The Angevin Empire* (London, 1903).
— *The Foundations of England* (London, 1898).
RATHBONE. *See* Kuttner.
Regesta Regum Anglo-Normannorum. Ed. H. W. C. Davis, C. Johnson and H. A. Cronne (Oxford, 1913, 1956).
Registrum Antiquissimum of the Cathedral Church of Lincoln. Ed. C. W. Foster and K. Major (Lincoln Record Soc., 1931-).
RICHARD OF ELY. *See Dialogus*.
RICHARDSON, H. G. *Bracton: the Problem of his Text* (Selden Soc., London, 1964).
— 'Business Training in Medieval Oxford' in *A.H.R.*, xlvi (1941), 259-80.
— 'The Coronation in Medieval England' in *Traditio*, xvi (1960), 111-202.
— 'The English Coronation Oath' in *T.R.H.S.*, 4th Ser. xxiii (1941), 129-58.
— 'The English Coronation Oath' in *Speculum*, xxiv (1949), 44-75.
— *The English Jewry under Angevin Kings* (London, 1960).
— 'Gervase of Tilbury' in *History*, xlvi (1961), 102-14.
— 'Glanville Continued' in *L.Q.R.*, liv (1938), 381-99.
— 'Henry I's Charter to London' in *E.H.R.*, xlii (1927), 80-87.
— 'Letters of the Oxford *Dictatores*' in *Formularies which bear on the History of Oxford* (Oxford Historical Soc., 1942, vol. ii).

Richardson, H. G. 'The Morrow of the Great Charter' in *B.J.R.L.*, xxviii (1944), 422-43, xxix (1945-46), 185-200.
— 'A Norman Law Suit' in *Speculum*, vii (1932), 383-93, viii (1933), 80.
— 'An Oxford Teacher of the Fifteenth Century', reprinted with corrections from *B.J.R.L.*, xxiii (1939).
— 'Richard fitz Neal and the Dialogus de Scaccario' in *E.H.R.*, xliii (1928), 161-71, 321-40.
— 'Roman Law in the *Regiam Majestatem*' in *Juridical Review*, lxvii (1955), 155-87.
— 'The Schools of Northampton in the Twelfth Century' in *E.H.R.*, lvi (1941), 595-605.
— 'Year Books and Plea Rolls as sources of Historical Information' in *T.R.H.S.*, 4th Ser., v (1922), 28-70.
See *Memoranda Roll.*
Richardson, H. G. and Sayles, G. O. 'Early Coronation Records' in *B.I.H.R.*, xiii (1936), 129-45.
— *The Early Statutes* (London, 1934).
— *The Governance of Mediaeval England from the Conquest to Magna Carta* (Edinburgh, 1963: reprinted 1964).
— *The Irish Parliament in the Middle Ages* (Philadelphia, 1952; reprinted 1964).
See *Select Cases of Procedure without Writ.*
Riesenberg, P. N. *Inalienability of Sovereignty in Medieval Political Thought* (New York, 1956).
Robert of Torigni, 'Chronica' in *Chronicles of the Reigns of Stephen, Henry II and Richard I*, ed. R. Howlett (Rolls Ser., London, 1885-90), iv. 81-315.
Robertson, A. J. *See* Liebermann.
Roger of Howden. *Chronica.* Ed. W. Stubbs (Rolls Ser., London, 1868-71).
— *Gesta Regis Henrici Secundi et Ricardi I.* Ed. W. Stubbs (Rolls Ser., London, 1867).
[Erroneously attributed to Benedict (abbot) of Peterborough.]
Rotuli Curiae Regis: 6 Richard I-I John. Ed. F. Palgrave (Record Comm., London, 1835).
Rotuli de Dominabus. Ed. J. H. Round (Pipe Roll Soc., London, 1913).
Rotuli Litterarum Patentium, 1201-1216. Ed. T. D. Hardy (Record Comm., London, 1835).
Rotuli Parliamentorum [*1278-1503*]. (London, 1783; Index, 1832).
Round, J. H. 'The Date of the Grand Assize' in *E.H.R.*, xxxi (1916), 268-69.
— 'Domesday Survey' in *V.C.H., Essex*, vol. i (1903), 333-426.
— *Geoffrey de Mandeville* (London, 1892).
See *Ancient Charters*; *Rotuli de Dominabus.*
Royal Writs in England from the Conquest to Glanville. Ed. R. C. Van Caenegem (Selden Soc., London, 1959).

Salisbury. *See* John.
Saltman, A. *Theobald Archbishop of Canterbury* (London, 1956).
Savine, A. 'Bondmen under the Tudors' in *T.R.H.S.*, New Ser., xvii (1903), 235-89.
Sayles. See *Select Cases.*
Scriptores XV. See *Historiae.*

SEEBOHM, F. *The English Village Community* (4th ed., London, 1905; reprinted 1915).

Select Cases in the Court of King's Bench. Ed. G. O. Sayles (Selden Soc., London, 1936-).

Select Pleas of the Crown. Ed. F. W. Maitland (Selden Soc., London, 1888).

Select Pleas of the Forest. Ed. G. J. Turner (Selden Soc., London, 1901).

Select Cases of Procedure without Writ. Ed. H. G. Richardson and G. O. Sayles (Selden Soc., London, 1941).

SIMEON OF DURHAM, *Historical Works*. Ed. T. Arnold (Rolls Ser., London, 1882-85).
[Vol. ii: *Historia Regum*.]

SOMNER, W. *A Treatise of Gavelkind* (London, 1660; 2nd ed., 1726).

Statutes of the Realm, vol. i (Record Comm., London, 1810).

STEIN, SIMON. 'Lex Salica' in *Speculum*, xxii (1947), 113-34, 395-418.

STENTON, D. M. *English Justice between the Norman Conquest and the Great Charter* (Philadelphia, 1964).
See *Pleas before the King*.

STENTON, F. M. *Anglo-Saxon England* (Oxford, 1943; 2nd ed., 1947).

— *The Latin Charters of the Anglo-Saxon Period* (Oxford, 1955).
See Kent.

STUBBS, WILLIAM. *Constitutional History of England* (Oxford, 1896-97).
[vol. i: 6th ed., 1897; vol. ii: 4th ed., 1896; vol. iii: 5th ed., 1896.]

— *Select Charters and Other Illustrations of English Constitutional History to the Reign of Edward I* (Oxford: 1st ed., 1870; 9th ed., by H. W. C. Davis, 1913, reprinted 1921).

— *Seventeen Lectures on the Study of Mediaeval and Modern History* (Oxford, 3rd ed., 1900).
See *Councils*.

SUTHERLAND, C. H. V. *Anglo-Saxon Gold Coinage in the light of the Crondall Hoard* (Oxford, 1948).

— 'Coinage in Britain in the Fifth and Sixth Centuries' in *Dark-Age Britain* (q.v.), 3-10.

TANCRED. 'Ordo Judiciarius' in Pilii, Tancredi, Gratiae *Libri de Judiciorum Ordine*. Ed. F. Bergmann (Göttingen, 1841).

Textus Roffensis. Ed. T. Hearne (Oxford, 1720). Facsimile edition by Peter Sawyer (Copenhagen, 1957-62).

THOMAS, PAUL. *Le Droit de propriété des laïques sur les églises et le patronage au moyen âge* (Paris, 1906).

THOMAS OF ELMHAM. *Historia Monasterii Sancti Augustini Cantuariensis*. Ed. C. Hardwick (Rolls Ser., London, 1858).

THOMAS OF WALSINGHAM. *Gesta Abbatum Monasterii Sancti Albani*. Ed. H. T. Riley (Rolls Ser., London, 1867-69).

Thómas Saga Erkibyskups: a Life of Archbishop Thomas Becket in Icelandic. Ed. E. Magnússon (Rolls Ser., London, 1875-83).

THORPE, B. See *Anglo-Saxon Chronicle; Diplomatarium*.

TORIGNI. *See* Robert.

Tournai. *See* Hermann.

TREHARNE, R. F. *The Baronial Plan of Reform, 1258-1263* (Manchester, 1932).

TROMBELLI, G. G. *Memorie istoriche concernenti le due canoniche di S. Maria de Reno e di S. Salvatore* (Bologna, 1752).
Tours. *See* Gregory.
TURNER, G. J. See *Select Pleas.*
Two of the Saxon Chronicles Parallel. Ed. C. Plummer (Oxford, 1892-99).

VACARIUS. *Liber Pauperum*. Ed. F. de Zulueta (Selden Soc., London, 1927).
VAN CAENEGEM. See *Royal Writs.*
VINOGRADOFF, P. *English Society in the Eleventh Century.* (Oxford, 1908).
— *Roman Law in Medieval Europe*. Ed. F. de Zulueta (Oxford, 1929).
— *Villainage in England* (Oxford, 1892).
'Vita Oswaldi Archiepiscopi Eboracensis' in *Historians of the Church of York* (q.v.), i. 399-475.

WALLACE-HADRILL, J. M. *The Long-Haired Kings and other studies in Frankish history* (London, 1962).
Walsingham. *See* Thomas.
WALTER OF COVENTRY, *Memoriale*. Ed. W. Stubbs (Rolls Ser., London, 1872-73).
WARNER, G. F., and ELLIS, H. J. *Facsimiles of Royal and other Charters in the British Museum* (London, 1903).
WEBB, C. C. J. *John of Salisbury* (London, 1932).
WEINBAUM, MARTIN. *London unter Eduard I und II* (Stuttgart, 1933).
WHEELER, R. E. M. *London and the Saxons* (London Museum Catalogues, no. 6: London, 1935).
[reviewed J. N. L. Myres in *Journal of Roman Studies*, xxvi (1936), 87-92.]
WHITELOCK, D. 'Archbishop Wulfstan, Homilist and Statesman' in *T.R.H.S.*, 4th Ser., xxiv (1942), 25-45.
— 'Wulfstan and the Laws of Cnut' in *E.H.R.*, lxiii (1948), 433-52.
See *English Historical Documents*, Wulfstan.
WILLIAM OF MALMESBURY, *Gesta Regum Anglorum*. Ed. W. Stubbs (Rolls Ser., London, 1887-89).
— *Historia Novella*. Ed. K. R. Potter (London, 1955).
— *Gesta Pontificum*. Ed. N. E. S. A. Hamilton (Rolls Ser., London, 1870).
— *Vita Wulfstani*. Ed. R. R. Darlington (Camden Ser., London, 1928).
WILLIAM OF NEWBURGH, 'Historia Rerum Anglicarum' in *Chronicles of Stephen etc.* (q.v.), vols. i-ii.
Worcester. *See* Florence.
WRIGHT, JOSEPH, *Grammar of the Gothic Language* (Oxford, 1954).
WULFSTAN. *Sermo Lupi ad Anglos*. Ed. D. Whitelock (London, 1939).
See William of Malmesbury.

Year Books:
30-31 Edward I. Ed. A. J. Horwood (Rolls Ser., London, 1863).
33-35 Edward I. Ed. A. J. Horwood (Rolls Ser., London, 1879).
1 and 2 Edward II. Ed. F. W. Maitland (Selden Soc., London, 1903).
See *Eyre of Kent*.

INDEX OF PERSONS AND PLACES

INDEX OF SUBJECTS